SEVENTEEN SEAS

Bronwyn Elsmore

Seventeen Seas is a work of creative non-fiction.
The events are based on real happenings, but the characters
are fictional. Any resemblance between the characters and
actual persons, living or dead, is coincidental.

© Bronwyn Elsmore, Auckland, 2012

This book is copyright. All rights reserved. No part of this work may be
reproduced or transmitted in any form or by any means, electronic or
mechanical, including photocopying, recording, or any information storage
and retrieval system, except for the purpose of fair reviewing.

The Author asserts her moral rights in the work.

ISBN 978-0-473-22003-7

Published by Flaxroots, Auckland
www.flaxroots.com

Design and cover by Aaron Elsmore

Contents

Halfway Around the World	1
The Other Side of the Tasman	9
Water Water Everywhere	22
Walking Forward	36
Too Many Ports?	51
Looking Alike	62
Hand it to the Brits	69
Ten Thousand Taxis	80
Selamat Datang	91
Cobweb in the Canopy	98
Another Language	111
All the Same in Kerala	120
Guests of the Goddess	137
Arabian Days and Nights	153
Ripples Aboard	165
The Colour of Water	170
Respect Our Beliefs	188
The Price of a Free Keffiyeh	206
Justice Human and Divine	232
The Gods Must be Angry	249
Lucky to be Here Today	261
Separate Ways	269
Time To Say Goodbye	276

— CHAPTER 1 —

Halfway Around the World

Only a small proportion of the more than 1800 passengers aboard the cruise ship stood on deck to see the city of Auckland recede, and to view the harbour – later to be referred to by one of the officers as almost the most beautiful in the world, in that it was "second only to Sydney's".

Even fewer were gathered on the wharf to wave goodbye as the ship cast off its links with the city and moved out into the harbour. It seemed the glamour of overseas journeying had faded into the jet stream created by the forty thousand flights that fly in and out of New Zealand each year to move the twelve million travellers arriving and departing.

One family, however, was part of the small group waiting on Princes wharf to see the ship depart. Several storeys above them a couple hurried along the Promenade deck and stopped at the most forward space open to the outside. They called to the family below and threw down coloured streamers, tying their ends to the rails. A wharf worker grinned as the children caught the end of the paper strips, which were the only ones in view. Clearly this was another practice that had been forgotten in the previous several decades. Or, more likely, abandoned through increased awareness of city standards, water pollution, destruction of rainforests, carbon footprints and other environmental issues.

As departure time neared the few on the wharf grew to a

small crowd of about fifty people and one large spotted dog. Some looked on curiously, perhaps wondering at the size of the white cruise liner in a time when they had thought such a mode of transport was over. The enthusiasm of the waving between the family and the couple on board increased as the vessel began to move outwards, and the two groups remained connected till the growing distance between hull and wharf forced the paper to break. An alert crew member who had been hovering, awaiting the moment, moved in to detach the flying strips from their anchor points and thrust them into a waste container.

Within minutes the Auckland Hilton Hotel that shares the wharf with the departure terminal, the taller buildings along Quay Street, then even the dominating spire of the Skytower had shrunk in size.

Mr Bradford Yorkshire was one of just a few people on board the liner who stood on deck for the departure. As the ship moved out into the harbour he shifted his spot to stand next to the couple who had farewelled their family and the three got into a conversation.

"That's Devonport, and the area where you can see one frigate is our naval base," Glen Henderson said, pointing.

"'Ow big's yer navy, then?"

"You're looking at a sizable part of it," said Glen.

"We spend too blumin' much on ours," growled Bradford.

Lynn Henderson steered the talk to safer waters, pointing to the distinctive island they were approaching.

"That island's called Rangitoto. It's a volcano."

"Active or extinct?"

"Dormant probably. It's only six hundred years old. It erupted from the sea – must have been quite a sight to the locals."

Bradford whistled. "It could go up again?" He'd taken the one-day excursion to Rotorua and was impressed at how New Zealanders lived comfortably with what seemed to him the lurking danger of natural disasters. In fact, there was a lot about this country he admired.

"That's t' trouble with having colonies," said Bradford after half a minute's silence during which he gazed at the peaked island, "at home tis all t'ones with blumin gumption that pack up thar stuff and move out t'new country. Then years on that's t'place that's moved ahead and t'home country's still back where t'was."

A few others joined those at the rails, watching as Auckland harbour receded into the distance and the growing grey of the end of the day. The Hendersons waited till they could see no more before familiarizing themselves with the ship that was to be their home for the next forty-six days.

The bulk of the passengers were no doubt still in the dining room enjoying dinner or resting from the day's exertions, particularly those who never let a port pass unshopped to the full. Since this was day 36 of an 81-day voyage for the eleven hundred of them who were in it for the long haul, Southampton to Southampton, by now there was a degree of ho-hum ennui about yet another departure from yet another port.

After all, over the past five weeks their senses had been fully exercised by the heady sights, smells and sounds of Madeira, Barbados, Margarita, Bonaire, Panama, Acapulco, San Francisco, Honolulu, Pago Pago and Nuku'alofa. And, one had to appreciate, one's energies had to be reserved for the fourteen further ports of call to come.

British tourists, it seemed to the Hendersons, had come a long way since the days of the 'Ten Pound Poms' – the million plus migrants who left the United Kingdom in the twenty-five years following World War Two in order to make a new life in the relatively unscathed countries of Australia, Canada and New Zealand. Several events over the next six weeks were to remind this Kiwi couple of Mr Bradford Yorkshire's observation that the migration period of the nineteen-forties and fifties had drained some of the pioneering component out of the British gene pool.

On a long haul trip such as this one not everyone could afford the extravagance, either financial or time-wise, to take the entire trip. Passengers left and joined the ship at each sector. The majority of the part-voyageurs were Brits who either flew out to one of the stops to join the cruise, or disembarked to fly back home. Some even left one ship and joined another.

A few hundred of the less fortunate passengers – those who had constraints of employment, finances, stamina, any or all of the above – repacked their evening clothes and left their cabins at Auckland, being booked on only the first half of what was advertised as a classic circumnavigation of the globe, and which promised experience of more destinations in one holiday than many people experience in a lifetime.

Their places were replaced by an equal number of second-halfers who flew out in order to enjoy a more leisurely return trip. Some of these had arrived in New Zealand in the weeks ahead, and spent the time between exploring. To a person, they exuded elaborate enthusiasm for places visited and people encountered.

HALFWAY AROUND THE WORLD

Some had seen a surprising amount of the country in an average of two to three weeks. Memories of travels in North and South Islands were overwhelmingly positive – in fact, not a negative word was forthcoming. At least not in the presence of the Hendersons or the few dozen other Kiwis who embarked in their country's Queen City.

Visitors Miss Leicester Secretary and her companion Ms Thankfully Divorced told of taking a local bus, not a tourist coach they stressed, between two points in South Island's prime tourist area the southern lakes. Riding along with them was just a handful of other travellers. In a tone approaching wonderment the pair told of how, when the driver heard the British accents of the women, he addressed the other passengers on board suggesting he turn the trip into a tour for the overseas guests. And so it was, with the driver giving commentary on local history, details, and explanations. Photo stops were made – the Church of the Good Shepherd, and the statue of the collie dog at Lake Tekapo – so the women, in addition to getting to their destination, had a customized tour thrown in. The other passengers moved forward to sit near them and add their knowledge along the way. The long distance coach took on the atmosphere of a party bus with all on board joining in. The wonderment in the women's tones reached the point of awe when they told how, at the end of their day the driver refused a tip despite the women's pressing him, and would not even accept the offer of a beer in the pub that night.

Even those with just the day in port raved about what they had pressed into twelve hours. The helicopter ride over the city's volcanoes was assessed as amazing, the "diving gannets and countryside" option rated excellent, and those who spent the full day and eighty-eight British pounds on the Rotorua thermal experience pronounced it prime – "except for the smell," of course. Ngaio and Lyall Wellington, another couple who embarked at Auckland, also intending to travel all the way to Southampton, found themselves at a point mid-Tasman explaining tactfully to a pair of sisters from Bristol that in New Zealand 'guysers' is always, but always, pronounced to rhyme with risers not with tweezers. Call them geezers, Ngaio thought to herself but was a little too polite to say aloud, and heads all around the thermal area will turn in order to spot the unfortunate old men you're referring to.

The score or so of Kiwis who boarded, booked on shorter or longer sectors of the remaining voyage, were warmed by the enthusiasm of the reactions. According to all the experienced travellers they encountered over the term of their various cruises their country was spectacular, varied in its offerings, and its people invariably friendly. As a further tangible recommendation, from this point of the journey tee-shirts and caps bearing kiwi and silver fern motifs were sported by people with accents from a good proportion of the UK counties from Avon to Worcestershire.

Other stops on the voyage so far had not been judged as favourably. This ship full of Brits was bent on skipping the northern climate and they weren't slow to express their disappointment in a full range of accents if their expectations were met with anything less than complete fulfilment. After all, it was mid February down-under, the height of the southern summer, and they had spent a lot to avoid winter at home.

"Mind you," one admitted, "we've mostly brought poor weather with us so far."

HALFWAY AROUND THE WORLD

'So far' covered the voyage beginning at Southampton early in the year, making its way "out" via the Panama Canal, weathering the waters of the Pacific to reach the City of Sails. On the way south there was a brief respite at the capital of American Samoa, referred to by all as "Pay-go Pay-go". It took Ngaio Wellington a few embarrassed moments to identify what she first thought to be a lamentable lack in her own knowledge, especially as she took some pride in referring to her homeland as a Pacific nation.

"Paygo Paygo?" she questioned Sally Sale from Somerset as they shared a table at lunch in the self-service Orangery on the first full day out. It took a further few exchanges before she identified the location, and found herself correcting again.

"Parng-or Parng-or," she instructed, "and you don't sound the 'g.'"

As she spoke she was aware she sounded like a schoolteacher, a role she'd never aspired to. However, as one who'd not only encountered, but enthusiastically embraced, her fourth generation New Zealander status when required to take a cultural safety course as part of her continuing education as a health professional, she felt duty bound to pursue the matter. She remembered an occasion many years before when an expatriate Brit had corrected her on the pronunciation of Leicestershire – and that after the man had butchered her own name. At the recollection she felt moved to add a further piece of instruction –

"And it's **Sar**mor-a, not Sa-**mower**."

Next stop on the outward trip had been Nuku'Alofa, but no one even attempted to voice that one – the ship's tours advisor had told them it's unpronounceable. Instead they resorted to the safer option of Tong-gar, remembered mainly as the place they encountered the most torrential rain they've ever seen. Ngaio repeated her lesson about the silent 'g'.

A small crowd of about fifty people and one spotted dog.

— CHAPTER 2 —

The Other Side of the Tasman

It took two days for the 76 thousand tonne island to cross the Tasman Sea at cruising speed. This came as something of a surprise to a good number of the guests aboard whose feet generally trod lands in the opposite hemisphere. The Wellingtons had encountered this miscomprehension before, as has almost every New Zealander and Australian. The experience of antipodeans and/or antisciians of northern habitat holding the belief that the two countries are the same, or at least joined by a short causeway, is legend down-under.

"How long does it take to drive between Wellington and Sydney?" a distant cousin of Lyall had written some months before. At the time he'd thought of a handful of possible answers along the lines of "about the same time as it takes you to drive from London to Madrid or Stockholm, from Brussels to Belgrade, or from Rome to Istanbul." Even more accurate, given that it's water all the way, is the comparison from Paris to Reykjavik.

You had to hand it to these intrepid travellers on this twenty-first century cruise liner, though. They took the news in good grace, moving to lay out their towels on the loungers on the Sun deck before settling down for a couple more days.

The Wellingtons and the Hendersons spent the time getting to know the vessel that was to be their home for more than six weeks and adjusting to its routine. On the first full day at sea, after the ship rounded the northernmost tip of their country and was starting its run across that part of the Pacific Ocean more often called the Tasman Sea by those who live on either side, the two couples met in the casual dining room known as the Orangery.

Lynn Henderson had noticed Ngaio Wellington during the boarding process partly because of the rich colour and sheen of her dark brown hair, but more because of the size of the matching suitcases she and her partner were guiding towards the loading trolley. In comparison to their own they were modest, and the single item the Wellingtons each pulled seemed to be all they had – she and Glen had much larger cases and another softer bag between them. The third bag was packed with more disposal items to be used on the voyage, then it would no doubt be pressed into duty as an extra to cope with overflow acquired on the way. The other couple must be making just the trip across 'the ditch', she decided, mentally using a term used by both Kiwis and Aussies to refer to the space between the countries.

Ngaio and Lyall had both noticed Glen because he wore a Black Caps supporter's tee-shirt. A fellow enthusiast, thought Lyall – he'd watch out for him on board and they could swap cricket stories over a drink. He had wondered if he would find any ally aboard. Otherwise it was going to be a long voyage in the company of fans of the English and Australian teams.

Now, meeting in the Tasman, the two couples from cities that often found themselves as rivals immediately felt the bond of fellow nationals in a foreign country. Other New Zealanders they'd talked to already were travelling as far as Sydney only. It was good to know there was another pair going the whole way to the other side of the world.

Lynn looked at Ngaio then, to a lesser extent, at Lyall, trying to assess the ages of the other couple. She decided they'd be very close to their own vintage.

"Did you take early retirement like we did?" she asked, with a slight emphasis on the last two words to reinforce the point that though she had crossed the sixty barrier she'd like it recognized that she wasn't yet eligible to receive national superannuation, which didn't come in till sixty-five.

Ngaio could appreciate that and responded that neither she nor Lyall had retired fully, but they'd cut back from full time the year before and were now taking several months off. How much work they'd resume on their return would depend on how much they spent on this trip.

"And how well we can settle after it," Lyall added.

Lynn looked around the dining room and confirmed what she'd already noticed in her exploration of the various decks.

"It looks as though, if you're not entitled to be in possession of a seniors' discount card, then you're under the average age of the passengers on board," she had commented to Glen earlier that morning.

Now she came to a further, and satisfying, conclusion that the two couples looked a good deal fitter than most others around them. Lyall laughed as she voiced it.

"Enjoy the feeling while you can," he replied. "We've taken trips like this before, and believe me, on any cruise ship you'll find constant reminders of what's on the horizon and steaming towards you."

Over the weeks to come, Lynn was reminded of that

conversation time and time again. Aging was a frequent theme with the comedians and fewer comediennes employed in the evening shows in the Curzon Theatre – their gibes made more acceptable by the fact that most of them were themselves of an age that allowed them to mix with their audiences without looking out of place.

"I've just reached sixty – you've been there sir, haven't you, but you probably don't remember it – it's when you start to realize you can do without sex, but you can't do without your glasses."

"It's the Captain's reception tonight. He usually holds it at the end of the voyage, but seeing some of you lot, he thought he'd better get it over sooner."

"Have you noticed that the older the man the higher the trousers? Some have to open their fly to blow their nose."

Despite the statistics, as Lynn pointed out to Ngaio when the two women returned to the subject a couple of weeks later, there was a lack of blue rinses to be seen, not a lot of twin sets, and pearls seemed to be on the endangered list above the water line. You had to hand it to a lot of the septuagenarians and beyond, they agreed. Men appeared to be happy to abandon their long strides to show off a pair of pale pins below the khaki knee-lengths, though a good number displayed patches of colour in the knots of veins exposed as they did so. The northern women showed even fewer inhibitions, not hesitating to don sleeveless tops that bared crepey arms, and pulling on pairs of shorts that put their cellulite on full display. Lynn, tugging at the short sleeves she now insisted on to hide a degree of flabbiness that paled in comparison to many around commented,

"They're a game bunch. I'll give them that."

THE OTHER SIDE OF THE TASMAN

"They're game for everything except shortening their bra straps," added Ngaio, whose fingers almost itched to be permitted to help some of the more elderly women to raise their profile.

The years of wear and tear also showed up in the variety of walking styles, the two couples agreed.

"And that's not even when the ship is rolling," said Glen.

"When it is," laughed Lyall, "some find the effects are cancelled out and they walk straighter than they do on land. Perhaps that's why they come back for cruise after cruise."

Joking aside, the four allowed, the ones who could walk were the lucky ones. A good number on board were not. Wheelchairs, walkers, frames, or sticks were frequent sights in corridors and elevators. The wheelchairs varied from custom-made Bentley-quality models that glided the passageways noiselessly, to ship-issued Lada-types that were propelled and turned with difficulty by the dutiful spouse, especially when pushing against the swell.

On day thirty-nine of the full round the globe voyage, day four for those who embarked in Auckland, what had been billed as the "most beautiful port in the world" acted with uncharacteristic coyness, hiding herself beneath rain and chill winds as the ship arrived in Sydney. It was not what Mr Liverpool-Lancs had looked forward to and, braving the open deck in short sleeved tee-shirt, he engaged in an extended grumble along the lines that since he'd shelled out a right bloody fortune to come to Australia during their summer, it was downright inconsiderate of the place not to make more of a bloody effort to see him right.

All the same, the cruisers poured ashore to make the most of this first day of opportunity in the lucky country. Harry and Zelda Hampshire, who could appreciate seascapes every day at home, took the "escape Sydney for the natural surrounds of the Blue Mountains to experience the unique solitude of the Australian bush" option and returned amazed at the scenery, though a little shaken at the versatility of the 4 wheel-drive vehicle and its driver in whose hands they'd placed their trust. The coach option that offered the chance to view a variety of antipodean wildlife might have been the better bet after all, thought Zelda, though she was still uncertain about gliding 900 feet above ravines and waterfalls on an glass-floored Electro-Scenic gondola, state of the art or not. The final clincher in the choice had been the cynical snort of a friend at home who'd spent some years in New South Wales.

"Friendly kangaroos and cuddly koalas? Believe me, there's no such thing as a friendly roo or a cuddly koala. Keep your distance from both of them."

Over the following days, however, they viewed snaps on digital displays that amounted to proof that some of their fellow cruisers had indeed enjoyed close-up encounters with creatures that not only fitted those descriptions but also with others that seemed to show that the Creator of this land down-under had clearly possessed a great sense of humour.

The Norwich Norfolks kept to their usual habit and signed up for the half-day "best seller" tour of the city, and drove past what was billed as the most celebrated sights – King's Cross which looked completely innocuous in the morning light but where they were assured it hots up at night, Chinatown that seemed to be a smaller tamer version of such ethnic areas elsewhere, Bondi beach which had to be admitted left the best of the stretches of their home coast way in the shade, and Mrs Macquarie's Chair the width of which suggested the early Governor's wife might have eaten more than her share of the fruits the new colony had to offer. The sights of the famed opera house and the equally familiar lines of the harbour bridge now among their memories, the Norfolks could truly claim to have visited the place that the once infamous Botany Bay had now become. Mr Norwich Norfolk could return home and quietly share with his nearest and dearest that should the family skeleton, in the shape of one Henry Edward Norfolk accused of having pilfered a fish, ever emerge from the proverbial closet they could take some consolation in that one of their own had a small part to play in the expansion of the empire and the formation of this great country. In fact, he felt tempted to add, it was a bit of bad luck that others in the family who were no doubt just as deserving had escaped the justice that would have eventually proved to be to their advantage.

To meet the expectations of those who chose to do their own thing in the city, Sydney warmed up during the day, but a pall of air pollution lingered, making eyes and throats sting. On the next major leg of the voyage, the passage to Hong Kong, its legacy the Sydney cough was heard all around the ship.

Australia redeemed itself partially with a perfect day in Brisbane. After a few grumbles about the fact that the wharf allocated was a distance from the city, passengers poured into the buses and set out in different directions to enjoy the sights of the River City and beyond.

Since she had vetoed Harry's choice of trip at Sydney, Zelda

Hampshire gave way to his desire to see a live crocodile show. The thought of being close to creatures that she believed should have joined the dinosaurs on the extinct list, without the barrier of a television screen between them and her, filled her with revulsion, but she was curious to see Australia Zoo. As the coach travelled north, she wondered if there was any chance of getting a glimpse of one of the Irwin family and, if so, whether she should give her condolences at the loss of the crocodile hunter. It was a question that lay still unresolved as they turned in to the park. It was just as well the chance didn't eventuate, she thought on the return journey. By then she'd come to a new understanding, albeit uneasy, about the place of these prehistoric creatures, even if they still topped her 'why-did-God-create' list – followed closely by all varieties of venomous snakes, then giant sting rays. Under the circumstances, she felt she'd coped extremely well.

Others arriving back at the ship's side in the late afternoon had gone in the opposite direction and viewed the marina developments, high-rise skyline, and tourist attractions of the Gold Coast. The groups who had gone inland in a 4x4 adventure came back equipped with boomerangs. After receiving a lesson as part of their bush experience, they were determined to master the art of the return throwing. None, however, were confident enough to practise at the rails.

Glen Henderson also sported an iconic item of Australiana. He and Lynn had seen the major sights of Queensland several times before, and on this occasion had taken the shuttle bus into the city to meet with a relative. The three had taken a ferry trip along the Brisbane River, then walked through the South Bank Parklands – unrecognisable, they all agreed, from the area that was formerly an unsightly industrial area before it was cleared to provide the World Expo site. It was a little later, as they were making their way back to the shuttle stop, that Glen spotted the hat. Now there was a hat a man could wear. Better than that, this broad-brimmed hat designed for outdoor men had become even more suitable over the years as the hole in the ozone layer had increased to record size – a much publicized topic in the southern nations. Along with a good proportion of south pacific residents over a certain age, Glen had previously received treatment for solar keratoses. As did every citizen of down-under he had noted the constantly repeated advertising encouraging the population to slip-slop-slap quantities of sunblock cream on every piece of exposed skin. And like a good number of southern males he rejected the advice if it meant adopting a head-covering that suggested he was either a potential wall-tagger armed with spray cans in his backpack, or off to the bowling green with a set of bowls in a vinyl carry case. Glen entered the store and surveyed the display. The crocodile range made a good no-lawn-bowls-for-me statement, but the addition of rows of croc teeth on the band might be a little over the top for one with no real connection with such wildlife. Giving the neighbour's cat an occasional pat hardly qualified him as a Mick Dundee. He passed by the kangaroo collection on the basis of a similar lack of familiarity, together with a tinge of regret that the creatures he still thought of in terms of Skippy were put to such prosaic purpose, and finally chose a drover cooler in dark brown. The mesh sides would also accommodate its being packed into a suitcase. There was no doubt, Glen told himself, this was a hat for a man. The sort of man it implied, he would find out in six countries time.

During the following day the rain set in, putting paid to many planned events. Anticipated trips to the Great Barrier Reef were cancelled, the day on Hamilton Island drenched. For those who had highlighted this part of the cruise and had their diving gear and underwater cameras laid out ready, the lucky country came in for a deal of what its inhabitants would refer to as being given a gobful. Even those passengers who hadn't intended to do more than head ashore to the nearest bar, also in local parlance spat the dummy and threw a wobbly. Mr Liverpool-Lancs was joined in his dissatisfaction by Mrs Coventry who had boarded in Sydney for her first cruise, and even more particularly by Mr Norwich Norfolk whose blustering disappointment vocalized in Champions Bar threatened to surpass the force 5 on the outer side of the hull.

A finer sky the following morning had passengers queuing to go ashore in the ship's small boats for a day in Cairns. Mona Coventry surveyed the shore, which seemed to be an unacceptable distance away. She noticed the tenders being lowered and blanched. From her vantage point at the rail of the Lido deck the small vessel looked even more miniscule than when seen hanging from the usual place above the Promenade deck. The first boats filled with passengers and set out. As they crossed the expanse towards Yorkeys Knob they shrunk even more till they morphed into mere dots. Bert appeared at her side. He saw her expression, but he'd been expecting it.

"Come on, love," he said, taking her elbow, "it's time to get on the tender."

"I think I'll stay," said Mona, "you go."

"You didn't go ashore yesterday, and it's another six days at sea after this. You've got your seasick patch on. It'll be all right, love." Bert steered her to the elevators to go below.

The couple joined the line of people waiting for the next tender. A man ahead of them, leaning on a walking stick, grumbled to a member of the crew standing by.

"Why do we have to go down to deck five? Why can't we get off from the Promenade deck?"

"Sir, if you can get into a tender from the Promenade deck, then the ship is sinking."

Mona felt her panic level rise. She closed her eyes when it was her turn to step into the bobbing boat and allowed the seamen to guide her across. As they waited for the craft to fill up, she noted that others around her seemed to be actually enjoying the experience. Laughter rose as someone asked a question that occurred to her also.

"Why is it that only the crew members are wearing life jackets?" The difference was, everyone else apparently thought the query was funny.

Tender number 10 was running very rough. It slowed right down then graunched and ground forward again throughout the three-mile trip from ship to shore. If the officer at the controls was having a difficult time operating the service, it wasn't for lack of advice from those seated in the cabin.

"Put a drop of oil in the gearbox."

"Pull out the oars."

Suggestions from the male passengers came thick and fast. With each renewed effort from the straining engine a thick cloud of black smoke erupted from the rear, all but obliterating the sight of the liner receding astern.

"All those notices around asking us not to throw anything overboard, and to reuse the towels in the bathroom," sniffed

Ms Poll Ution, "so much for the company's concern for the environment."

Mona stepped from the boat to the wharf with a lot more enthusiasm than she had boarded.

"There you are, love," said Bert coming after her, "that wasn't so bad, was it?"

It was, almost, she thought to herself. Now she was on shore she could figure out how to stay there. Bert took her arm and led her to the shuttle bus that would take them into the town of Cairns. He had felt her anxiety during the trip across the water and had come up with a plan.

On the return journey Mona sat at the front of the tender with her eyes fixed on the white ship that grew larger as they approached. Bert, his arm linked with hers, relaxed. The couple of brandies he had ordered for her after their lunch at a café seemed to have helped. She wasn't one to drink more than a shandy, and normally he wasn't one to encourage her, but this occasion had been an exception.

Others around them were not so pleased. A woman called Sally, whose accent suggested she was from Somerset grumbled to her companion Tania at the paucity of the shopping in the town. Despite their efforts the pair had managed to return with only three plastic bags between them. Norwich Norfolk was also vocal. On the one occasion when he'd planned to do something a little more adventurous – if a trip into the hill country could indeed be classed as adventurous – the news was bad. Flooding in the hinterland meant the cancellation of most of the booked excursions. Norwich Norfolk renewed his complaint.

"What's all this we hear about drought in 'Stralia?" he

boomed, "Here's me feeling I'm blimmin Noah on me bloody ark."

The shore seemed an unacceptable distance away.

— CHAPTER 3 —

Water Water Everywhere

In the face of six straight days at sea, it was with somewhat reduced good grace that the pool towels were again laid out on every available sun-lounger and deck-chair.

There had been some further defections and replacements among the passengers in both Sydney and Brisbane, and the eighteen hundred cruisers who settled in for the next leg, were ninety percent Brits. Fourteen Kiwis, more than one hundred Australians, and single-digit numbers of a few other nationalities helped fill the 935 cabins.

For the majority this was the beginning of the journey 'home'. The ones on board for the full round-trip didn't get a chance to change cabins so, unlike the ideal held by their globe-cruising forebears who liked to travel 'portside out starboard home', there were no passengers on this voyage who could claim the 'posh' label.

By this time in the course of the full voyage some habits and habitats had become established to the point of being almost unchallengeable. A particular table near the Pennant Bar on Lido deck was claimed by a group of men from the northern counties who spent a good deal of each sea day, glass in hand, working on obtaining a permanent imprint from their chairs. Their wives were in no such danger as they hurried from one activity to another – making novelty items out of tissue boxes and scraps of material in a corner of the Crow's Nest, learning

French or Spanish from a pair of multi-lingual sisters in the Uganda Room, and adding to the jackpot pool building up daily in the Bingo session in Carmen's lounge.

Notices displayed on the outside decks to the effect that sun-loungers could not be reserved and if vacant for more than thirty minutes deck staff would remove belongings from them, were ignored – apparently interpreted by the dedicated tanners who made their selected spots extensions of their staterooms in all but the most inclement weather as constituting no real threat. Caroline Coolangatta, a sarong tied above her bust to cover her swimsuit, cancer society approved hat on her head, and with approved 30+ sunscreen lotion and book in hand, made two laps of the areas around the Riviera Pool searching for an available recliner. About half of them accommodated bodies – the others were marked as occupied by the fact that they had towels, bags, and other items laid conspicuously on top. Only two people were actually in the water. She settled less comfortably on the raised rim surrounding the pool to wait, but neither this time nor any other when she repeated the action did anyone come to retrieve their articles. Neither did any staff member move to free the space.

Caroline didn't feel like making an issue of it. She and her cousin Briar Melbourne had boarded at Brisbane so were among the most recent to join a group that they realized had already established patterns of behaviour. At 45 and 42 they were also among the younger passengers on board. This had become clear immediately from the prevalence of people holding sticks and walkers – the women seemed to be held up by slow walkers in the passageways each time they emerged from their cabin. One who always appeared to be ahead of them pushed a wheeled walker with a card hung on the front displaying a red printed 'L'. At least she had a sense of humour.

Most of the old ones did, it seemed.

"I didn't know if I was having a heart attack or an orgasm. When you're past sixty you can't tell the difference," a man at lunch had shared.

"Did you ever meet Elvis Presley?" a comedian asked a woman with a good head of white hair. "Never mind dearie, it won't be long now."

Even though lunchtime in the Medina Restaurant was designated free seating, a group of five, by means of coordinated times of arrival, usually managed to sit together at a table for eight. The other three places were filled by casuals who provided both entertainment and an audience for the regulars. The fact that the five also served to deliver at least equal amusement to each day's new tablemates did not occur to them.

One of the couples, known quietly to the others as 'Basil' and 'Sybil', though not actually bearing those names, could hardly escape being compared with the fawlty pair. With just a little stretch of the imagination, considering 'Basil's' height and 'Sybil's' lack of it, even their physical appearances weren't dissimilar. Given that the couple hailed from Plymouth, just a crow's flight from Torquay, it's a wonder they showed no sign of being aware that their dining companions found the parallels so obvious especially when, on occasion, those names were let slip.

A further couple at the table Mr and Mrs Liverpool-Lancs were, in their physiques, the mirror images of 'Basil' and 'Sybil' – Mrs LL at a lean 1.78 metres stood a good dozen centimetres over her thickset husband, who compensated by being quick to offer her a chair at every chance.

The fifth of the regulars, Joe, encouraged the use of a description rather than a name – "That's me, Jovial Joe from Jersey". He was a veteran of many cruises who collected stories he took delight in relating. If an opportunity was slow to arise, Joe wasn't above manipulating a situation to suit.

"Hello, I haven't met you before. Your first time on this ship, is it? You're not likely to make the same mistake as an old fellow I met on my last voyage, then. He said to me 'I've been on several long cruises before.' And how are you enjoying this one?' I asked. 'I'm all right now,' he said, 'I always feel much better after I've got the first leg over.' Well, he was eighty-five if he was a day. 'Good for you, Grandad,' I said."

Others conducted to the group's table were the main target of Jovial Joe's anecdotes, particularly if they admitted to being first time cruisers.

Rich and Liz, from a small town in the hills of New South Wales "about a hundred k from Sydney", met the Medina lunch group when the ship was forging through the Banda Sea. The couple watched in growing amusement as the pair from Plymouth argued over whether couscous was pasta or a grain.

"It's pasta," ruled Susan aka 'Sybil', "now do hurry up and order, you're holding up the waiter."

Liz nudged Rich's knee under the table and murmured "Poor Manuel." He leaned towards her to whisper in her ear, "It could have been Waldorf salad." Later, as they climbed the stairs to the Promenade deck to do the circuits needed to work off the dessert, Rich asked "What did they say their names are?"

"Bruce and Susan," responded Liz.

"Who are they trying to kid?"

'Basil' sometimes attempted to retell Jovial Joe's jokes to their table companions at evening dinner in the Alexandria restaurant, but with rather less success, causing 'Sybil' to cluck her tongue and add an explanation.

"Bruce forgot to say that the man who the actress was talking to was actually the captain. That makes all the difference, doesn't it?"

At their table for ten in the first dinner seating in the Alexandria, 'Basil' and 'Sybil' were joined by three further couples – Harry and Zelda Hampshire, Glen and Lynn Henderson, Bradford and Yvonne Yorkshire – together with travelling companions Miss Leicester Secretary and Ms Thankfully Divorced. By the time the latter two left the ship in Singapore in order to fly home to their jobs, the marital status of each was not likely to be up for renegotiation, at least in the short term.

Despite knowing that over the next six days they would travel from Australasia to Asia, many on board still found it hard to get to grips with that much water as the ship moved through a succession of seamless seas.

Mona Coventry, seated next to Ngaio Wellington at their designated table in the Medina Restaurant, made it known that there was good purpose behind the fact that she chose to live in the English city sited the furthest from the ocean. When she met her Bert on a trip to Blackpool with friends going on fifty years earlier she'd looked out into the Irish Sea and felt discomforted by the lack of substance. If he was interested, she told him, he'd have to follow her to Coventry. After two weeks of weighing it up, he had, and instead of developing the marine side of his interest in motors Bert had enjoyed a career with the motor industry. What her husband didn't know about Rovers, Peugeots Aston Martins and Jaguars wasn't worth knowing, Mrs C often told people. In his retirement years Bert was restoring a 1976 Triumph Stag, though most of his forty years service was to do with a much more prevalent vehicle that everyone could readily recognize, the British taxicab.

Given his wife's aversion to the sea, Bert had worked hard to have her agree to coming on this cruise. Mona had studied the planned route of the full itinerary and decided that the initial stretch across the Atlantic, then the later even more daunting expanse of the Pacific Ocean was too much to contemplate. In an act of compromise the couple agreed to fly to Sydney and join the ship for the second half of the round the world voyage. On the map, this section of the planned route seemed to Mona to require navigation through passages between a succession of island groups. After that it would be a matter of hugging coastlines around Asia, to the safety of the Mediterranean, and then following the Spanish and French coasts back home. The first shock that came on the leg from Sydney north was discovering that cruise ships, far from sailing within hailing distance of a shore, steamed safely many miles out to sea. Now she found that since they had rounded Cape York at the northern tip of Australia days were passing by without as much as a hint of a hill showing above the horizon. Even had there been a tall mast for a cabin boy to climb he would rarely have been able to raise the call land-ho. Mona began to empathize even more completely with the desperation of Kevin Costner and his co-characters in Waterworld, and seldom ventured onto the open decks. She checked the small patch of plaster behind her left ear daily and was cheered to find the anti-nausea medication was apparently working – even when others commented on the small chop she made her way through the interior passageways with comparative confidence.

For the next five days sea followed sea. The Tasman was followed by the Coral Sea, through the Arafura, Banda, Ceram, Molucca, Celebes, Sulu, and into the South China Sea.

At a spot en route an extra diversion took the cruisers away en masse from the usual leisure activities. They left the deck-chairs, shuffleboard and tennis courts, they abandoned the bars, library, and card games, though probably not the more serious procedures occurring in the health and beauty spa.

The sister-ship to their own vessel, was to pass by on her voyage south. Most of the Brits seemed to know of the event in advance, but in case anyone was still unaware of the pending encounter the captain himself took responsibility for dispelling their ignorance. The ship-wide loudspeaker system broadcast frequent updates from the bridge. When it was announced that the sister-ship would be passing a half mile off to port at 11.40 a.m. the atmosphere took on an air of anticipation. The Hendersons, the Wellingtons, Rich and Liz, and no doubt most of the other New Zealanders and Australians aboard, wondered at the change of mood around them. The next bulletin advised that the other vessel was now just fourteen nautical miles away, and the open decks filled as passengers lined the railings. Those with balcony cabins on the port side settled themselves in comfort to observe. The travellers who called the southern countries home looked up from their various activities to witness, with some wonderment, hundreds of their fellow shipmates making for the outside doors, many of them gripping small Union Jacks on sticks.

At the following update, that the ship's sister was visible from the bridge, every square foot of the promenade was occupied. No doubt below decks the Chief Engineer was busy pumping water into the starboard tanks to avoid the ship passing the point of no return at 65 degrees list.

Now the public address system came alive again and the stirring notes of *Rule Britannia* sounded through the salons and passageways, prompting the few people still inside to scramble for access to the open deck. Ngaio and Lyall, their curiosity finally aroused, not by the prospect of seeing another ship but at the exodus from the public areas, rose and followed.

The members of the entertainment staff were clearly well prepared, and ready to make the most of this break in the routine of an otherwise uneventful day at sea. From a stack of cartons of supplies, they were handing out hundreds of flags to those who hadn't brought their own. The loud speaker burst forth with *God Save the Queen* and then *Land of Hope and Glory*. The two white liners passed by, doffing red ensigns in acknowledgement of their sorority. A roar went up and a thousand Union Jacks waved.

As the two sisters drew apart again, heading in their opposite directions – their own northwards and the other to the south – the crowd dispersed. Flags were replaced in the cartons, and those who had waved them returned to their various pursuits accompanied by the strains of marches reflecting the pomp and circumstance of the occasion, not a few dabbing at their misty eyes. A group of Kiwis and Australians, both of whose nations were anticipating their inevitable if not imminent switch to republic status, was left on deck, gaping in amazement at the display of nationalism just witnessed. Not that any would have voiced it aloud, given that they were outnumbered more than twelve to one.

Apart from the antipodean contingent a minority of the passengers were of nationalities other than British, most of whom had joined at their home port along the route. No matter where they called home, while aboard they found themselves subject to UK norms. The journey from Southampton to Australia was invariably called the voyage 'out', with Australia to UK the 'homeward' leg. Ms Coolangatta and Ms Melbourne, admitted to being confused when first asked "Are you on the ship all the way home?"

"No," responded Caroline, "the ship doesn't go back again, so just to Southampton."

On day four of the six days at sea, while passing through the Molucca Passage, the cruise liner slipped over the Equator with barely a reference being passed. The event had been well celebrated on the southward journey in mid-Pacific Ocean so this time across the zero latitude mark Neptune and his court were left to rest on their marine beds, and any later-boarding pollywogs remained uninitiated.

Willy Wolverhampton and Billy Brighton however, occupying their usual table near the Pennant Bar on Lido deck, saw the occasion as a chance to revive the debate they'd started on the voyage out and which had lain unresolved since. Now they spent two more hours and four further beers apiece arguing over whether or not water going down a plughole switches its

WATER WATER EVERYWHERE

flow clockwise to anticlockwise, and the reverse, on different sides of parallel zero. They could have taken the opportunity to conduct their own experiment, but inertia intervened. Besides, that might prove one of them right and the other wrong. Rather than a need to know the truth, it was the debate itself that was more important.

It was also around this point in the voyage that Glen and Lynn stepped into one of the midship elevators on their way to a later-than-usual breakfast to be greeted by smiles from another couple and a cheerful "Good morning". The man's accent reminded them of past neighbours who, some years before, had sold their property and returned with great reluctance to their former hometown in Herefordshire or Hertfordshire – the Hendersons couldn't remember which.

"We'll be back," the departing neighbours had vowed, "when Mum passes away." Mother must still be holding on, they assumed, because the pair had not reappeared.

"Lovely day," said the man after he'd pressed the up button. He grinned, gave them what appeared to be a meaningful look and added, "The Germans have already reserved all the deck-chairs."

He and his wife were still laughing as they alighted at Arcadia deck. By the towels they carried it seemed they were destined for the Riviera Pool. Lynn was puzzled.

"What did they mean by that?" she asked.

Glen shrugged. The door slid open at Lido deck and they walked aft to the Orangery, the episode forgotten at least for the time being.

Lyall Wellington passed by their table ten minutes later, greeting them then passing on. He had a busy day planned. The ship's daily schedule offered a good programme of lectures, and having spent the last twenty years of his life in sales and training he was happy to sit and listen to someone else doing the talking. This morning he was on his way to learn more about the founding of the British Empire, and after lunch he'd attend another talk in a series about British military operations, then a further address on the topic of ships that changed maritime history. Ngaio had looked at the list. It was usually she who took up opportunities to increase her knowledge on a range of subjects, but there was nothing there to interest her – she'd give those ones a miss.

Besides, she had spotted a competing offering that appealed more. Vanderbilt's card room was usually inhabited by groups of four dealing and bidding with a seriousness that warned her to keep away. At designated times on sea days, however, the chairs were vacated to make room for another crowd – many of them equally competitive, Ngaio realized. From the first time she joined the regulars at the daily quizzes something was clear to her. She had no trouble holding her own with the general knowledge questions. On literature she could compete with confidence, and she scored well in geography. The Pacific and Asia were her forte but the opportunities to benefit from it proved limited. The problem was the over-representation of very British-centred questions – she wished a few on the premiers or significant buildings and institutions of New Zealand, rather than English kings and queens or their residences, would figure more. All the same, she continued to take her place at the tables.

In a closed community, such as on board ship, rumours are

WATER WATER EVERYWHERE

bound to spread. And they did. With the half-way mark of the complete round-the-world voyage past, one piece of gossip that went the rounds concerned the number of people who had died on the trip so far. The Cruise Director, addressing a capacity crowd in the Curzon theatre before the evening's entertainment, was happy to assure those who were no doubt considering themselves lucky to be among the survivors that the passenger list had retained its original number, one hundred per cent, to date. To this point the ship had been death-free. At this reassurance an expression of relief that was both audible and visible rippled through the crowd. Pleased sighs could be heard throughout, and the shoulders of some of the more year-laden cruisers relaxed a little.

The most circulated item of tattle, however, was about the makeup of the staff on board. The ship was served by 850 officers and crew, and the captain had already reported that they came from seventy different countries. Throughout the passenger decks, however, a further important piece of information was exchanged freely. It was passed from diner to diner across the starched white linen as the entrée dish was expertly replaced by the plate for the main course. It was shared between loungers on the Sun and Lido decks aft as drinks were delivered by smartly dressed bar attendants. And so the message, invariably uttered in tones of quiet satisfaction, spread.

"They may be from a lot of different countries, but all of the staff on board are Christians."

In case this was not enough, the imparters of the intelligence added a further assurance. It was a policy of the company to employ only baptised members of the brethren of Christ.

When the scoop was passed on to Mr Napier, a retired Kiwi

journalist, he put his book aside and leaned back to think about it. It didn't take him long to decide that if there was any truth at all behind the hearsay, then those in the personnel recruitment suite, and a good number of the staff themselves, were surely enjoying a joke at the expense of the cruise company. Even more, it seemed they had managed to fool a good proportion of those whose food they prepared, whose cabins they cleaned, and those they were piloting through the world's waters.

They were doing it brazenly too, thought Mr Napier, who had flown the Tasman Sea to Sydney to spend a few days with a daughter then joined the cruise at its berth close to the famous coat-hanger bridge. After all, each member of the staff wore a name badge that clearly declared their name, in many cases giving strong clues to their family's affiliation. If the Pratiks, Sachins, Sandeeps, and their fellow believers on board attended Sunday service when they're at home, he mused, it's a fair bet it would be to the extreme surprise of their friends and neighbours in the various towns and cities of the Indian subcontinent. And if that were so, it seemed a very remote possibility indeed that the parents of some would have named them after Hindu deities, as he'd found more than one of them proud to admit was the case.

Likewise, if Abdul, Iqbal, Muhammad and the like remembered their baptisms and confirmation ceremonies with affection, this would be a real talking point in the Friday services in many mosques spread throughout a number of countries.

Even if it was perhaps not surprising that such speculation started, particularly given the age group of most of the passengers on board, thought the former sub-editor, it's hard to see how the shipboard grapevine could keep it going around considering the makeup of neighbourhoods in the United Kingdom at present, and the inclusive religious education programme followed in that country's schools for a good time now.

Perhaps the spreaders of the conjecture chose to notice just the Alberts, Rosalies and Valentinos and to turn a convenient blind eye to the Sultanrajs, Rakiprakashes, and Virajs. Mr Napier, shaking his head at the thought, picked up his book and opened it at the bookmark. No doubt to many of them it was more comfortable that way.

A roar went up and a thousand Union Jacks waved.

— CHAPTER 4 —

Walking Forward

Every morning the Third Officer announced the ship's position, giving the present latitude and longitude, then adding the distance to some spot in Dorset – Charminster, Corfe Mullen, Crossways or somewhere else about as far from Waipukurau, Waitakere, or Wanganui as one can get.

One of the passengers with an alternative affiliation, lurked in the passageway leading to the entry to the bridge and accosted the Officer at an opportune moment.

"Please could you, just once, mention Devon," Mr Newton Abbot pleaded, but the Officer was unmoved. So it was that each morning all aboard the cruise ship continued to be told how far they were from places such as Piddletrerthide or Puddletown.

With a further thirty days to go before she docked at her home port of Southampton – just a short bus ride from the much publicized Dorset – for most of those on board anticipation of a more exotic destination was high. Hong Kong lay dead ahead.

It had been a long stretch between ports. Six and a half days and 3261 nautical miles of water had passed by since the last stop with only the occasional glimpse of land in sight. For the dedicated shoppers aboard, it proved a particularly hard time. With only the shops on Promenade and Ellora decks to satisfy them, and with legends of the wonders of oriental markets in their minds, they were desperate to get ashore.

WALKING FORWARD

On the awaited day, as the liner cruised slowly into 'the fragrant harbour', the ship's Ports Advisor broadcast a running commentary over the public address system. Perhaps his purpose was to keep the retail-deprived ones occupied while the goal came closer at tantalizing slow pace. His efforts, however, did provide amusement for one passenger – male, sixty-something – standing at the rail.

"There are seven million people living in Hong Kong. Ninety eight per cent are Chinese," came the broadcast advice.

"Is that right," stated Mr Napier, in the tone used by Kiwis when informed by foreigners for the ten thousandth time that their country has a fair few sheep.

"There are about five hundred thousand Christians."

"That means about six and a half million Daoists." Dick Napier was quick on the uptake. The retired journalist and sub-editor had absorbed more than a few facts over his working career.

"As you can see, there are several other cruise ships also here in the harbour."

"Yes, I had spotted that. Hard to miss, I'd say." Dick was onto it again.

"There's a brown bird flying away on the port bow. Does anyone know what it is?" At this point Mr Napier offered a suggestion, best left unrecorded.

Passengers who had balcony cabins on the port side found themselves with a fine view of the Ocean Terminal building. Lyall Wellington reckoned he and Ngaio could just about reach out from their balcony and help themselves from the plates of those dining in the restaurant named inappropriately California Pizza Kitchen.

"That reminds me of a man on our last cruise," offered Jovial Joe, always ready to respond to such a promising lead-in line. "We'd just boarded and were unpacking our bags before the ship left port and got under way, when I heard the fellow from the cabin next door berating the steward in the passageway. 'Where's the purser's office?' he was demanding. 'I paid for a cabin with an ocean view, and all I can see is the bloody wharf.'" Jovial Joe paused, looking around at his audience for effect – he knew how to tell a story. "The steward, he was a little guy from Manila, Fernando his name was. Well, Fernando was quick, and right away he said 'Never mind the Purser, I can see to that for you, Sir. I'll have it fixed for you by the time you come back from dinner.' Sure enough, after dinner everyone on our side of the ship had a sea view. I reckon Fernando earned himself a good tip on that voyage."

There was a day and a half to spend in Hong Kong. For a good number on board that was a fact they were planning to take literally. Cash, travellers' cheques and credit cards were at the ready.

Rhoda Retail had taken time the day before to prepare. It took her the best part of an hour to ferret through every bag, purse and pocket in her stateroom in a search for notes and coins left over from previous ports. When the resulting hoard was sorted and counted Rhoda found that as well as pounds and euros she had currency in four different varieties of dollars. In addition, she was also the possessor of a good assortment of balboas, bolivars, Netherlands Antillean florins (understandably otherwise known as NAFIs), pa'angas and pesos – thanks to shop keepers and stall holders in a variety of places most of which she remembered only barely, who had accepted American dollars with eager efficiency but returned any change in the local equivalent while insisting they had no dollars in small notes. She surveyed the cash arranged in small piles on the bedspread and experienced a rare moment of altered perception. Rhoda was the owner of a medium size retail business, and hopeful proprietor of another when she returned from this holiday, otherwise referred to as 'buying trip' for tax purposes. She was on record as opposing any move to a change from the British pound to the euro – a position she had argued many times. Now, for the first time, she could appreciate the feelings of European arrivals in her own country and had a twinge of doubt about her former stated stance. Perhaps, it even occurred to her now she was on the other side of the counter, there should be even more sweeping reform. Imagine being able to go anywhere in the world and not have to deal with matters of currency exchange. This, however, was not the time for further examination of the issue – it would wait for her return to her place behind the cash register. She cut strips from the previous day's copy of *Britain Today,* which was delivered to the cabin daily, and wrapped each pile, labelling the rolls with the relevant currency and amount. Hong Kong, of all ports, would be the place to get it dealt with. First stop would be one of the money exchange booths she remembered from a past visit to be perched in the frontages of tightly-packed buildings. No doubt she'd receive nothing like a market rate for the coins, but if she could find someone willing to take them it would relieve her of a sizable package and its weight. That done, Rhoda reviewed her shopping list and readied her bags so as to be able to get an early start.

The gangway had barely breached the gap between the deck and the wharf when the charge of the heavy brigade of serious shoppers began. Having been commercially curtailed for the past six days, things had to give. The acknowledged heavyweights – sisters Savvy and Serial Shopper, Mrs Bling Festooned, Tania Trade, Sally Sale, Bert Buyer and Con Sumer – led the wave that swept through the stores in the Ocean Terminal out into Canton Road, then surged down Peking Road towards Nathan Road, before spilling out into further streets of downtown Kowloon.

Others with less concern for consumerism followed at more sedate pace to explore the attractions of mainland and island.

"It's eight years since we were last here in Hong Kong." Lynn Henderson spoke in the tone of wonderment she usually employed when watching the Animal Channel and wondering aloud about the way eels found their way from the creek near their property in West Auckland, all the way to the sea, then swam more than two thousand kilometres to Tonga to breed. "How could they have made such changes in so short a time?"

"Because they don't have to deal with our local body authority." Glen had locked horns with the planners in the council offices more times than he cared to think about.

Whatever the fact, there was agreement – in the time between visits the streets and shops in downtown Kowloon and the island's maritime rim had been transformed into monuments of modernity.

At least, that was the case till you looked upwards, Lynn realized after she had experienced some moments of nostalgia for the scenes she remembered. Above the glitzy façades that housed the premises of the world's top fashion houses – some

WALKING FORWARD

so exclusive she had never heard of them – she could see evidence that the old buildings remained, with crowded floors rising into the jumbled skyline. Exploring further, the Kiwi couple found that away from the harbour rim it was clear that the former Hong Kong still existed. Narrow streets of little shops and local markets continued to cater for the needs of the Special Region's residents. Worshippers still offered incense and petitioned the deities in busy backstreet temples, and sounds of chanting children wafted from within the walls of neighbourhood schools.

If the spenders on board were anxious to hit the shops, the locals were equally ready to assist them to do it. Many of those manning the stores had also been transformed it seemed. In parts of Peking Road one could be excused for confusing it with Colaba Causeway. Over the intervening years there must have been mass immigration to Hong Kong from India, and as many Indian as Chinese accents now clamoured for their attention.

"I thought we were in Mumbai next week." Glen came back on board on day one a little earlier than anticipated in order to escape being asked for the twenty-fourth time if he wanted a new watch, for the twelfth time if he'd like to be fitted for a suit and, on turning down those resistible enticements, receiving numerous offers of discounts on further items of tailoring. Under the circumstances, Lynn was happy to bring him back. Not only had she refused countless invitations for her to purchase handbags, jewellery, cameras and cell phones, but she'd had to intervene on occasions when she felt that Glen didn't appear quick enough to turn down the many offers of massages.

Mrs Bling Festooned also appeared to have met her match – a first in her experience.

"I've always said shopping is cheaper and more effective than a psychiatrist, but after today I think I need one."

Happily, she soon found a solution. Considering that any time taken up by dealing with touts in the main streets added up to hours not profitably spent, she decided to restrict her area of operation to the Ocean Terminal where assistants mainly waited politely at their counters till approached. The decision proved no real hardship since the complex accommodated more than seven hundred shops.

One of them, not far from the passage from ship to shore, featured a colourful window display with a couple of long-eared furry creatures cavorting by means of hidden mechanics across a flower-bestrewed meadow. The bucolic scene was set off by a large sign that read "Spring is in the Hare". Even Bling believed it was absurd.

"Harebrained," corrected Mr Festooned.

The Australians and New Zealanders also viewing the display, thought of the damage that had been dealt to their countries by members of the Leporidae and Lagomorpha families – a matter of incalculable cost – so were even less impressed, and mentally aimed shotguns at the leaping leporids as they passed by the offending window. Bling, who had nothing against bunnies herself but had done some research on the Chinese calendar as she was planning to purchase an appropriate pendant for a grand niece, gave good justification to support the general judgement.

"It's not even the year of the rabbit," she said.

Before the ship departed, however, she had reason to look upon the display with somewhat more benign eyes.

Other passengers, who ventured further afield into the

suburbs of the city, had different stories to tell. Several of them involved the unfailing courtesy of locals when asked to give directions and answer questions, the helpfulness often enhanced with such delightful language –

"Go this way, down escalator, walking forward, turn left."

Cousins Ms Coolangatta and Ms Melbourne decided to make their own way around the city, including a visit to the latter's home state's namesake, Victoria Peak, but soon found themselves a little confused. They were consulting a map, turning it first one way then the other, when a local woman came to their rescue then willingly went out of her way to help them reach their destination.

On day two, the Hendersons avoided the shopping streets around the Ocean Terminal and came back marvelling once more, this time at how efficiently thousands of people were moved from place to place in minutes by way of the expanded mass rapid transit system. Lynn's wistful comment regretting the lack of something comparable at home – "why not rail-tracks down the length of the motorways?" – resulted in a reprise of her husband's condemnation of their own local body authority.

A recent innovation could be accessed without even stepping off the ship. Each evening, as the passengers were informed, the city turns on a spectacle of laser lighting, billed as *A Symphony of Lights*, from dozens of the tall buildings that line the harbour. This "wonderland of dancing lights set to music", as it is recommended enthusiastically by the Hong Kong Tourism Board, "a stunning multimedia show that is best viewed from the harbour itself!" was a bonus for some. Those who had balcony cabins on the starboard side found they had exclusive boxes from which to watch.

On the first evening in port, the open decks were crowded. Right on the billed time of 8 p.m. the promised show began with every colour of lights playing on the surfaces of the variously shaped buildings. On and off, zig-zag up and down, star, and revolve. Beams of bright colours reached upwards piercing the night sky. At the same time ferries and floating restaurants decorated with strings of flashing and static lights crisscrossed the water adding to the sight.

On evening two in port, the starboard decks were even more crowded as diners left the restaurants to see the spectacle recommended by those who had watched the night before. On and off, zig-zag up and down, star, and revolve. The display had barely started when Mr Liverpool-Lancs snorted, "It were better last night," and stumped off. Mrs LL followed a few steps, then returned.

"'E's a daft apath," she said, settling herself back at the rail.

At the end of day one Ms Coolangatta who found the population of her home town, combined as it was with its twin town Tweed Heads, was at the upper edge of her comfort zone, and wasn't looking forward to another day in the midst of the seven million residents plus that day's share of the annual thirty million visitors likely to be adding to the clamour of the streets. Her cousin, on the other hand, was buoyed by her eventual conquest of the city's bus system and favoured further exploration. Ms Melbourne had heard about Stanley market from Tania Trade whose travelling companion Sally Sale found day one brought on a relapse of the cough she thought she'd shaken off. A visit to the medical centre, Sally decided very regretfully, then a quieter day, was all she could cope with on day two – there were more ports coming up that required her full strength. Tania, however, given that the market was a good distance away on the far side of Hong Kong island was dubious she could make it on her own. She had entertained no illusions about her abilities with an unfamiliar map since an encounter with the diagram of the London underground had proved beyond her comprehension when she'd visited that city. The solution was simple – Tania and Briar Melbourne would team up for the day. With Briar's navigational expertise combined with Tania's bargaining skills, a trip to Stanley Bay would no doubt prove a profitable use of the day.

Caroline Coolangatta was of course more than welcome to join them, the pair assured her, but while her cousin and Sally had been coming to the arrangement Caroline realized she could be free to follow up on something that just a half-hour before had seemed out of the question. She looked into Anderson's lounge on Promenade deck and found Dick Napier in the same spot she'd left him after a discussion they'd had a short time earlier about his plan for the day.

"Would you like a companion on your trip to Lantau Island?" she asked, not meeting his eye in case her offer was about to be turned down. "It would be good to get out of the city, and the climb would do me good."

Dick, caught off guard by the unexpected offer, failed to find the right words of refusal so the arrangement was made.

At this stop on the full round-the-world itinerary, more people who had been forced through circumstances to book only as far as this destination, packed their bags and made their way to the airport. 'Basil', coming back on board to see suitcases waiting outside a good proportion of doors along the passageway and a new batch of passengers finding their way around with the aid of small maps of the ship, was in his element. This made him a member of the old hands club, and he was quick to help out with directions.

"Carmen's lounge – go down two floors and right down that end."

"Are you quite sure, dear?" queried 'Sybil' as the enquiring couple disappeared down the stairs. "Carmen's seven aft, isn't it?"

"Ah…" 'Basil' was never fazed for long. "Never mind, they'll find it. And they look as though they need the exercise."

A day and a half in the economic Eden of the orient had those who wanted to stretch the spending power of the pound working hard. They returned from the happy hunting grounds at frequent intervals on both days bearing bags and boxes, sometimes wheeling new travel cases that looked as though they were already laden. A quick stop aboard for lunch, and they were off again.

At a table near the Pennant Bar a glass-holding group from the northern counties competed for the most accosted award.

"Six offers of watches, seven to have clothes tailored to suit either madam or gentleman…"

"You were lucky. Eleven for t' watches, twelve for tailoring, and 'nother dozen for ladies' handbags."

"That were nothin'. After gettin' away from the small stuff I were bothered by three men trying to sell me diamonds. I ducked into a nearby shop to get away and came out a half hour later with three pair of new eyeglasses."

"We had it really tough. First we had to get away from twenty-two people beating us over the head with handbags, then we were set upon by a gang of gorillas who tried to rope us

WALKING FORWARD

and drag us into a place where they were offering massages…"

"Massages – luxury!"

On the second day, barely an hour before they were due in the dining room for dinner, Mrs Bling Festooned experienced a flash of inspiration, closely followed by a flush of frustration that the significance of something she'd seen on her morning foray had escaped her till this time. What if, she shuddered at the thought, the realization had been delayed till the following day when they were in the South China Sea and out of shopping range – then their Emma's forthcoming walk down the aisle would be ruined for the lack of the most perfect neck ornament her gran could ever hope to find. Grasping her bag, which was always kept prepared and at hand, she leapt to the door of her stateroom uttering an uncharacteristically brief explanation that was missed entirely by Mr F who was anticipating the climax point that his seven centimetre thick paperback novel was at long last approaching. Seventy-five minutes later when the steward entered the room in order to replace the barely used towels for the second time that day and leave the customary, though unneeded, chocolate on the pillows, he found Mr F fast asleep.

"I'm sorry, I thought you'd be out. You're not at dinner?" he asked, rather unnecessarily.

Over the next half-hour Mr F hurried around searching each of the decks in turn, checking and rechecking the dining room and the regular meeting spots, in growing fear of being berated for missing yet another important instruction. There was no sign of his wife. At the same time, Bling was completing further laps of the various floors of the Ocean Terminal and also growing more frantic as she looked for the passageway that led back to the ship. Just as she was about to resort to asking for assistance she rounded a corner and a welcome sight met her eyes. A pair of bunnies bobbed up and down beside a board proclaiming that spring was in the hare. A sense of both relief and triumph washed over her. Bling was confident she knew her way from here. She went past the window with the designer shoes. Yes, next was the display of leopard-print flight luggage she'd stopped to look at and, tarr-ah, there it was – the exit manned by a crew-member checking passenger cards. Bling showed her identity card and crossed the walkway to the ship just under two hours after she'd left.

"It's not very difficult," said Mr F when they were reunited, and he was feeling very relieved it wasn't he who was doing the apologizing this time. "There are overhead notices leading you to the ship terminal. And didn't you see those plaques showing a ship that are set into the floor?"

"I navigate by the shops," responded Bling.

Dick Napier and Caroline Coolangatta arrived back on board a little after Bling's reappearance. They made straight for their respective staterooms to shower and change, then met again in the Orangery for dinner. In response to Caroline's questions, Dick told her about his hometown. During the day they had established a few points in common between their places of origin. Both were situated on the east coasts of their respective countries; and though the small town on the southern rim of Queensland that she called home had only a few thousand residents if she crossed the street into the New South Wales city of Tweed Heads, as she did every day to work, the populations of each were comparable. Neither of them, each realized much later, had made any reference to a partner. Each of them was happy to leave it that way.

"More Kiwis?"

The ex-newsman was describing the waterfront stretch that was his familiar territory – tall Norfolk pines, steep shingle beach, a row of tourist amenities – when a voice interrupted. Ngaio and Lyall Wellington stopped by the table and introduced themselves, then Lynn and Glen Henderson who were following. After a few minutes Caroline excused herself and the five New Zealanders moved aft to the Pennant Bar where they could see ferries and other small boats crossing the harbour as they talked. They were all pleased to find fellow Kiwis on the passenger list, and even more relieved to learn the others were on board for the rest of the voyage to Southampton. As Glen put it, it was good to be able to greet someone with the phrase "How are you going?" and not have them answer confusedly "by ship."

A little after that, Briar Melbourne and Tania Trade made it back up the gangway, the former helping the latter with her evening's haul of plastic bags. Tania had found during the afternoon that Briar could indeed find her way without mishap, even without resorting to turning the map upside down, so had pressed her into a further trip to the night markets in Temple Street. As a consolation intended for her usual shopping mate, one of the plastic bags held a shoulder bag purporting to be a Gucci original, purchased after what Tania considered a smart piece of bargaining for fifty-eight Hong Kong dollars. Briar deposited the pile of plastic bags at the door to Tania's cabin and made her escape while the other was locating her key card. It wasn't as though she regretted acting as her new friend's guide for the day – she'd seen more of the city as a result – but she was determined it was a one-off.

By the time the bow thrusters moved the ship away from the berth at midnight it seemed to Rich and Liz standing at the rails on Lido deck aft that the ship was lying much lower in the water than when it cruised into the harbour the morning before. As they stood standing shoulder to shoulder watching the lights of the city recede they pondered whether the extra water displaced would threaten the small islands in Victoria Harbour.

The liner steamed back into the South China Sea then turned her bow to the west. With another month of the voyage to go, there were a further seven seas and more exotic ports to come before heading into the European spring.

Meanwhile, all aboard were reliably informed, the ship was 6071 nautical miles from Dodds Cross in Dorset and closing.

A couple of long-eared furry creatures cavorting by means of hidden mechanics.

— CHAPTER 5 —

Too Many Ports?

Three further days on the ocean lay ahead. With several changes of bearing – southwest, to west, to northwest – the South China Sea morphed into the Gulf of Thailand.

The cruising crowd settled again to rest, recuperate and regain some energy for the next stop, making the most of their enforced captivity for a further three days. The ship was noticeably quieter than on the previous sector as by now the Sydney cough had largely abated. All the deck-chairs and sun-loungers were occupied for the full extent of the daylight hours on the Sun deck – referred to as "melanoma deck" by Ngaio Wellington who also wondered aloud if the occupants had never heard of the hole in the ozone layer, a much publicized topic down-under.

For destination cruisers, however, sea days are the intervals between ports. Many of those who considered themselves in this group filled in the time on the move as much as possible.

On their first day on board Lyall and Ngaio had spotted a notice on the promenade deck that stated 3.2 times around equals one mile, and had paced out several miles each day they weren't ashore. Since their temporary home was effectively a British ship, despite its registration in Bermuda and ownership based in Miami Florida, they found the imperial system still reigned unchallenged, so they and other passengers who meas-ured in metrics had to do the maths. They got to recognize those who walked the mile regularly in an effort to fend off the years and the kilos – pounds for the Brits. The fits and would-be-fits strode out suitably clad in neat sneakers, the not so nimble got around in a less lively fashion wearing a variety of footwear that, to Ngaio's concern, included heeled scuffs and jandals. The really serious exercisers were not to be seen – they were in the gym, suitably togged, hard at work on the treadmill, or straining at the rowing machines.

The nine passenger decks and the ship's overall length of 270 metres ensured there was a fair amount of walking to be done even for those who were not intent on working off the kilojoules. The Wellingtons, who were accommodated in a forward cabin, felt they had an advantage in being forced to walk the length of the vessel to the restaurants aft, though not all around them agreed. As a further aid to counteracting the effects of the frequent and copious meals served in the dining room they made a habit of avoiding the elevators and taking the stairs. This usually had the additional benefit of being faster as the lifts invariably stopped at each floor, and those entering or exiting were likely to be assisted by a walking stick, zimmer frame or wheelchair.

The count of the infirm aboard increased by one on the second day out from Hong Kong. Ngaio Wellington was on lap five of the promenade track and about to overtake a younger woman when she had to break her stride and take a wide step to the left to avoid the falling figure in front.

"Are you all right?" she stopped to ask.

Mrs Brisbane raised herself and winced as she straightened her leg.

"I've hurt my ankle," she said. "It was my thong."

TOO MANY PORTS?

Ngaio removed the twisted piece of rubber from Mrs Brisbane's foot. As a maternity nurse the lower extremities were not her forte but she didn't need any specialist training to be able to pinpoint the cause.

"You've gone over on your jandal," she said.

"It was my thong," repeated the other.

In Kiwi idiom, a thong is a garment worn right in the area of Ngaio's expertise – one that she herself avoided for reasons of comfort. Her knickers were chosen for their very disinclination to ride up and become lodged between the buttocks, and she couldn't imagine how others apparently found underwear designed to disappear in such a disconcerting manner at all preferable. However, cross-Tasman interaction and the existence of an Australian branch of the family meant that Ngaio was not under any misapprehension for more than a moment. She made the mental translation and concentrated her attention on Mrs B's ankle rather than the lower abdomen. One of the crew hurried towards them and took in the situation at a glance.

"Flip-flops," she diagnosed, "they're not the best for walking – we get quite a few of these mishaps."

Another member of the entertainment staff arrived to help and the two crew members, with Mrs Brisbane between them, made their way in the direction of the nearest door. Ngaio was left holding the broken jandal, or the broken thong, or the broken flip-flop – or whatever it was called.

It seemed it was in the company's interest to keep the able ones fit for as long as possible, so a programme of exercise was laid on for those who liked to work at their leisure. Even those who gave the various mechanical devices in the gym a miss were prompted and abetted by the full schedule offered for a day at sea. Lynn Henderson consulted the advertised programme and found she could start with "Walk a Mile With a Smile" at 8 a.m., progress through a session of pilates, move on to social tennis, line dancing class, a deck quoits competition, shuffleboard competition, dancing class covering tango, mambo and salsa, then compete in tennis and table tennis competitions, yet still fit in a lecture on "Understanding Your Metabolism". And that was just before lunch.

The afternoon brought the possibility of a game of cricket, more deck quoits and table tennis, social football, and another dance class – ballroom this time. If all or any of that was not to her taste, a golf pro on board could help her with her game in the practice nets or the electronic simulator. If she'd been of a mind to bring a set of clubs along with her, or failing that if she hired them on board, she could take advantage of golfing shore excursions at thirteen of the twenty-eights ports the ship visited on this voyage.

Even if a person engaged in only a few of the organized activities they should be nicely warmed up for a full evening of dancing and partying.

One of the youngest and most attractive women on board was about half the average age of the full complement of cruisers. She was also the thinnest. She was often to be seen power-walking up multiple flights of stairs, without the slightest hint of panting or pausing at the landings. As she did so, she encouraged others to match her pace – a tad insensitively given the differences in ages.

"Come on ladies," she called out to those gathered in front of the elevators, "use the stairs – it's good for you."

TOO MANY PORTS?

"How do you keep so thin?" asked Mrs Chubb, resting for a breath mid flight on the aft staircase as Ann O'Rexia passed her at a faster rate of knots than a tea clipper with a force six tail wind.

"I don't eat and I go to the gym," replied Ms O reaching the top and disappearing at a jog down an adjacent corridor. Mrs Chubb and Mrs Panting Heavily continued pulling themselves to the top, cast a brief glance upwards to the next floor and headed to the lifts.

Another group of passengers who reasoned that the very nature of a cruise, either in intent or definition, was in direction opposition to the idea of effort, settled for the leisure alternative. Some became members of the lobster club by settling almost permanently on the sun-loungers on Lido deck.

A couple from County Durham best illustrated the two approaches. Emma ordered her days with a serious list of commitments recorded each day in a small notebook, which she consulted frequently as she moved from one to another. When two or more selected activities conflicted she attempted to switch between venues, so could often be seen hurrying between the Curzon Theatre and the Playhouse, or the Oasis Spa and Masquerade. Her husband Dave, most often found around the Terrace Pool or in their cabin, had quite different habits.

"I'm vertical to eat, horizontal to sleep. Most of the time I'm horizontal."

Not all passengers considered themselves destination cruisers, however. With the coastline of Thailand approaching one of the all-the-way-rounders, clearly a card-carrying member of club recumbent, expressed some dissatisfaction with the itinerary. To Ngaio Wellington's question "Are you enjoying the cruise so far?" the man she had addressed offered a considered response.

"Yes," he didn't sound completely convinced, "but there are too many ports."

Ngaio cast a look at the chair across from her and found it well occupied. Though the lounge chairs in Carmen's were ample in size there was very little gap between the body of the man and its sides, and its seat was barely visible under the one that covered it. The chair and its occupant were well matched, she decided, both could be described as well padded. From their first days aboard she had noticed a correlation between the amounts of food piled onto plates in the self-service Orangery and the size of the bottoms on the dining chairs. The higher the mound of food, the more the overhang. As the days passed, and she observed further, she realized her first assessment had been a trifle simplistic. The equation needed to factor in the relative kilojoule and glycaemic index ratings of the offerings laid out in the various serveries. From then on, along with Ann O'Rexia though the two did not meet, Ngaio avoided all but the salad bar at lunchtime, and didn't settle for long in one place.

An exception she allowed herself was the time spent sitting in Masquerade some afternoons. This nightclub area on the Promenade deck was billed as the place to go for late night action but Ngaio, as an early riser, didn't appreciate any activity that took place in the extra late hours. She and Lyall headed off to their stateroom each evening after the second show in the Curzon theatre. On sea days, however, Masquerade assumed its alternative role as venue for the art auctions.

TOO MANY PORTS?

The fine arts presented an area that had always interested Ngaio, but had been relegated to the one-day-when-I-have-more-time part of her life. Before she had left home, in her months of preparation for the tour of Europe to come, she had sought advice on the mustn't-miss museums and galleries. One of the first things she noticed on boarding was the amount of artwork that hung not only in the area designated the art gallery, but also on every available wall throughout the public areas. Within days of joining the cruise she was delighted to find that by means of the art lectures and the accompanying auctions she could kick-start her knowledge and appreciation of the artists and their work while on board ship. Already she was finding she could pick a Picasso from a Pino at twenty paces, and had managed to insert a few educated comments into dinner conversations – at least, she was confident they were more educated than she could have managed pre-embarkation. She now identified specific places on their Europe itinerary as "Dali country" or "Monet's Normandy".

Lyall was also taking the opportunity to extend his knowledge during this forty-six day time-out period of his life, by going to the series of lectures offered on sea days, though he thought of it more as entertainment rather than life enhancement. After sitting through the first dozen he adapted his opinion somewhat. It was good if you were a Brit and you were interested in the history of the empire's military, wars, or its shipping and aircraft industries. There was also the drawback that Lyall had advanced through the levels of the Toastmasters educational programme. He held the Distinguished Toastmaster Award and could not avoid making judgement. The elderly male speakers, he had to conclude, had an appalling lack of presentation skills and an even worse understanding of their supporting technology.

"Then don't go," advised Ngaio after hearing yet again about the use of a power-point display to show a single illustration. Lyall continued to attend but took a book along as well.

Caroline Coolangatta was another who jumped at the chance to benefit from the days at sea. She and Briar Melbourne discovered the language classes and agreed to take advantage of them, since they were free. But which of the two, French or Spanish, should they choose, since neither felt confident of challenging themselves to the extent of taking up both? Briar reasoned she would find either useful in her work as receptionist for a rental car company, and Caroline vacillated as to which would hold her in greater stead during her forthcoming bus tour through Europe. Both of them would be useful, since she planned to visit both countries in the three weeks following the end of the voyage. From schooldays some decades before, boosted un peu by occasional study of a phrase book, she could claim some knowledge of French, though she was quick to admit "mon français est très pauvre" when threatened by the possibility of any test. She could use the sea day classes to brush up, or she could try to become equally inefficient in Spanish. The ship's itinerary included a stop in Barcelona, and she was looking forward to that particularly. Finally she chose the second option, reasoning even a few words of Spanish might help to keep her out of trouble – if it didn't prove to be the cause of getting her into it in the first place.

While her Queensland cousin was still deliberating, Briar came to a quick decision. Since she could arrange only limited time away from work, her cruise was ending at Singapore. That meant she could fit in just a few lessons. It was better that she use them to build on the two years of French she had taken in secondary school – not that she remembered much, but there was always the hope something would resurface. The pair agreed to attend separate sessions – Briar taking français in the morning and Caroline going to español in the afternoon.

The Australian cousins didn't reach agreement on another matter, but chose not to make it an issue between them. As they had grown up in separate states and spent limited time together during childhood, the decision to travel together was based more on expediency than a particularly close bond.

When Briar first suggested a night at the casino, Caroline's eyebrows lifted in surprise. As she understood it, her uncle Caleb was even stricter than her own father about such pastimes. In fact – she searched back nearly a decade and a half in her memory – didn't she remember her aunt at the funeral blaming his death on the chill he received picketing in the rain against the opening of the first such den of iniquity in the city?

"I've never been to a casino," Briar explained, "and if I did it at home, it would be bound to get back to Mum – there's no point in upsetting her."

Caroline understood that perfectly. All the same, the suggestion wasn't one she wanted to take up.

Ms Melbourne didn't push it. With this trip stretching her budget, given the fact she was making an effort to get her mortgage paid off, she didn't want to put herself in the position of losing money either. She just wanted to sample the experience, and any trips to the Riviera or Monaco to observe the real thing were only to be dreamed about, for a few years at least. She had passed through the Monte Carlo Club, billed as the ship's "own slice of sophisticated glamour from the Riviera", on the way along Promenade deck to Carmen's many times. She'd noticed that most evenings, and even more so during the day, the gaming tables were not heavily patronised and staff were standing around waiting. The slot machines did somewhat better, with rows of people sitting and feeding them hour after hour from super-sized paper pots of coins. That didn't appeal to Ms Melbourne, but there was something magnetic about a spinning wheel, and croupiers pushing stacks of coloured chips across to dinner-suit clad players. In her mind they all looked like Daniel Craig. A notice in the entertainment guide gave her an idea.

There were six people, three women and three men, who showed up for the learn-how-to-play session. The croupier who greeted them was dressed neatly in a waistcoat. He didn't display much enthusiasm. No doubt he had done this many times before, answered the same questions, and knew the odds of payback were low. A barman appeared and handed out the promised glass of champagne, and the six seated themselves around the Blackjack table for lesson one. Two more quick lessons followed.

An hour later, her head a confusion of the rules and techniques of Blackjack, Roulette and Three Card Poker, Briar and the others rose to go.

"Now you know how to play, can we expect to see you all here?" asked their tutor.

A couple replied positively. They must have caught on to the different hand movements better than Briar had – she was concerned she'd signal to be hit with another card when she should stand, and the only bet she'd consider making on the

TOO MANY PORTS?

roulette table would be a simple choice between black or red.

"What about you?" The croupier was looking at Briar.

"Perhaps," she answered. Unlikely, she thought. When she had sat at the gaming tables with chips in hand, she'd had a sense of her father jogging her elbow, and a vision of her mortgage payments disappearing. The waistcoated one, no doubt an expert in reading body language and even the finest facial movements, turned back towards the positive pair. As Briar moved away she heard his comment.

"Most people just come to these sessions for the free champagne – we don't see them again."

— CHAPTER 6 —

Looking Alike

The coastline of Thailand was drawing closer and the professional shoppers, having been forced to rest from their favourite occupation for all but a day and a half of the last eleven, were raring to go. But go where?

Sisters, Savvy and Serial Shopper, were in a dilemma. Serial consulted her list of items to be purchased on behalf of others and found that a requested item was to be sought at a specified shop in Bangkok's Siam Centre. Savvy, though, had done some research and learned that the capital was about 110 kilometres from where they'd be docked at Laem Chabang. Given the notoriety of Thai traffic, to sit on a coach for several hours in either direction, she argued, was not a good use of their talents. Bert Buyer agreed. He had begun his retail career with a market stall selling almost anything, but particularly household utensils, then moved up in several steps – from a small backstreet shop to being the owner of a moderate empire of three shops in the main streets of three smaller cities. This impressive background marked him as a senior in the world of merchandising. Bert was deferred to by a good number of the bargain-hunters brigade.

The alternative, a trip to Pattaya less than half an hour's shuttle away, was judged a better choice by a good number of the shoppers. Sure, they'd heard about the main attractions of Bangkok in the pre-port briefing and, yes, the buildings and

LOOKING ALIKE

gardens of the Royal Palace complex looked wonderful, and the Temple of the Dawn undeniably stunning, but the fact was they wouldn't have long enough at them to do them justice anyway. In that case, they reasoned, they'd have to come back another time to see them. Con Sumer, a retired plumber from Portsmouth, was equally as definite and persuasive as Bert.

Whatever their destination, the inveterate spenders changed their pounds, their American dollars and any remaining Hong Kong dollars into baht which, at an exchange rate of more than 50 to the pound caused at least a brace of Brits to return to their cabins to collect their wheeled shopping bags. When the ship was alongside the dock at Laem Chabang the hardy band waved goodbye to one of their sworn squad, Sally Sale, who was pronounced not fit enough for a day ashore. Sally's chest infection had lingered longer than most, and it was only on doctor's orders that she didn't join the rush for the gangway. She stood on her balcony, starboard forward, waving forlornly – the cannula by means of which she was receiving daily doses of antibiotic still inserted in her forearm. To her travelling companion, Tania Trade, to whom Sally had given frequent counsel, "Anyone who thinks money can't buy happiness doesn't know where to go shopping," it was a deeply moving moment. But a moment only, as Tania found a single seat on a departing coach and turned her full attention to the task ahead.

A series of small problems presented when the shuttle service deposited the early-bird buyers in the town. The large hotel in North Beach Road, which was the drop-off point, proved a prominent landmark for pick-up later in the day, but the position provided an immediate disappointment for the lack of perceivable shops nearby. Serial Shopper on hitting the pavement protested loudly.

"I told you we should have gone into Bangkok."

Savvy accosted a pair of passing locals, two look-alike young women wearing Armani and Versace camisole tops which, given the reputation of the local manufacturing industry, were most probably look-alikes too.

"Where are the shops?" she demanded, apparently taking it for granted that the Thai schooling system had already bowed to the pressure of acknowledging English as the language of international commerce. Fortunately, for whatever reason but more likely as result of language lessons given to the local lasses by the Shopper sisters' visiting countrymen, she was rewarded with smiles and hands pointing southwards.

"That way."

Serial and Savvy set out without further delay, but more disappointments soon became apparent. A little distance on they came to a site of excavation fronted by an immense banner promising the opening of "Asia's Largest Natural Beachfront Shopping Complex" with a date yet ten months in the future. After a longing look, and sighs of regret, they passed on.

Some minutes later, Serial and Savvy, attended by a retinue of mercantile middleweights, reached the first shopping mall. They raced to the door to find it locked. The mild irritation experienced when deposited by the ship's shuttle some minutes walk from the central shopping district now escalated when it was realized that the present predicament was due to even more inconsiderate cruise planning. After three days at sea they had reached land, at a renowned place of retail rapture, on the very day the nation was holding its parliamentary election.

"I thought they had a king," wailed Serial, apparently not

LOOKING ALIKE

appreciating that monarchies were not incompatible with democracy even though the sisters were born and bred in Essex.

According to Thai law, the success of the electoral process was to be encouraged by ensuring that the population had increased opportunity to cast their votes – hence, shops were instructed to open later on this one day of the year. With no choice in the matter, the habituated buying brigade settled themselves on the steps outside the entrance to the mall to wait for opening time.

That was not the only bad news to come, as the statute-makers also decreed that attendance at the ballot boxes would be boosted even further by a ban on alcohol. In addition to the delayed opening of shops and saloons, those who had left the comfort of the various bars aboard ship now found they were faced by the horrors of a dry day.

This was a double blow to the couples Brighton and Wolverhampton who brought up the back of the bunch. Billy and Willy had planned to park themselves at a beach bar for the day, relying on their wives to pour them back onto the shuttle home when Belinda had bought the Bencharong porcelain commissioned by a collector friend, and Wilma had selected the length of silk in exactly the right shade of mauve for the mother of the bride outfit needed in September. Plus, if possible, handbag and shoes to match. The two men were disgruntled at the thought of supping soft drinks all day, but shuffled over the road to sit on striped deck-chairs beneath red white and blue beach umbrellas emblazoned with the words "Bangkok Hospital Pattaya". From this vantage point they could watch the various activities taking place in the waters of the bay, respond to offers of food, cold drinks, sarongs, and all manner of consumer goods at the rate of three per minute. Or they could observe the passing parade along the promenade walk.

"All the couples are holding hands," commented Billy, taking the straw out of his glass of cola so he could get direct access to the rim of the glass. "Good idea, that. You let go of a woman's hand and she shops."

"There ya go," said Willy, indicating a couple walking past, "see that man? I reckon he's no younger than we are."

"I've been thinking that," responded Billy. "There've been a few who'd give me a couple of years, I was thinking."

"And the women, they'd be…"

"Girls," said Billy, "Our Paul's eldest 'd be about the age of that one there in the brown tights."

"They're all European men, and Thai girls."

"None of 'em look very happy, I was thinking."

The pair sat silently for a few minutes.

"Ya reckon ya'd be up to it?"

Billy's eyes were still on the retreating form of the girl scuffing along in gold sandals.

"If that one had fair hair," he said, "it could almost be our Katie. Nah. It wouldn't be worth the grief."

"Me neither."

The two looked across the street to where the mall doors were finally swinging open to allow entry to the newly activated band of buyers. They settled down again and ordered another round of colas.

Bert Buyer, meanwhile, had managed to deposit his wife with the mall crowd and strike out on his own. Away from the seafront the town was buzzing with local life. On all five levels of a jam-packed IT centre it was hard to move, and even harder

LOOKING ALIKE

to hear as each store selling audio gear blasted out its selection of music. Bert progressed through a whole floor of cell-phone shops on his way to an upper level where he found his goal in the racks of look-alike computer software. He entered, pulling a list from his pocket. Some hours later when he had retraced his route through the now-busy streets and found the waterfront, he came across Billy and Willy, still at their beachside spot, and still distressingly sober. He put down two large carry bags and called for a coke.

"No sign of the girls yet?" he asked.

"Nah – what ya got there?"

"Computer stuff."

"Ya inta that?"

"Not me. But I'll sell it when we get home. This lot oughta pay for all she's spending today."

Meanwhile, back at the boat, Sally Sale found the day was not completely lost. In order to accommodate cases such as her own – those who for one reason or another could not venture into the town areas – a group of enterprising local merchants set up a makeshift bazaar, shipside on the dock. The stalls were amply supplied with shirts, shoes, shawls, and scarves lavishly embroidered with birds and elephants. Sally set about gratefully rewarding their thoughtfulness. In the dining room that night she appeared looking like an extra from *The King and I*.

Back into the Gulf of Thailand – referred to as the Gulf of Siam by some of the old-timers who either hadn't caught on, or refused to be converted – the ship continued on a course south-south-east.

They settled themselves on the steps outside the entrance to the mall to wait for opening time.

— CHAPTER 7 —

Hand it to the Brits

This time there was just a single day between ports – the ideal in cruise itinerary planning. On such days the most active shore-goers, whether their choice is swinging a five-iron at yet another new golf course, climbing to a vantage point to take in a wide view of the area, or beating a path around the shopping streets, have a chance to recharge their energy to peak capacity without it having time to deplete again. Even those who elect to sit in a tour-bus at each stop get a break between local tour guides. This is an advantage, as the most entertaining some of the guides get is when they remind their passengers at the end of the trip how well they and the bus driver have looked after them; and the most animated they become is when they stand saying farewell, their hands at the ready to receive a top-up to their fee.

Just as important on a day between ports is the chance to catch up on clothes washing, especially the items designed for wearing on days ashore. It was abundantly clear to everyone on board that the ship's laundry offered a great service – all the crew-members, particularly the officers in spotless white uniforms, always appeared kitted out in impeccable fashion, and the table cloths in the dining rooms were whisked away between sittings at the mere hint of a spot. No doubt some of the passengers could afford or be willing to have their garments dry-cleaned or laundered for the advertised fees, but for the majority of the passengers the preferred option was doing it oneself.

On many cruise ships this is done by rinsing out one's singlets, shirts, skirts and shorts each day and hanging them in the bathroom where the air-conditioning assists the drying process. This ship, though, being designed for the British market, catered for its guests by providing two self-service laundries. At almost any time the dedicated spaces on Arcadia and Canberra decks were meeting places that were patronized as well as some of the lounge areas, though not as enthusiastically as the deck-chairs on a good day. In order to minimize any inconvenience to cabins nearby operating hours were set, and as the morning opening time neared a line of people toting bulging bags with sleeves and legs protruding waited to claim first the washers then the dryers. Later in the day, and particularly when the social schedule declared it was a formal night, it was the ironing boards that were fully employed. People waiting for their spin cycle to finish leaned against the machines and chatted. Those with more experience of the white-ware offered useful tips to others –

"That dryer's extra hot – I'd keep it set to medium if I were you."

"Did you get that soap powder at the shop? It's very expensive that way. Pick up a packet next time we're ashore."

Ngaio pushed open the door of the laundry on Canberra deck aft, holding a plastic bag of washing in each hand. The Wellingtons had packed as lightly as possible, and the summer-weight clothes they'd each worn the day before in Thailand had to do duty again tomorrow in Singapore. She was initially surprised to see nearly as many men as there were women attending to the task, and adjusted her preconceptions of British gender roles. These had been based mainly on two expatriate couples who were former neighbours. Tom, at number 21, had once told her in a confident tone while his wife looked on with a benign expression,

"I said to Eliza on the day we were wed, 'I make the big decisions, you make the small decisions' and that's the way it's always been."

On another occasion Gwen, who lived on the other side of the photinia hedge that separated the Wellingtons from the Chichesters, had regaled her with a lengthy and amusing account of the one time her Bennie had taken on the weekly wash, given that she was laid up under orders not to leave her bed and her mother-in-law was also 'poorly'.

"That's the one and only time he's been near the washing machine," said Gwen, "and I barred him from ever touching it again."

The first time Ngaio had visited the laundry this judgement seemed to be confirmed. Two women piling washing into adjacent machines were sharing their frustrations.

"I asked my husband to empty his pockets – now look what I find. There was this pen in his pocket all the time."

The second woman nodded, her several chins swaying sympathetically,

"Aye, they're not very good. We have to do for them, don't we?"

Now, however, Ngaio was surprised to find that, apart from herself, the room contained males only. As she loaded a vacant machine she observed men who were lads during the Battle of Britain attending to the tasks. One was bending to pull a load from the washers, another folding his into a basket, and a third was running an iron over the pleats in his dinner shirt with acceptable expertise. In the face of this evidence she was only too happy to revise her opinions. Okay, she resolved, it was time for a talk with Lyall.

There was another thing the Brits did very well, the Wellingtons and the Hendersons agreed over lunch. The couples had now been aboard for half the forty-six days of their journey from one side of the globe to the other, and three weeks in the company of these northern residents had confirmed several conclusions. Observation of behaviour aboard revealed that, without a shadow of doubt, the art of queuing had reached its peak in the United Kingdom. Lines, short to lengthy, seemed to form spontaneously around the ship whenever three or more people arrived at the same destination at any given time. Couples wanting a table in Café Bordeaux at lunchtime waited in order till escorted by the maitre d' to an available space. Passengers wanting to ask a range of questions of long-suffering staff manning the reception desk on Formosa deck stood behind the roped barrier until called. Even those anxious to get ashore for fear of coaches departing without them, or shops closing early, took their turn. Of course people queued in New Zealand too, but it seemed to the Kiwis that the lines they encountered on board each day were more regimented. Perhaps, suggested Glen, it was to do with the countries' different military traditions. He'd heard stories from his father and grandfather, who had served in the second and first world wars respectively, about how over-officious officers trained in the British tradition had been brought down a peg or two by the

HAND IT TO THE BRITS

Kiwi troops. It was that, agreed Lyall, mixed with the antipodean rejection of a class structure. Whatever, all four continued to take their cue from the majority. In most cases the system worked well.

They found it a little more difficult to come to grips with another of the habits of the bulk of their fellow passengers from the north.

One evening early in the cruise Lynn and Glen, replete from dining at their designated table in the Alexandria Restaurant, walked forward to the Curzon Theatre for the scheduled entertainment. They entered the 660-seat auditorium and looked to find a pair of unoccupied chairs. That was odd, thought Lynn, spotting a curious pattern. Though there was plenty of room still available, all the seats along the aisles were filled by people already seated – with twos, fours, sixes at the most on each side. The spaces in the middle of each stretch, the majority of the seats in each row, were vacant. They picked a row and indicated to the people on the aisle that they'd like to pass.

"Excuse me. Pardon me, do you mind if we…thank you."

They seated themselves in the middle of the row. The remaining seats either side of them filled slowly. Each time further people arrived those already sitting at the ends of the rows would stand to make way for the later arrivals.

The pattern repeated itself night after night. The front row and all the aisle seats were snapped up by the first arrivals.

"Why don't the early ones sit in the middle of the rows?" wondered Lynn. On the occasions when they were early, or the offered entertainment wasn't attracting such large numbers, she and Glen made their way to the centre of an empty row. The next people to arrive would take the aisle seats and the pattern of filling from the sides would resume.

The Hendersons entered the theatre from the port side door one evening a week or so later as the Wellingtons came in from the starboard. The couples found themselves negotiating a passage into the same row. They met in the middle.

"Why don't they fill up the centre of the row first?" asked Lynn.

The custom was odd, agreed Ngaio and Lyall.

The lights dimmed.

"It's a comedian tonight," whispered Ngaio to Lynn, "I hope he's better than the last one."

"I prefer the musical shows put on by the company," agreed Lynn, "they're always good."

The comedian started his routine.

"There was a Yorkshire couple took a cruise. At their table was a Frenchman. The first evening when their dinners were served the Frenchman looked at his fellow diners. Bon Appetit. The Yorkshireman held out his hand. Charlie 'Ardcastle, he said affably. Every night for a week it was the same. Bon Appetit, said the Frenchman. Charlie 'Ardcastle. The waiter tactfully took Mr Hardcastle aside and told him the meaning of his dining companion's greeting. So the next night as the meals were served he volunteered, Bon Appetit. The Frenchman replied. Charlie 'Ardcastle."

A few rows forward in the centre block of the theatre Jovial Joe scribbled a note on a small pad he kept in his pocket. He could adapt that one nicely – it would find a place in his repertoire for cruises to come. With himself featuring in the place of the waiter.

In this area too, you had to hand it to the Brits, the Kiwi

HAND IT TO THE BRITS

couples agreed some time later – they do know how to relate to performers. At least, to the ones who are making the grade on stage. With the English tradition of variety theatre behind them, the ship full of cruisers had come prepared to enjoy themselves, and they were willing and quick to provide the expected responses to the entertainers' cues.

"I come from a poor family..." a comedian would begin, and a sympathetic chorus of "ooohh," on a declining note would come from the seated rows. Arms waved back and forth in unison during appropriate musical numbers, or clapping would accompany the beat. When a singer or musician paused at a key point in a number, the appropriate words – "tequila", "doodly-ah-bah", "white cliffs of Dover" – would be supplied by a willing chorus throughout the theatre.

What's more, this ship full of senior citizens seemed more than happy to provide the straight-man role to the comedians' banter – which also explained why the front rows always filled first, Lynn realized after some nights of observation. Passengers from the southern climes, whose tradition was more in the line of singing to guitar accompaniment around a campfire or barbecue, kept a more comfortable distance back in the theatre. But those from the British Isles appeared to vie for the positions where they could be addressed and potentially embarrassed.

"Is that your second husband, Madam? Yes, I thought so, he wouldn't have been my first choice either."

"You're not a complete idiot, are you Sir? No – I can see there are still some parts missing."

Ngaio resisted an urge to put her fingers in her ears when the music began. It helps if you're hard of hearing, she thought. It was the same in the Playhouse movie theatre, she'd found.

SEVENTEEN SEAS

Perhaps the entertainment crew had a policy of catering to an aged audience – or maybe it was the sound technician who was the one with significant hearing loss. She could be joining their company by the end of the cruise.

Now as she sat there, the second part of the entertainment, provided by a male singer, was reaching its end. True to form, this one had presented the usual list of numbers. What is it about the singers they hire, she wondered? They all seem to choose the same songs. Already, they'd been treated to the Tom Jones classics *Delilah, Green Green Grass of Home,* and *It's Not Unusual* by three different singers. Frank Sinatra hits were offered at least as frequently, with *Mack the Knife* coming in multiple vocal as well as instrumental versions. And every, well almost every singer, male or female, as well as groups and the company chorus, chose the same one for a climactic finale. There was no doubt that *Con Te Partiro, Time to Say Goodbye* was a great number for a closing piece, but it was in grave danger of suffering from over-exposure on this voyage.

The singer was still assuring his love he would go with her on ships across seas when those seated on the aisles started to rise and make their way to the aft doors. By the time he was taking his bows the number had risen to several dozen, and when the MC swept onto the stage the defectors were forming a small stream heading towards the exits. That was another thing about these audiences, thought Ngaio. She'd noticed on other nights that as so many people started to leave early there was danger of some artists thinking they were getting a standing ovation – at least until half the house started making for the doors.

"They're off to Carmen's," explained Lynn, "they want to get a seat for the entertainment on there."

76

HAND IT TO THE BRITS

Ngaio had looked at what was offered in the late night sessions. Both ballroom and country dancing were not the Wellingtons' thing, karaoke didn't appeal, and comedians tended to make up for a lack of good material by offering a more 'adult' routine than those in the earlier shows. Overall, she and Lyall found nothing to tempt them. Looking at the ages and mobility of some of those making their way out of the theatre and heading aft to the nightclub lounge, she wondered how some of them were up to it. No doubt a good number of them were the ones she noticed while she walked her circuits of the outside decks – recumbent, eyes closed and mouths open, fast asleep for a good deal of the day. With her walking, the art lectures, and the quizzes she enjoyed attending, by this time of night she was ready for bed.

For some, this sea day was their last full day on board. The following morning would see them docked at the next of the exotic Oriental ports – one that so many had looked forward to eagerly and others reluctantly as it meant the end of their voyage.

At each major stop on a long cruise fewer or larger numbers of passengers vacate their cabins and leave to make their way onwards or homewards. Others come on board to take their places. When some Kiwis disembarked after taking just the trip across the Tasman, Rich and Liz from New South Wales boarded to travel two sectors, which included five ports. They joined the ship in Sydney, "the most beautiful port in the world," enthused the captain, and even though they were really 'bushies' who lived a good drive north, they had to agree.

With each passing day, however, their glow of pride

77

diminished a degree, and the thought of ending their cruise at Singapore grew a little less regretted. As soon as the last of the Australian stops was no longer reached by a ripple in the wake of the liner, sales tables had been erected on Devanha deck to sell off the memorabilia said to represent down-under. "Your last chance to take Australian souvenirs home – good presents for family."

Liz and Rich cringed at what was on offer. From among the usual suspects – key rings, fridge magnets, and tea towels with aboriginal designs – Rich picked up a water ball featuring a dreadfully crafted Sydney tower and skyline and could hardly contain his disgust. Liz was more upset by quantities of small koalas portrayed in colours never seen among the real ones that clung to eucalyptus trees. Had Liz and Rich walked away from the display then all might have been forgotten, but the couple tarried a moment too long and spotted an even more heinous crime. When found by Glen and Lynn trying to drown their indignation in the Riviera bar, the Australians were ready to take on the boutique buyers over their lack of taste.

"Did you see those plastic kangaroos dressed in blue boxing gloves and head guards?" they moaned into their bottles of Fosters.

Their Auckland neighbours were sympathetic at the same time as being relieved that the offerings said to represent their own country were not as offensive. But their empathy extended to a certain degree only, as for them other points of contention had arisen.

Like all Kiwis who travel anywhere outside the south pacific region they'd already been asked repeatedly on this voyage if they were Australian. Even worse, in the estimation of New

Zealanders, is the claiming of their distinctive symbols by the land 'over the ditch'. They can laugh when expatriate Kiwis make up a good number of 'the lucky country's' entertainment stars, and when one is named Australian of the Year, on the grounds that those figures are exports who can speak for themselves. But they are quick to repel attempts at appropriation of true long-term cultural icons such as the late great racehorse Phar Lap, and the dessert phenomenon the pavlova. Here, on board ship, they'd encountered plenty of instances of ignorance already. In one of his patters introducing the evening show the cruise director had already erred unforgivably by attributing the phenomenon of bungy jumping to Australia.

However, in a principle similar to that contrived in Hollywood blockbusters when the world's warring nations cooperate to defend the planet against alien invaders, the twin countries of the South Pacific recognise they have more in common than in opposition and, faced with attack from outside the region of Australasia, band together in a latter-day Anzac alliance. Lynn and Glen could feel for their trans-Tasman neighbours and stayed to offer a further few words of sympathy.

After what seemed a decent interval Lynn excused herself. She'd been on her way to find the perfect place to read her novel – a warm spot protected from the sea breeze, yet with enough shade to avoid her having to use too much sunscreen. On her way up the stairs yet another person had told her she was too late – the Germans had already taken all the deck-chairs, and she wanted to check out that curious claim.

— CHAPTER 8 —

Ten Thousand Taxis

In the event that the retail areas of Hong Kong and Bangkok or Pattaya were not sufficient to sate the shopping appetites of some of the cruisers, a third Asian port was plotted and now lay dead ahead of the bow.

With a mercantile tradition that reached back almost two centuries to when one of their enterprising countrymen established a port and trading centre on the island, it was no wonder that the roar of the Lion City held a strong attraction for the best of Britain's browsers and barterers. What's more, none of the ports of call to come after this stop offered so much purchasing promise, so Singapore was to be exploited to the full.

Those who favoured the researched approach to retailing already had notes on recommended areas. Nevertheless, they attended the pre-port lecture in the Curzon Theatre, considered by Con Sumer as equivalent to the all-important team talk before the test match.

"Good 't know," he pronounced when told of the thousand dollar fine for littering.

"I can remember when it used to cost a penny to go," Con added at hearing the fact that followed – not flushing a public toilet could cost 150 Singapore dollars, and that was just for the first offence. "That's a bloody pricey pee."

Further advice followed. Anyone with a supply of chewing gum must be certain to leave it on board ship, for fear of a fine

TEN THOUSAND TAXIS

of thousands of dollars or even a gaol term for smuggling it ashore. Smokers, who experienced some moments of panic, were assured their habit was still legal, but with an energetic smoke-free campaign under way they should watch where they lit up, and remember that a carelessly discarded butt constituted littering.

On the morning of the Kiwis' twenty-third day aboard, the ship was docked in Keppel Harbour at the overseas terminal of the city named for an animal that had never paced its ground till the formation of its world-class zoo. Though the legendary Sumatran prince almost certainly misidentified the animal he saw streaking through the undergrowth, the resulting name of Singapura proved a popular choice with later settlers – City of the Lion no doubt presenting a more dramatic image than the more prosaic Seaport equivalent it replaced. In modern times, however, the marketing advisors of the Singapore Tourism Board outdid even the prince's flight of fantasy when it crossed the lion with a fish. As a consequence, by the end of the day the image of the Merlion was destined to come aboard the ship in the form of postcards, plastic models, soft toys, fridge magnets, key-chains and a myriad other consumer items that the prince, even given his imagination, could not have dreamed of six centuries earlier.

Early on Tuesday morning Ngaio stood at the city-side rail on Lido deck and looked skywards. Only a little above the funnel stretched the cables of the aerial ropeway, with suspended gondolas moving to and fro between the islands of Singapore and Sentosa. She could see people inside the cabins. Lyall, she knew, would like to do that. Their only trip to Sentosa was made decades earlier when the island lacked the amenities it had now, but she had no wish to return. At least not that way. She remembered the chill she felt only weeks after their visit when she heard of the accident – about the derrick of an oil rig breaking the cable, and the cabins with their passengers plunging more than fifty metres to the water. The thought filled her with horror. She sent a silent wish of safe travel in the direction of the moving gondolas, and joined Lyall on the way down to the shore exit.

If Liz and Rich, Briar Melbourne, Miss Leicester Secretary and Ms Thankfully Divorced who were leaving the ship in order to fly home to work, or any of the others who were departing for the airport, had paused by the gangway at the time of disembarkation with the intention to bid farewell to friends made aboard, their sense of loss would have been compounded, and any thoughts about their abandoning the vessel would have been reconsidered. With all the enticements of this modernised, hygienised, indeed fully sanitised orient waiting, those continuing the voyage were already ashore, being unwilling to delay sampling the wealth of attractions the place had to offer.

Caroline Coolangatta had been torn between making a show of accompanying her departing cabin-mate to the airport, and exploring the various streets of the city by means of a rather extraordinary map she had spent many hours studying. *The Secret Map of Singapore*, a hand-drawn guide to the "bizarre, mysterious, intriguing, exotic" places with "every nook and corner revealed", had been purchased by a friend who had visited the island state years before, and entrusted to Caroline with the repeated insistence that, even though it was no doubt out of date, it must be returned to its owner on her return.

TEN THOUSAND TAXIS

Briar, aware of her cousin's quandary, insisted that she could get herself to the airport. She'd take a taxi to Changi from the terminal, and there wouldn't be long to wait for her midday flight out. With only token argument Caroline conceded. That left her free to get "off the beaten track", as the guide advised and throw herself into the "temple hopping, fortune telling, bargain hunting and food sampling" it promised.

There was not even the pretence of regret among many of the others waiting at the rails for the gangway to be set up. Sally Sale, now cannula-free and pronounced fit enough to resume her place among the incurable addicts, led the rush to the coaches waiting to shuttle the pack of purposeful purchasers to the malls. Without a backward glance towards their disembarking friends, the true-blue band of buyers, spurred on by the thought that to the truly dedicated a mere ten hours devotion was somewhat sacrilegious, girded their loins with their money belts and went forth with purpose and zeal.

Orchard Road with its mass of stores, mini to mega, came out a distinct winner, though mainly because the majority of those who emerged from the shuttle at the corner of Scotts Road never thought of making their way to any other destination. A few, however, found the MRT and relived their recent Hong Kong experience by visiting Chinatown, or anticipated what was to come by going to the area known as Little India. They too made it back to the ship bearing a quantity of plastic bags that threatened to scuttle any environmental concerns either the cruisers or the shipping company took pride in promoting.

Some coach-loads of senior men, and fewer women of similar vintage, also took a trip in the direction of Changi, though not with the purpose of going to the airport. For Richard and Vera, residents of a balcony stateroom on Canberra deck, it was a sentimental journey though, as Richard commented, sentimental was not really an accurate term for a period in his youth he had spent the rest of his life trying to forget. In the prison museum Vera identified a photo of her Uncle James, a chaplain in the Allied forces, and at Kranji War Memorial at the north of the island the couple searched for his grave. In the rows of more than four thousand plots, it was a fruitless search in the time available, leaving Vera both disappointed and somewhat relieved. She didn't know how the actual encounter would have affected her.

As was their habit at most stops, Bradford and Yvonne Yorkshire had opted for the Highlights of the City tour – "best seller, the ideal way to get an overview of the destination without effort". This had the advantage, according to Bradford, of viewing what was promoted as "the heart of Singapore's sophisticated hotel and shopping centre", Orchard Road, through the windows of the coach – safe proximity, given there was no opportunity for Yvonne to get out and disappear into Tangs, Wisma Atria, or the Far East Plaza. But it was something much less commercial in nature that impressed itself on Mrs Y, "lady-wife" to Bradford, and provided her most vivid memory of Singapore. After a drive through the old colonial area of the city Yvonne experienced some sort of epiphany following the viewing of a trinity of sights. That might be putting it a bit strongly, she admonished herself some days later when recalling her reactions, but it was certainly a moment of insight. The tour passed by the Supreme Court building – rectangular, fronted by Corinthian pillars and topped with a green dome, it would have fitted into the London landscape without an eyebrow being raised. The cricket club, so their guide informed them as they drove past, was a centre of colonial social life during the century before the Second World War. Then came the Anglican cathedral, its Early Gothic architecture presenting a stately sight admired by the coach full of highlights habitués as it stood tall and white in the centre of an area of lawns and trees.

"We could almost be back home in Salisbury," came a voice from across the aisle.

That was it, Yvonne explained to Lynn Henderson at dinner that evening. She didn't make sense of her feeling of unease till the tour had moved on across the Singapore River into Chinatown. In contrast to the earlier spots, these streets were teeming with life as people went about their daily work. The Indian temple where they stopped couldn't have looked more different from the cathedral. The tower entrance, right on the busy street frontage, was covered with images of brightly-painted deities. Inside, people were engaged in individual acts of worship. She didn't understand any of it, but the thought that came to her was that it fitted with the area. In contrast, the British buildings belonged elsewhere. They were lovely, Yvonne assured Lynn, but in such a overall setting she couldn't help thinking they were, she paused, incongruous.

Meanwhile, Caroline, *The Secret Map of Singapore* in hand, was exploring streets that were reminiscent of her hometown in no way at all. She walked, taking in the sights, enjoying her aloneness amid the crowds. Medical halls were busy, with their attendants ladling scoops of dried ingredients from bins and drawers onto sheets of paper for customers presumably with a variety of needs. Barbers trimmed hair and music shops blasted noise. This store, she discovered, still traded in frogs, fish, and turtles as indicated on the map and, true to another note she read, a man sat making mah jong tiles in a small shop nearby. One couldn't go down any street in the area without being tempted by the scents of spices, perfumes, or smells wafting from small bakeries. If she felt the need to have her fortune told, to buy any goods she could possibly imagine including ginseng and crushed pearls in bottles, exquisitely ornamented screens, or a brightly painted lion head for a street parade, there was a choice of traders ready to supply.

Caroline rounded a corner and saw a line of coaches disgorging hundreds of people onto the pavement. Many wore distinctive lanyards around their necks, with familiar boarding cards hanging over ample bosoms and bellies. Too many tourists, this isn't what she wanted. She looked around, spotted a local bus at a nearby stop and hurried to catch it. Eleven minutes later, having passed multiple sights that fairly screamed out for further exploration she alighted in a street of which she neither then nor later learned the name. Nearby, a single-storey building backed by high-rise office blocks caught her eye. The railings outside were hung with bright red banners with gold writing. As she watched, people came and went through the open gateway. She took twenty or so paces towards it. It didn't look to be private. She moved even closer. An elderly woman sweeping the narrow courtyard between the fence and the building looked up and apparently appreciated her hesitance. She waved her arm towards the door, clearly inviting her to enter.

The interior exceeded Ms Coolangatta's expectations many times over. Large pictures of a dragon and a tiger flanked the entranceway. A woman walking in behind her lit a handful

TEN THOUSAND TAXIS

of incense sticks and placed them in a large brass urn filled with ash. Caroline walked through the several rooms taking in the sights. A variety of cats of different colours also wandered about. A white one with some ginger markings reminded her of a previous pet long since gone. There appeared to be a ceremony taking place. Caroline kept a distance and wondered if she was intruding but no one seemed to take any notice of her. She stood and watched as some large models were placed near the group – a bed, house, dining set of table and chairs, and then a car, all crafted artistically from coloured paper. Two large figures, a man and woman, also sculpted in paper seemed to be at the centre of the ceremony. It looked almost as though a wedding was in progress, but a woman in the group was weeping.

She moved on. Two images on a side altar might have escaped her attention, despite their colourful clothes and the offerings heaped in front of them, except for the sign displayed beside them. Written in English, it instructed worshippers to –

"Please use cigarettes in place of prohibited items as your offerings to the gods."

Caroline stood puzzling over the intention of the request, which seemed at odds with the state's strong discouragement of smoking, till she noticed the black tar-like substance smeared around the mouths of the figures, and recalled a reference in a novel about the Australian gold fields and a woman addicted to opium. Really, this was turning into a great day. If she was looking for something completely outside her own experience, she was finding plenty of it.

All in all, the foresight of Sir Stamford Raffles the founder of the Lion City, himself born on board a ship in exotic waters, was well rewarded by the homage paid in Singapore dollars by his countrymen and their commonwealth associates that day. A good number of them even fitted in a rite of communion, downing a glass of the now legendary Singapore Sling in the Long Bar of the Raffles Hotel before hailing one of the city's ten thousand taxis to get them back to the overseas terminal.

Dick Napier was among the hundreds who took advantage of the shuttle from the ship into the city in the morning, but was distinguished from all others by being alone among the passengers to return in the afternoon with no more bags than he took ashore. The one that hung from a wide strap over his shoulder held his laptop. He walked about for ten minutes before he found an acceptable place to sit – a small garden area with tables at the rear of a shopping mall. It was as far from road noise and canned music as was possible to get in the heart of the city, and what little intruded was partially neutralized by the sound of a small fountain, commonly now called a water-feature. Most important, a sign fixed to the wall indicated it was a free Wi-Fi hotspot. With a tall coffee beside him, he set up the computer and settled down to a period of serious news reading. Old habits were hard to break.

In the main, international news didn't get past the bow wave of the ship, and even in an age when information bombards the airwaves, perhaps penetrating every unsuspecting pore, the majority of the cruisers seemed content to keep to the metal cocoon and let the outside world wash by with the wake. Lest the ignorance about the rest of the globe become too intense perhaps, a four-page folded sheet with *Britain Today* proudly displayed on the masthead, was delivered to each cabin daily.

TEN THOUSAND TAXIS

The first 2 pages gave truncated accounts of news at 'home' – typically, the death of an apparently well-known television personality, flooding and power-cuts in the southwest of the United Kingdom, and bad news to the cruising class as the budget forecasted a slashing of economic growth. All pretty much as it would be in the Kiwi newsman's own home town, really. An article on the costs of Britain's military operations in their Iraq and Afghanistan war zones – Dick noted they didn't hesitate to use the 'w' word – stated that efforts there were to double. That was, thankfully, a major difference between the countries.

The more newsworthy stories in the news-sheet were balanced by a sprinkling of quirky items – buxom belly dancers had caught the eye of the Queen's consort, more than a thousand people dressed as Robin Hood gathered in Nottingham in order to smash a previous record, and Camilla was reported to dance to a Marley beat when a Jamaican military band entertained royalty. All were eclipsed, however, by the barely believable news that the BBC had sold the television series 'Allo 'Allo to Germany.

The remaining two pages of the ship's daily could be dismissed quickly – market data from the London Stock Exchange, international rates for the pound sterling, the latest Lotto results, and a page of sports that didn't have much relevance to those without affiliations to specific football teams – except for one shining exception when the Black Caps achieved a resounding success over the English cricket team touring New Zealand.

To a career journalist it was frustrating to be so out of touch for days at a time. Internet access provided by cyb@study situated on Sun deck near his favourite Crow's Nest sitting area was okay for minutes spent downloading email, but that merely whetted Dick's appetite for longer sessions online. Now in this small haven ashore he was in his element. He took a sip from his mug, and logged in via the complex's free access. For the price of a coffee or two he was set for the day.

As a shop-till-you-drop port, and it having been six days since leaving Hong Kong, with only restricted opportunities in Thailand between, Singapore had to be popular. If the ship's plimsoll line was under threat at Hong Kong it was even more of a concern that evening as the liner made her way back out into the Singapore Strait and turned northwest into the Malacca Strait.

Not for the first time, Serial Shopper came to a conclusion while checking off her list that evening. Shopping is better than sex. If you're not satisfied after shopping you can always take it back and exchange it for something you like.

A few relived their recent Hong Kong experience by visiting Chinatown.

— CHAPTER 9 —

Selamat Datang

Day fifty-nine of the full itinerary was not likely to be highlighted ahead on any of the passengers' calendars. On a list of can't-wait-for destinations Port Kelang couldn't hope for even an honourable mention.

As the crew negotiated the busy sea-lanes of the Malacca Strait on the ship's journey north, groups discussed the options. The day in Singapore was judged a great success, and the one coming in Penang two days later was full of promise.

This one in between, however, was regarded by many as something of an optional extra. Harry Hampshire, called upon to give judgement by fellow diners at their table in the Alexandria restaurant, launched into what threatened to be a full history.

"It used to be Port Swettenham in colonial times…" he began, but was stopped by Zelda before the lecture progressed further. He gave the place a rating of three.

"Three out of five, that's not too bad then," said 'Basil'.

"I think you'll find Harry's scale goes to ten," said 'Sybil'.

The coach trip to Kuala Lumpur, in Harry's estimation – and mind, it was only his opinion but they did ask – was akin to that between Laem Chabang and Bangkok because of the traffic congestion around both capital cities. There wasn't anything of note to see in KL anyway if you weren't into viewing mosques, and furthermore there was nowhere else worth going to in the

SEVENTEEN SEAS

area. This pronouncement brought a moment of two of silence, during which the Yorkshires thought they too should have decided to stay on board for the day, but they'd already booked the coach into the city.

Anwen Cardiff and her husband had boarded at Singapore taking over occupancy of both the stateroom and the Alexandria first sitting dining places formerly allocated to Miss Leicester Secretary and Ms Thankfully Divorced. Now Anwen nudged Aled under the table. The couple had light accents that deepened when they got excited.

"If you really don't want to go, we could take them off your hands. Al and I would like to go. We'd pay you for them, you understand."

The transfer was quickly negotiated and a bond formed between the couples, even though Al and Bradford were to share many a heated discussion in Champions bar between the relative merits of their favoured codes of football before the voyage was over.

"We'd rather hoped to get up the Petronas Towers," said Glen Henderson, with Lynn adding an explanation in case it seemed like an alternative offer for the newly reassigned tickets.

"We're not taking the coach – we hear there's a train from Kelang into KL."

"Are they the towers that were on that film with Sean Connery?" asked 'Sybil', seated on Lynn's left.

"Entrapment. That's right."

"Oh you wouldn't see me up there, dear." Yvonne Yorkshire gave a little shudder.

'Basil' added "Nor me."

"We wouldn't see you up a stepladder," said 'Sybil', "Now eat

92

SELAMAT DATANG

your starter before the waiter comes for your plate."

"If you want my opinion again," began Harry Hampshire. The Hendersons exchanged a quick glance, perhaps detected by Zelda who nudged her husband's arm and said something under her breath. Harry changed tack.

"The last time I was here there was nothing at all at Port Kelang, just a dock. We went into Koo-arla Lump-par on a coach. By the time we got through all the traffic it was almost lunchtime. They dropped us at a shopping mall that had nothing in it – nothing to speak of – we mooched around there for two hours and then it was time to get back on the coach. And all the time it poured with rain. You know Koo-arla Lump-par gets its name for the muddy rivers."

"It was a long time ago, Harry," said Zelda.

"Don't you remember? It rained cats and dogs. Didn't it?"

"Yes, it rained." She looked across the table at Lynn. "The towers weren't built then, dear."

"I'm stopping on board," said 'Basil'. "I don't want this. It tastes like fish."

"It should do. You ordered the salmon." 'Sybil' met Zelda's eyes. Both women raised their eyes in a gesture of sisterhood.

The following morning the Hendersons, in the company of Caroline Coolangatta, were among the first group to make their way past the signs reading "Selamat Datang" to the waiting shuttles. In the town of Kelang they took a taxi to the train station, a further taxi ride on arrival in the city, and reached their goal in good time. They looked up at the twin towers.

"Spectacular," said Glen.

Lynn found herself remembering the movie and hoped on behalf of Catherine Zeta-Jones that the actress had a stunt double. Caroline wondered aloud about the name Petronas and tried to relate it to classical literature. Surely he was a son of Zeus. Glen agreed it would be fitting, but the truth was much less romantic. He didn't bother to add he'd looked it up just the night before. Caroline was disappointed – a petrol company didn't have anything like the appeal of a deity or hero.

The trio approached the building, anticipating the view from such a height. The counter attendant at Tower Two was sympathetic, but didn't they know that admission to the Skybridge was limited and viewing times restricted? They'd missed out for the morning, and tickets for the afternoon session had already gone. They walked away, disappointed. Some time later, after they had rounded several blocks and returned, they noticed the queue forming for the afternoon viewing.

"C'mon," said Ms Coolangatta, "Let's give it another go." She led the way and greeted the attendant, "Selamat datang."

The man smiled, and Caroline explained their dilemma. They were here for the day only, they had to get a train back to Kelang within the hour in order to rejoin the ship. Was there no way…?

"Wait here," they were instructed. The attendant walked off a distance and had a word with another man. He returned shaking his head. Caroline chose not to notice.

"Selamat datang," she repeated. "Can we go up?"

The man smiled again.

"I'll try to get you in. Wait here."

Some time later still, with the allotted time almost up, Ms C again greeted and pleaded. With a shake of his head accompanied by a grin, the attendant allowed them through.

The three made it back to the ship just in time. Lynn

SELAMAT DATANG

Henderson, pausing to read the signs at the beginning of the raised roofed walkway back to the ship read "Selamat datang ke Malaysia".

"Doesn't that mean 'Welcome to Malaysia'?" she asked. "In that case selamat datang means welcome."

"Looks like it," agreed Glen.

"Shall we tell her?" asked Lynn, looking at Ms C walking ahead.

"Why bother? It worked, didn't it!"

The Hampshires and the Plymouths were already seated and examining the menu when the Hendersons and the Yorkshires arrived in the dining room simultaneously that evening. Harry was in full flight informing his tablemates of what was obviously the high point of his day.

After they left Hong Kong some days before he had regaled them with an account of the time, many years before, when he and Zelda had taken a memorable cruise out of Singapore. Over the full course of one evening's meal, he'd given a full account of the destinations. The climax of tonight's story was that the smaller liner that had been moored on the other side of the cruise terminal today was the very same as the one in which they'd sailed on that earlier occasion to several exotic spots.

"She just cruises out and back from the harbour on take-your-secretary-away-for-the-night casino trips. Sad really."

Tonight Harry was in his element, being able to add a further chapter in his series about where old cruise ships go to die.

"I thought I recognized her," he claimed with an air of triumph, pausing a moment to draw the newcomers into his story by explaining he was talking about the small cruise ship anchored on the other side of the wharf alongside to starboard. "And sure enough, I found we've been on her. It was more than twenty years back, when she was a ferry sailing out of Stockholm. She was the *Stockholm Star* then. The *Wasa Queen* she is now – that put me off the track for a while, but of course it's for Vaasa in Finland. Now she does just casino cruises – in and out of the harbour, twelve hours return. I thought I recognized her, and I was right – can't be too much wrong with the old grey matter."

'Sybil' reacted with the air of one reassured of deliverance as Yvonne took the chair beside her.

"Had a good day, did you?" she asked, and without waiting for an answer volunteered that she and Zelda had taken the shuttle into Kelang.

"We had a great time, " agreed Zelda, with a glance at the men. She pulled out a digital camera, turned it to view and passed it around.

"We met this man at one of the temples we saw. He was making an offering at the altar. 'I've been praying for a lucky day,' he said to me. I asked him 'Is there a god or goddess for this temple?' And he said, 'I don't know, I just pray.'"

Basil snorted.

"We did enjoy it, didn't we?" Zelda looked to her companion for support and 'Sybil' smiled her agreement. Both women picked up their menus. Whatever they could have done for the day it had to be better than stopping on board.

Anwen Cardiff began to offer their experiences on the coach trip but to little effect. Between ordering and eating Harry and 'Basil' were revisiting various ports remembered from past voyages. Instead, Anwen and Lynn resorted to sharing anecdotes about their respective days, just managing to hear each other over the men's conversation. From then on they tried to seat themselves side by side each evening.

He said, "I don't know, I just pray."

— CHAPTER 10 —

Cobweb in the Canopy

Lyall and Ngaio Wellington were particularly looking forward to the next day's destination even though it was their third trip to Penang. The port lecture had reminded them of what they'd seen and done before – admired the botanic gardens and the butterfly farm, photographed the picturesque shop-houses and clan temples, enjoyed a rickshaw ride through the streets of George Town, posed with the Buddhas at the Kek Lok Si and the pit vipers at the temple of the Azure Cloud, bought copies of designer watches at Batu Ferringhi – all the usual suspects.

"It seems the population doubles each time we visit," said Lyall on hearing the count for the island was now more than 700 thousand, "I remember it as smaller."

The pair's other dominating memory of their previous visits to Penang was of sky high temperatures and even higher humidity. In that case getting out of the city would be a good choice. Or at least above it. This time, they decided, they would seek the heights of Penang Hill, for its views and added comfort.

On disembarking, Ngaio and Lyall walked some blocks from the wharf and sought advice from the city's Public Relations Officer, a young man whose enthusiasm for helping foreigners come to grips with the features of the Pearl of the Orient seemed boundless. He advised taking a taxi to Bukit Pinang.

"There is a bus you can take," he told them, but all agreed that for the day tripper time is more important than a dollar or two.

"The taxi should cost twenty ringgits," he cautioned. "The driver may ask for more so settle on the price before you set out."

A taxi pulled into the kerb at the first raise of a hand. A good start, thought the Wellingtons.

"How much to go to Penang Hill?"

"Twenty ringgits."

That was easy. They were reassured. So much for all the warnings, which were amply backed by their remembered experiences from an earlier trip. They climbed into the rear of the car.

This driver was unlike those anywhere else in the world – he didn't try to talk, and ask where the latest occupants of the back seat were from. That was good too – it meant there was time to look at the sights.

Within a few blocks, however, a slightly disturbing observation materialized. Ngaio noted that the driver was yawning at worrying intervals. He also kept removing one hand from the steering wheel and rubbing it over his head in an early morning clearing-the-mental-fog gesture. On more than a few occasions he jerked the wheel to bring the car back on an even course.

Yawn, rub, jerk.

Ngaio was a veteran of countless taxi rides in places all over the world. Though some of the journeys had proved to be white-knuckle jobs, so far they'd all resulted in her being delivered to the desired destination without any serious mishaps. She relaxed and looked around with interest. This street they were in seemed to specialize in wedding houses – very upmarket establishments offering hi-fi receptions by the look of them.

Yawn, jerk, rub.

A variety of churches appeared. Each one morphed into another a short distance on – Baptist, Methodist, Anglican. Were there ever sufficient Christians on the island to justify the number and grandeur of these edifices? she wondered.

Jerk, yawn, rub.

As the car got further from the shore and closer to the interior of the island, churches were replaced by the more exotic architecture of Chinese and Hindu temples, and mosques.

Rub, yawn, jerk.

Maybe that's why taxi drivers elsewhere talk to their passengers, Ngaio found herself thinking – to relieve the boredom and stay awake. She spotted two small figurines of buddhas on the dashboard. Maybe the driver, and hopefully those he ferries, had the blessing of the Enlightened One – she hoped so.

Jerk, rub, yawn.

The front seats of the cab had covers over their backs and it took Ngaio a minute or two to register what they were. The one on the driver's side was a blue tee-shirt with its front featuring a promotional scene of the island, turned to brighten the view of the passengers in the back. The back of the front passenger seat had a grey knit tank top stretched over it. In each case the armholes were positioned at each side of the chair. She was appreciative of the idea. It seemed a good recycling initiative.

Rub, jerk, yawn.

It was a relief to reach the hill. The driver took the 20 ringgits Lyall offered without asking for more – clearly he was less of an opportunist than the taxi operators remembered from a previous visit. Perhaps he was too tired to consider that some revision of the pre-negotiated rate was worth a try. More likely, given his ethnicity, this was his first fare of the morning and it was therefore subject to the belief that the day's business hinged on the success or failure of the first sale.

The couple followed the signs that indicated the way to the funicular rail and Ngaio looked up at what seemed like an almost vertical rise to the top of the hill some eight hundred metres above. She was not particularly keen on being hauled up, lowered, or transported across by means of cables of any composition or diameter, but the alternative was clearly not an option. Lyall noted her hesitation.

"Just like home," he said, "it'll be like going on the Kelburn cable car."

The Kelburn hill isn't vertical, thought Ngaio, and somehow she had more trust in her own local body authority and its by-laws than one she didn't know, but she followed to the place where the downwards crowd was disembarking.

The pair entered the last of four carriages. The front three seemed to be stacked above it. Unlike the range of seats she knew accommodated passengers at home, this one had just one form on one side of the small cabin. It was already occupied. A sign on the wall, apparently intended for tourists given that it was in English, read –

**SEATS IN THIS TRAIN ARE FOR PHYSICALLY CHALLENGED PEOPLE.
PLEASE OFFER YOUR SEATS TO THE HANDICAPPED, OLD FOLKS, PREGNANT LADIES AND CHILDREN.**

Ngaio settled herself with her back against the leading wall, her feet a little apart to form a stable base. A young man, one of the seated locals, stood and offered her his place on the end of the perch. She hesitated. Did she look pregnant? No, she prided herself on keeping a reasonably flat midriff, and her grey hair should rule that out anyway. She wasn't obviously handicapped. That left only – grey locks aside she wasn't ready for a concession on those grounds. Besides, the vacated space looked extra slim. Ngaio, a former maternity nurse, who had often regarded with wonder the slightness of the oriental physique, estimated that if the bench seated four Malaysians, it would take only two Europeans with comfort, three with overlap. She shook her head, but the young man motioned to the vacated seat again. Hang it all, this was no time for pride and he mightn't offer again. She smiled her thanks, and moved to take his place. A further busload of people appeared on the platform and the cabins filled.

The train ground upwards for close to fifteen minutes. Ngaio kept her eyes on the vegetation that clung to rocks passing perilously closely to the window. Looking for orchids growing in the spaces, she told herself. The station appeared and the standing passengers vacated in a rush. That wasn't so bad, she thought, somewhat relieved the ascent was over. But wait, it seemed she had relaxed too soon – everyone was heading over to board an identical train. She looked up to see a further stretch of track disappearing into the clouds. The morning smog anyway.

Again the train creaked and ground slowly upwards, for a further quarter hour. They drew into the top station just as Ngaio was thinking the lush vegetation would give way to tussock and alpine daisies any time now, and she wouldn't be at all surprised if the locals appeared in Heidi costumes and lederhosen with ornate braces. At more than four times the height of her home city's vantage point, Mt Victoria, there'd have to be a great view. She went to the viewing platform overlooking the city ready for an overview of the Pearl of the Orient. Some of the major features of George Town could be glimpsed palely through the smoky haze. The rest of Penang Island could only be imagined. So much for that. Now they were here, what would they do?

Among the signs leading to various amenities was a notice advertising a canopy walk. Ngaio remembered negotiating an impressive timber-top walk in Australia with only a modicum of unease, and drew its attention to Lyall. In doing so, she missed the first warning sign. The notice also read "Now reopened".

They walked two kilometres along the road indicated. The going was mainly uphill, but the route looked down on rainforest and the road itself was lined with trees. Gardens set around large and obviously expensive houses were lush with hibiscus, gardenia, croton, bird of paradise. It was a good choice after all. This on its own was worth the walk.

On the way another couple, younger, a lot fitter and pacing it out much faster, overtook and passed them by. That's okay, thought Ngaio, we're out for the stroll not training for the Olympics. A little before they reached the advertised spot Mr and Ms Fit came striding back on the return journey.

"Is the canopy walk worth it?" Lyall called out to them.

"We got there, but we didn't go on it," was the reply. The pair continued their power walking around the next bend, perhaps to avoid any follow up questions.

That was the second warning – also ignored. Ngaio and

SEVENTEEN SEAS

Lyall went on. Just when they were beginning to think the advertised two kilometres were more promotional than actual, they reached a small booth. Ngaio stopped short. The promised apparatus that was the canopy walk looked like a cobweb strung across huge gulfs between impossibly tall trees.

That was the third warning.

But they'd come all that distance. And the price was only the equivalent of two New Zealand dollars. That should have been a fourth warning, but everything's so cheap in Malaysia, Ngaio told herself in an attempt at justification. It wasn't entirely successful so, making a further effort to convince herself this was still a good idea, she questioned the ticket seller.

"Are you sure it's safe?"

"Of course, madam. Two hundred and twenty metres. I went over it twice myself this morning."

Considering he either owned the enterprise or at least kept himself in sarongs and satays by manning the booth, that mightn't mean a lot under the circumstances.

"What do we see? Trees? Monkeys?"

"Yes," he agreed. "Write your names on this register, including passport number, or some form of identification, phone number for notification."

"Why do you need that?"

"Just in case."

"But you said it's safe."

"Just in case."

That was definitely the fifth warning. But Lyall was prodding her from behind, and had already handed over the ringgits. Ngaio stepped aboard.

A board was pretty much what it was. A narrow board at

that, but placed over what she hoped were wire cables. At the sides of the swinging walkway were rope walls of a partially reassuring height. She thought of Indiana Jones taking the step of faith, she talked to God, and stepped out. Clinging onto the side ropes, hand over hand, foot after cautious foot, Ngaio traversed the first chasm. Would the trees below break her fall if she dropped a hundred metres through them, she wondered, or prove a further hazard?

At the end of the first section there was a solid platform, onto which she leapt in relief, not stopping to see how it was anchored. It felt stable. That was enough to reassure herself, momentarily.

From there the route dropped to another level by means of two vertical ladders. Going down was good, she reasoned – there'd be less distance to fall. The lower platform provided a view of the rest of the cobweb – further spans slung between trees, their middles dipping, and with gaping drops beneath them. At this point she considered making her way back up the ladders she'd just descended, and back across the plank the way she'd come.

"Yes, I know there's no refund," she would assure Encik Ticketseller, "that's fine, keep the money. Here, I'll give you more money – all the ringgits I've got. I'll throw in my watch – sorry I'm right out of steak knives or you'd get half a dozen of those too. I just want to be back on terra firma."

But the next sky-walkers were already beginning the traverse, Lyall was telling her to get a move on, and this was very definitely a one-way bridge. She had to press on.

Several more expanses followed – without the benefit of solid platforms between them. Step after step, eyes fixed rigidly on the end of each span, Ngaio moved on, still talking to God. Silently. The sign affixed to the spans ruled that those intrepid enough to venture forth should maintain silence. Was that in order to help preserve the pristine sacredness of the nature experience? Or was it to stop those infinitely less intrepid from calling heavenward in panic? That one she could understand. She hoped it wasn't for fear that the sonic waves generated by conversation would cause stress effects that might tip the balance. She was dimly aware that a party of walkers well ahead were ignoring the rule and conversing loudly. How could they walk and talk? All her energy was concentrated on the step by step, metre by metre crossings.

With ten paces to go she all but hurled herself forward to attain the promised land and collapsed, almost sobbing with relief. She sat for a while, thinking that she'd never before really appreciated the truth of the saying about legs turning to jelly. She'd have to take an overdose of calcium before even considering attempting that feat again.

Trees? Well, yes, those were the things the cobweb clung to, and which waited with outstretched arms to welcome her so far below. Monkeys? Not a sign, but despite her fascination with the creatures, if one had offered en route to share her precarious perch she would have frozen with fear that the additional few kilograms of weight and the movement might prove the tipping point. In view of the other plank-walkers who were venturing forth in groups it was an irrational thought, but valid at the time. You had to be there.

In the event, she'd seen nothing on the 220 metre journey except the next step ahead and each anchor tree that offered first the promise and then the goal of another section traversed.

Ngaio and Lyall started on the two kilometre hike back towards the cable train. It seemed someone had changed the road during their short sojourn because now it was uphill most of the way back. And Ngaio's knees were still suffering from a gelatine-calcium imbalance. But she was thankful. She was back on solid ground, with eight hundred metres of mountain under her sandals. At the end of the road, safely seated in a café, she appreciated the tropical trees and flowers all around.

"For someone named after a tree, you didn't do too well," commented Lyall.

Ngaio ignored him and talked to the long-tailed macaques that had gathered around to observe. Here they were – she hadn't needed to go in search of them at risk to life and limb, the monkeys had come to her.

"Leave the canopy stuff to us," was the message their wise faces seemed to be showing.

"Thanks," her still pale mask read in response. "I think I'll take your advice."

The return journey by cable train seemed completely risk-free in comparison. Despite the fact the fifty percent plus slope appeared to drop away beneath the descending carriages Ngaio felt relatively relaxed. She was standing on boards that felt solid. Some months later Lyall chose not to draw her attention to a news item that, just weeks after their visit, the railway was closed for six months due to a "protrusion of various wires from the cable". There were some things it was better she didn't know, he reasoned.

At the base of the hill, there was a row of about a dozen taxis waiting. That was always a good sign – there was bound to be competition and that meant a realistic fare could be negotiated. One of the drivers asked for thirty ringgits for the return journey.

"Twenty ringgits," countered Lyall.

"Thirty ringgits."

"But it was only twenty ringgits to get here."

"You can't get here for twenty ringgits. Not for less than thirty ringgits." The driver was adamant. He didn't seem at all inclined to interrupt his downtime unless it was excessively profitable. Lyall protested further on the basis of the established arrival price, adding in a rush of inspiration,

"Besides, it's downhill on the way back. It should be only half that."

"Thirty ringgits."

Tourists finding themselves further than walking distance from downtown were obviously in no position to bargain.

By this time other cabbies had joined the chorus. This was clearly a meeting of the taxi drivers' union and they were all staunch. Perhaps there were some non-members further down the road. Considering the principle and their duty to other tourists, Lyall and Ngaio set out on foot.

Fifty metres further on a single taxi was parked by the kerb. The driver leapt from his cab, and offered it for hire.

"Thirty ringgits," he quoted.

"But it was only twenty ringgits to get here."

The taxi driver paused for a moment, then motioned to the friend with whom he'd been sharing a pack or two of cigarettes to vacate the front passenger seat. This man moved to the car behind and got behind the wheel.

"The price is thirty ringgits, but he'll take you for twenty ringgits."

"But that car is not a taxi."

"He used to be taxi driver."

"Used to be?"

You had to hand it to the first man – he was a quick thinker. "*Is* a taxi driver but now is changing cars and waiting for the new taxi."

If there was indeed a new car in the offing it was just as well. This one had seen better days – a lot of them. The gear stick graunched as it was pushed into first.

The first part of the trip ended a further fifty metres down the road at a Caltex station. Three attendants joined the driver at the pump. One man recorded some figures in a notebook, a woman delivered the gas, another man looked on. That was one way to solve an unemployment problem. The operation didn't take long. Five-point-two litres were transferred to the tank, at a cost of ten ringgits. It should be enough to get back to the wharf.

Once more the gears complained and the car started down the hill. The open windows that revealed a lack of air conditioning provided an efficient system nevertheless – they allowed the noxious gases to pass right through the car without hindrance. Any misgivings the couple held about the driver's ability dissolved during the rest of the fifteen minute drive. Though the traffic had increased many-fold since the morning's trip up the hill, the return journey was negotiated expertly. Perhaps their substitute taxi driver was indeed awaiting his new car.

Ngaio and Lyall were delivered back to the wharf, the twenty ringgits handed over, and they alighted. The car and driver, whoever he was, would now return to his patch, they assumed.

Not so. They watched as he pulled in among the taxis and sat there waiting for a further fare.

It seemed only the first of the taxi drivers they encountered in Penang that day was not an opportunist.

Hand over hand, foot after cautious foot, Ngaio traversed the first chasm.

— CHAPTER 11 —

Another Language

For the full round-the-world trippers the journey was three quarters over, and for a good number of them there was just the least looked-forward-to part ahead. A pre-depression lethargy came over some of the cruisers.

With one group on board, however, the smiles became broader as the ship made her way towards what every travel brochure ever printed refers to in clichéd terms as "a land of contrasts", promising that every journey to this "incredible", "history filled", "mystical" land will prove to be "the trip of a lifetime". Of the hundreds of members of crew who comprised the ship's hotel department almost all hailed from India and for workers who get to go home only at the end of their contract rather than each evening it was a long time between visits.

Mumbai, the second stop on the ship's ports of call in India, is the location of the cruise company's training school for hotel staff so even many of those from other states had a connection with the city. Only some, however, could be spared from their duties for even a few hours in the afternoon, and though the crew cooperated to ensure that as many as possible of Mother Mumba's children could take a hurried trip home, for others it would be a case of so near and yet so far.

Sanjay, a waiter on his first contract, shared his delight with Anwen and Lynn when they asked about his plans as they rose from their table in the Alexandria restaurant. His mother would be coming to the ship to see him.

"Didn't you tell us you are married?" asked Lynn. She recalled his blushing confession some time before – an admission that astonished all the diners who had been speculating about his age. 'Sybil' had said he didn't look a day over sixteen.

"What about your wife?" continued Lynn, "You'll see her too, won't you?"

Sanjay shook his head.

"No," he replied. He didn't look at all disappointed and repeated happily that he'd see his mother.

As they left the restaurant Anwen whispered,

"Do you think they were married as children? Perhaps his wife's still a child."

"I'm not sure if they still have child marriage in India," said Lynn. "What do you think?" she asked her husband.

Glen took her arm and steered her towards the Curzon Theatre.

"He didn't seem too concerned about it, so let's leave it at that."

All the same, Lynn found her thoughts returning to the good looking young man and wondering.

On the first of the three days at sea that separated Malaysia from India Mr Napier spent long hours occupying one or another of the lounge chairs in the Crow's Nest lounge, Sun deck forward. He was very much at home in his own company but spent very little time in his stateroom during waking hours. As one of the few single men aboard – a state he had no intention of changing – he'd had to pay nearly the same amount for his room as did a couple, so had settled for an interior cabin on Ellora deck. He found the area was more than ample for one, especially as he had packed economically. Even with his shirts and suits hanging neatly there was still space in the wardrobe, and there were cupboards he hadn't even opened. The one drawback was the lack of natural light from a window. His ageing eyes required a good level of daylight, he was finding. During the day he made visits to his cabin only when they were necessary – usually to pick up a further book or deposit his reading and writing material when the volume made it too cumbersome to take to the dining room at lunchtime. His skin colouring made sunbathing a recreation that was not recommended, and the lack of prescription sunglasses made reading outdoors difficult, so he had learned to select one of the many lounge areas as his daytime home.

Trials conducted over his first week aboard showed him the Crow's Nest was the best place to sit and read, or fill in the day's journal page, and to indulge his thoughts. True, you had to choose your spot. The starboard side was often set aside for the craft classes and when one of these was in session the women working with needles, material, paper, glue, and an assortment of other items he barely looked at as he passed by, produced a fairly constant level of conversation. The port side of the lounge was designated the smoking area so that was to be avoided too. Along with most men who have spent their working lives in newsrooms, Dick Napier had once been a heavy smoker, but had given up what he now recognized and referred to as an insidious habit. He could no longer abide the smell of tobacco smoke, and was apt to be abrupt with those he encountered who offended his now resensitized nasal passages. Dick found that a seat in the centre of the lounge area reduced the sound from starboard to a level that was not obtrusive, and the fumes fouling the port side were sucked up by the air conditioning before they reached him. On previous days at sea he had also made a happy discovery that in the Crow's Nest he could get a cup of coffee that was halfway decent. Still only halfway, he thought as he sat down that morning, but that was a great step up from what was available in the dining rooms.

Today, his novel lay on the table still unopened some time after he'd settled in. He would usually have read up to ten thousand words by now. After recording a few lines in his journal Dick had leaned back in his chair, gazed out the curved front window and allowed himself to become lost in his thoughts. Before he had entered the lounge area he had stopped to examine the chart fixed in a glass case on the wall near the starboard entrance, and noted that the ship had passed the northern tip of the island of Sumatra during the night and was now in the Andaman Sea. Somewhere to the north of their present position lay the Nicobar Islands and further north again, the Andaman group. He thought back to recall details of maps and diagrams that he'd selected to publish on the international news pages just over three years earlier. It didn't seem possible that he was sitting here in such comfort, high above waters that had caused so much destruction to so many people. By the lack of comment, or even acknowledgement of the region's recent history by his fellow passengers, it seemed that he was the only one among them to make the connection. Eventually, however, light hunger pangs made him look at his watch. He'd have to move if he wanted any lunch. He picked up his book and walked aft to the Orangery.

The form of lethargy that gripped some of the passengers

ANOTHER LANGUAGE

during the three days at sea was good news for the bars and the sales tables set up outside the shops on Ellora deck and Promenade. Increased numbers of punters patronised the daily bingo session held in Carmen's lounge.

Ms Coolangatta, despite coming from the Australian state that has embraced gambling most enthusiastically, had to admit she had never played the game.

"I 'ad a coosin like you," said Nola moving her plastic tray to make more room at the table port side in the Orangery where the women met. "Not a big eater, then, are you? Or did you 'ave a big breakfast? I like to 'ave a good lunch, me. Don't eat mooch first thing in morning, only porridge and toast. So I like a good meal mid day."

Caroline mentally compared the amount on their respective plates and decided it was in direct proportion to the amount of stress being put on the chairs they occupied.

"Anyways, this coosin," Nola continued with barely a break, while she simultaneously made good progress on the plateful of curry and rice, lasagne, and cold cuts in front of her, "this coosin, Elsie 'er name is, she'd never been to the bingo neither, never 'ad till she came and stayed wi' me one autumn. I took 'er along and darn it if she didn't win the four corners straight off, and then one of the line prizes. Well, she wanted to go back the next day and there was no stoppin' 'er after that. Trevor, 'er 'usband, 'ad passed on by then, that's why she were staying wi' me, and it's just as well, because 'e wouldn't 'ave liked it. Not one little bit. 'Elsie', she said to me, 'why shouldn't we? It's good fun in our old age.' I said 'less of the old age, I'll thank you'. But she were right. So why don't you do the same and come along?"

Caroline estimated that Nola had the advantage of about a

quarter of a century head start on her, and it flitted through her mind that a sharp retort wouldn't be inexcusable. But it was clear that her new acquaintance meant no offence.

"What the hell," she thought, she'd come on this cruise to experience new things and there was nobody on board likely to send reports back home. So it was that the secretary of their church's focus group on problem gambling, found herself sitting in Carmen's later that day with a swatch of tickets, as a newbie under the tuition of Nola and three other Bingo buffs. It was just as well Briar had left the ship at Singapore, she thought as she arranged her cards. By now her cousin was safely back in Melbourne at work, so Caroline's minor indiscretion was sure to escape comment in the family.

It was another language being used, she decided as entertainment officers Jan and Steve called the numbers. She had already encountered Jan at the quiz sessions held near the Riviera bar, and Steve looked as though he worked out at least daily in what she'd heard was a state-of-the-art gym though she'd never even looked in the doors. Now they were speaking in Bingo lingo.

"Twenty-seven, a duck in heaven. Five and five, snakes alive. Thirty – dirty Gerty from cabin thirty."

"Forty-four, droopy drawers." The significance of that one wasn't clear. Caroline pondered about it and had to be prompted by the woman on her left.

"Mind out, you missed one. They just called seventy-two."

"Snow White's favourite number," called Jan, and Nola's table companions burst into song, 'Five oh, five oh, it's off to work we go'.

Bert Buyer, two tables over, called Bingo and the women sighed.

ANOTHER LANGUAGE

"The luck of the Irish, 'es got," the woman on her left commented.

"I thought he were from Sussex," said Nola, "'Ow did you do, then, loovie? Not bad for your first time. Just two off. Didn't we 'ave number sixty?"

"Blind sixty," confirmed Blue Rinse, "You have to watch them, love."

"Eyes down," came the order from the front as Steve began the next game. "Number twenty-two. Two little ducks."

"Quack quack," came responses from throughout the room.

"Thank you quackers," said Steve. His enthusiasm sounded forced, thought Ms C, but then he'd probably done this a thousand times.

"Number three, up in a tree." This time it was a chorus of "meows" that answered back.

"Five and nine, the P & O line," came the call. Caroline's mental question was interrupted by ship's whistle imitations from the players.

"Thank you fleeters."

"On its own, number four. Four on the fourth number. Spooky." A few notes from the X Files theme completed the call.

"Thirty-three. Dirty knees."

"Wash 'em," came the growled response.

Caroline, her mind reeling like car fifty-four going clickety-click down the sunset strip was nudged by Blue Rinse.

"You got it, love. Are you going to squeak? Bingo here," she called out, picking up Ms C's card and waving it.

"Just like my coosin Elsie," said Nola, looking perhaps a shade sorry that she'd once again provided herself with competition for the day's prizes. "I expect there'll be no stoppin' you now, neither, loovie."

The following day in the Orangery Caroline carried her lunch tray to a table on the starboard side. She didn't spot Nola, but just in case, she'd already put a mark by the movie showing on the day's entertainment sheet. She wasn't sure if she'd go or not, but it provided a useful excuse. It wasn't needed, fortunately. Twenty-five minutes later, walking forward on Devanha deck, she met Dick Napier outside the entrance to the Playhouse. He was looking at the board giving notice of the next screening, and comparing it to that day's sheet. As she approached he shook his head slowly.

"On one it says the film showing tonight is *Eye of the Dolphin*, and on the other it says *Eye of the Tiger*. Now which is it, do you think," he asked.

"Wouldn't have a clue," Caroline hadn't heard of either of them. "Dolphin, tiger – does it matter?"

"It would to the tiger, or the dolphin."

The pair walked on together sharing comments on the standard of language in the printed information on board. Dick, with his editor's eye for detail reeled off a list of complaints – poorly constructed sentences, punctuation, spelling errors and inconsistencies, capitalization, grammar.

"And they call themselves the mother country, home of the mother tongue," he despaired.

Caroline laughed.

"Don't they say ten out of two people are dyslexic?" She stopped in Raffles bar where she'd been heading for a cup of coffee.

"I've heard you can get a reasonable cup of coffee here,"

ANOTHER LANGUAGE

she said.

Coffee and literacy – here were two things an ex-newsman knew intimately.

"I'll join you if you don't mind," he said and the two found a table.

Over a long black, together with company from the same sector of the globe, Dick's mood mellowed. He even stopped hearing Caroline's rising inflexions at the end of sentences.

"Well," he conceded, "this ship has produced one literary masterpiece. Did you see that notice in the window of the shop next to the library?"

"It's just over there." She twisted around to point.

Dick didn't turn.

"It was a poem for Valentine's Day. It started –
A thought, A wish, A kiss by far
Spoil your Valentine in the spa..."

"Fair dinkum?"

"Go and have a look. It goes on for another six lines. They're just as stunning."

"Valentines was three weeks ago," Caroline was dubious.

"It's still there."

— CHAPTER 12 —

All the Same in Kerala

Lyall and Ngaio looked out over the next port of call from the balcony of their stateroom on the port side of the ship. It was not the first time the Wellingtons had visited what cricket commentators delighted in terming the subcontinent, but Kochi was a new experience. They hoped it would prove to be a good one, but so far the signs hadn't been favourable.

When they first pored over the cruise brochures before booking, one of the listed highpoints, they agreed, was the scheduled day in Colombo. Though they were experienced travellers, Sri Lanka was still on their 'to visit' list, hovering near the top.

Lyall figured that a nation less than one quarter the size of New Zealand, though admittedly with five times its population, which consistently produced cricketers the like of Jayawardena, Muralitharan, Sangakkara and more, had to have a fair bit going for it. His favourite story of dedicated watching at the Basin Reserve, was of Martin Crowe and Andrew Jones knocking up 467 test runs in their third-wicket stand against the visitors; nevertheless he held the small island nation in high regard.

Ngaio, who couldn't help but wonder how the man who couldn't be relied upon to remember details of any domestic matter could recall the innings on an almost ball-by-ball basis some seventeen years later, had her own reasons for wanting to visit Sri Lanka. Her own fascination with the location began

ALL THE SAME IN KERALA

even further back when she had read a novel set in Ceylon's colonial era. Viewing the National Geographic channel since had made her relatively knowledgeable about the top sites for exploration.

When the ship's confirmed itinerary surfaced as they paid the deposit for their trip, the couple noticed Colombo had been edged out, apparently due to political unrest that flared up frequently enough to threaten the country's safe status. They were both extremely disappointed at the change, even though neither reason for their desire to set foot on the island could withstand more than superficial scrutiny.

Colombo's departure from the lineup meant the nod went to "Cochin". The shipping line's itinerary planners had apparently missed the change of this city's name even though they'd picked up on the Bombay-Mumbai reversion that occurred in the same year. Lyall and Ngaio consoled themselves with the thought that they hadn't seen much of South India, and the fact that Kochi in Kerala was known in its heyday by such descriptions as the "Queen of the Arabian Sea", and "Venice of the Orient" promised this would be a worthy replacement.

In the days preceding their arrival at the substitute port Ngaio checked out Salman Rushdie's *The Moor's Last Sigh* from the ship's library. Regret over the missed opportunity had faded somewhat, to be replaced by the scents of cinnamon and vanilla, which became heavy in her imagination. The ship had cruised past Sri Lanka the previous morning, without her giving it much of a thought. Now, though, their first view of Kochi was a disappointment. The couple looked over the dull grey roofs of the buildings of the port to a brown mountain of rusting metal piled a little along the dock. The former thoughts

SEVENTEEN SEAS

of Sri Lanka's attractions resurged, and now the loss of Buddha's teeth reposing in gold-topped temples, and the green expanse of the CCCG, seemed even more regrettable.

Uniformed men guarded the gate between Kochi's port and city to keep the crowd outside at bay. The fleet of tour buses swept out the gateway unimpeded, transporting the tourists to exotic destinations – a cultural tour of the rural heartland including glimpses of the unhurried lifestyle of the locals, their simple homes and small workshops (soft drink provided); a canal cruise of Kerala's backwaters (tea, coffee or a soft drink served at a hotel); or Fort Kochi with its old colonial architecture (refreshments served at a local hotel). An even more impressive fleet of taxis and auto-rickshaws was gathered outside, denied entry. Passengers electing to do their own thing walked out from the isolated territory to be mobbed by drivers offering their services.

Ngaio and Lyall followed groups of others taking their chances.

"Taxi with air-con." From experience, they knew this wasn't a guarantee the equipment was in working order.

"Special price for whole morning. Only five hundred rupees."

"I have Ferrari. Take you to Old Kochi." Anyone impressed by this claim would be escorted to a three-wheeled auto-rickshaw where the legend 'Ferrari' sign-written on the back window would be pointed out proudly. It was a popular brand, it appeared – or rather rebranding – as a good number of the otherwise identical autos, described by some as a bicycle on steroids, had joined in on the joke.

Lyall and Ngaio had been pleased to find the name of the place where the ship was moored was marked on their map

ALL THE SAME IN KERALA

as Wellington Island, and assumed the victor of the Battle of Waterloo was remembered in this part of the former British Empire also. However, the country famous for illusions such as the legendary rope trick had more secrets in its repertoire. It wasn't till they looked, much later, at other sources that they found the area referred to alternatively as Willington, even though named for Lord Willingdon once Governor General and Viceroy of India. And the island, which now blended with the surrounding city as though it had existed forever, was in fact a man-made expanse constructed from sand excavated while deepening Kochi port. However, being ignorant of these facts at the time, and though this place looked nothing like home, to the Wellingtons the familiar name seemed a good sign. They set out prepared to make the most of their day in this historic part of India's southwest.

They decided to walk a distance to where their map mentioned a ferry service across to the old city, and began to brave their way through the clamour of the drivers, turning down all offers, which became increasingly more reasonable the further they progressed.

"You want a taxi?"

"No, thank you, we're walking to the ferry."

"Special price for whole morning. Only four hundred rupees."

"No, thank you, we're going to walk."

"Special price for whole morning. Only three hundred rupees." The further from the gate the cheaper the price. That was usually the case, they'd found in many parts of Asia. Then they heard a different line.

"This man, he's an honest man. You go with Abdul."

The man speaking indicated another – a middle-aged man

standing a little apart from the crowd. This was a new angle – one driver recommending another. Perhaps it was a pre-tested and proven approach perfected by a pair of friends, but it came at a good time. Lyall and Ngaio were already reconsidering their plan of walking any great distance. They were feeling the effects of the heat after going just a couple of hundred metres, and starting to think that by the time they reached the ferry it was likely they'd be ready to return to the comfort of the ship. That scenario wasn't an option, so they stopped to consider the recommendation made.

Abdul, though obliging when signalled forward by his sponsor, seemed more laid back, or perhaps less desperate, than the other hundred hopefuls around him. He'd take them to Old Kochi, show them the best of the attractions over the course of the morning for one hundred rupees. On the basis of other offers being made this was clearly a very good price. Previous experience, however, had impressed upon Ngaio and Lyall that the quote given at the commencement of a journey often bore little relationship to that demanded at the end, so they sought confirmation. Abdul assured them the quote was correct. One hundred rupees was the contract. In their home port of Wellington, this amount wouldn't buy them a cup of coffee. If it supported Abdul's family for even half a day, then Kochi had a lot to recommend it as a place for relocation to avoid inflation. What's more, Abdul's English was readily understandable, an important point for people whose Malayalam didn't reach past "namaskaaram". Especially when even that knowledge was redundant, given that "hello" was freely used here.

Abdul led them to his vehicle, a black three-wheeled auto-rickshaw almost indistinguishable from the millions of

ALL THE SAME IN KERALA

other such overgrown tricycles without which transportation throughout Asia would grind to a halt. This too bore the Ferrari claim. Abdul didn't draw attention to it but grinned as it was noted, then invited his charges to climb into the back, an area supplied with nothing but a single bench seat – minus doors, side windows, seatbelts, airbags, and any other refinements that might be expected to come with a model claiming to emanate from Maranello. He settled himself into the front compartment, grasped the handlebars, and turned the key. There was a noise that made Lyall wonder fleetingly if his son was indeed calling at their Karori house to see that the lawns were kept in check, and the mutant moped set off.

It was years since the last journey they'd undertaken in such a style and the advantages of tuktuk travel swept over them in reminder. It's certainly the way to get up close and personal with those you've come to observe, thought Ngaio as they narrowly avoided a mother carrying one child and leading another at an intersection on Indira Gandhi Road. Further on they were forced to a stop as a service truck ahead paused to pick up a load of refuse piled at the side of the street. Here we are, in a place famed for its spices, and we have to be here on rubbish day, thought Lyall, wrinkling his nose as the full range of relevant aromas passed through the cabin.

Abdul made a turn and slowed to negotiate a barrier half blocking a bridge approach. He'd take them over the old Thoppumpady bridge, he explained. There was a new one but it was further away, and this one was less busy as it was now closed to larger traffic. Less busy than the alternative this bridge may be, but they appeared to be making the crossing at the same time as what could have been a year's production to

125

roll off the assembly line at the nearest auto-rickshaw factory and, more worryingly, an additional quota of pedestrians and cyclists. For variety, a horse-drawn cart also added to the congestion. They bumped their way across the uneven surface that was laid down in the time of the British raj – a concerning sixty plus years before.

Abdul, though, proved to be not only multi-lingual, and an auto-wallah of sufficient skill, but also an accomplished tour guide. Stopping midway across the structure he turned around in his seat to explain that this middle part of the bridge went up to let ships pass underneath. Like London Bridge, he added. Ngaio, her preference for terra firma reconfirmed by the tree-tops experience in Penang, grasped the upright beside her and questioned if that feature was still used.

"Not any more," Abdul assured her, "ships go other way now."

All the same, she relaxed when the sound beneath the wheels of the autorick solidified.

"Look at that," she pointed to a sign at the entrance to the old city. It read –

KERALA – GOD'S OWN COUNTRY

A little further on there was a variation.

SMILE – YOU'RE IN KERALA, GOD'S OWN COUNTRY

For a couple coming from a place that also claimed the declaration "God's Own Country", frequently shortened to "God's Own" or even "Godzone", it was a pleasing thought. They were warming to this place.

ALL THE SAME IN KERALA

Perhaps Abdul caught the change of mood. He stopped again and put a request. Would they do him a favour and visit some shops he'd take them to? As experienced travellers in Asia, Ngaio and Lyall had met this one before.

"We don't want to buy anything," they told him.

Once again, though, there was a variation. They didn't have to buy a thing, Abdul assured them. He didn't receive a commission, but with the ship in port there was a special incentive offered for drivers. If he took his charges to five nominated shops, he would earn a free tee-shirt. In terms of Indian prices, a free tee-shirt seemed in the same league as a cup of coffee at home. They looked at each other. How could they deny the man that? If their driver could indeed guarantee they didn't have to buy, they could hardly refuse. He could, so they couldn't. Abdul pulled up in front of the first shop and went to the office to register his contract while the Wellingtons were welcomed by one of a line of waiting attendants, each one of whom looked to Ngaio as though he could be on leave from Bollywood and was just awaiting the call for the next part as male romantic lead.

They were given a glass of tea and shown around each of the departments. The quality of the goods and the manner of display had improved markedly since her first visit to India, thought Ngaio. All the same, they emerged thirty-five minutes later having managed to avoid pulling out their credit cards.

"Did you buy anything?" enquired Abdul. He seemed quite content with their reply – perhaps because there were four further stores to come.

The next shop was very much like the one before. The salesman, who was even more good looking than those in the previous place, began in the carpet showroom, unrolling rugs

127

of every size out on the tiled floor. Yes, agreed Ngaio truthfully, with Lyall supporting, they were beautiful, but the fact was they didn't need any more carpets. The young man, who Ngaio decided must have been descended from the Hindu gods, raised and lowered the hems of the mat to reveal the sheen of the silk. Yes, it was stunning, but their home in Karori already had wall-to-wall carpet. That was not a problem, they were assured – in that case you lay this carpet on top. But they were on the ship, on their way to Europe. The man must indeed have had divine ancestry – he had an answer to every human dilemma, and once again the solution was made clear. Their pick would be packed, sent, and waiting for them when they got home. With a tinge of regret they could not reward the quality of the salesmanship, let alone the evidence of divinity, they spent a further ten minutes moving through the other rooms making appropriate appreciative comments about bronze artworks, pashminas, jewellery, wooden crafts.

Abdul said goodbye to the friend he was talking to in the shade of a cashew tree, and after establishing that this place too had failed to make a sale, the motor mower sound started up again and the tour resumed.

"You want to see a church?"

The Wellingtons agreed, yes that would be good. At least they wouldn't be pressed to purchase. The would-be-Ferrari roared into the courtyard of the Santa Cruz Basilica and the couple looked up at the twin Gothic spires.

"Oldest church in Kochi," said Abdul, waving them towards the doorway.

A group of three sat in a pew near the front, their heads bowed. Tourists walked through the sanctuary with little regard for the would-be worshippers, discussing the features of the ornamentation and taking pictures. A priest was giving a small group of visitors a lecture on the art works that adorned the interior. The sales technique here was only a little less subtle than in the shops visited, for the cleric stood conspicuously near a copious receptacle with a slot in the top and a notice pointing out the price of maintaining this piece of history.

Abdul followed up the stop with a quick drive into the grounds of the residence of the Bishop.

"He's not here now," he announced, apparently interpreting some sign of non-occupation visible to those in the know. "We go on?"

The Wellingtons, who had not intended to request an audience with His Excellency anyway, nodded and Abdul whisked them to shop number three.

"No parcels," he noted as once more they left the luxury of the air-conditioned building and returned to the increasing heat of the outside air.

"No, we said we didn't want to buy anything."

"Now I'll take you to the Chinese fishing nets."

"Yes, we want to see those." The pre-port lecture had included that as a must-see, though Ngaio wondered at the time if something as prosaic as fishing nets could capture her interest and hold it for long.

A few minutes later, having walked through groups of children offering fistfuls of postcards for sale, she was standing on the beach looking at the famed nets and, somewhat to her surprise, found their design fascinating. Even an engineering ingénue could see that these were something to be marvelled at – even more so when she remembered the claim that the system was designed more than six hundred years before. She watched as the fishermen walked along beams suspended over the water and the nets dipped into the water, then were raised by a simple pull of a rope thanks to a finely balanced row of rocks serving as counterweights. She pulled the camera out of her shoulder bag and walked a few more steps towards the water. One of the team of fishermen called her forward – come, take photo – but she stood her ground. Not only was the whole structure in shot at this distance, but from her previous travels on the subcontinent Ngaio knew that a snap at close range would provoke a claim for some financial consideration. This was a land where even supposed sadhus didn't pose for free.

She replaced the camera in her bag and walked forward for a better look. The fisherman approached again. He indicated a metal bowl on the platform.

"Fish," he said, "come and look, take picture."

No, she assured him, she'd seen fish before.

"Take picture," he invited again. At her further polite refusal he dashed to the bowl, picked out a small polka-dotted fish and held it up by the dorsal fin for her to admire while it wriggled and gasped. She turned away. Other tourists walked up and Ngaio took the opportunity to retreat to the roadside, only to encounter the postcard pushers once more.

"You like gods? Pictures of Indian gods," said a pair of boys working in tandem. "Elephant-head god, monkey god, god with six arms…"

Polite refusals didn't work. Ngaio looked around for the auto and found that theirs was indistinguishable from the other fifty also parked nearby. Lyall was still on the beach by the nets engaged in a conversation with another tourist. By the

ALL THE SAME IN KERALA

illustrative movements made by their arms the two men were working out the mechanism of the structure.

"Here, Shiva god. You see, he have snake in hair."

"Maybe you like flowers. Have flowers here," Boy two riffled through a further set of postcards.

Ngaio's desire not to be rude to the children was second only to her desire to escape, preferably without a swatch of postcards that she really didn't want. She tried a new tack.

"They're all gods," she said "I want goddess."

"Goddess?" the boys stopped and sorted frantically through the cards.

"Yes," added Ngaio, "I want…" the memory of a friend back home telling her she was named for a goddess came to mind at the opportune moment, "I want Lakshmi."

The riffling stopped, the boys consulted in Malayalam, she assumed, then darted off in different directions to interrupt further small colleagues engaged in other negotiations.

"I be coming back," called the slightly taller one as he took off.

Ngaio also took the opportunity to take flight. 'Sorry, I won't be,' she thought in response and, gaining the road, walked quickly to the waiting fleet of three-wheeled Ferraris.

A couple, also from the ship, were making their way in the same direction, and discussing how they'd paid the price to view the mechanics of the fishing method. After being invited onto the platform to help pull on the rope that raised the net, the man found that, rather than being rewarded for his services, a monetary contribution was expected to be given for the experience. It seemed the small spotted fish and its companions were not the main catch from which the men at the nets expected to earn their income. The woman was holding a handful of postcards. She converted the cost of the stop, nets experience and cards combined, from the American dollars they had handed over.

"It's only two pounds all together," she said, "and I can give these to the children next door."

It was almost a relief to enter shop number four with its air-conditioning and a welcoming glass of iced tea. Again the salesmanship was superb. Ngaio wondered briefly whether the immaculately tailored young man who escorted them from room to room had served his apprenticeship in sales as a barefoot boy on Kochi beach. Or perhaps he had a psychology degree for he knew when to abandon one product and draw their attention to another.

Abdul was more than puzzled when they exited this store too minus shopping bags.

"Perhaps you'll get something at the next place," he commented. For one who had assured them it was of no consequence to him whether they bought or not, he looked a little dejected.

Lyall had seen enough of shops, especially as the four so far had stocked the same range of goods and there was no reason to suppose others would offer any variety. He voted to call a halt to that part of the tour. Ngaio, however, felt they should honour their promise. Besides, there was just one to go to reach the required five. She sought assurance from Abdul, who confirmed his original story – the tee-shirt would be forthcoming even if Fort Kochi's finest failed the final test to flush out their Visa cards.

By this time they could spot the difference between wool and

ALL THE SAME IN KERALA

silk carpets at a dozen paces and knew the words to use to comment admiringly on the superb quality, but to the disappointment of yet another hopeful Bollywood candidate they still saw no reason to overlay their present axminster with an additional layer.

"Nothing being posted?" asked Abdul, once more noting their bag-free hands. Ngaio suspected this might be the one and only time in his career as a rickshaw captain that he had witnessed such an event. She wondered how he'd relate the story to Mrs Abdul that evening – of how a couple from New Zealand turned the tables and provided the locals with an example of their own country's historic ideal of detachment from material things.

"You want to see Jews' church?"

The apparent incongruity of the presence of a synagogue in south India was well covered in the travel guides they'd perused in the ship's library, and also mentioned in the port lecture. As they alighted at the spot, however, Abdul spotted a small hitch. Lyall's shorts, even though approaching the knee, were unacceptable. For a country in which the millennia-long religious tradition of male nakedness was still sometimes observed it seemed a small quibble, but the ruling was clear. While her husband waited in the street redolent with the heady scents of a score of spice shops Ngaio, whose legs were covered and therefore not a cause for offence, was escorted to the entrance alone. She examined the interior hall of worship with its goldrailed pulpit and repository for sacred scrolls, its chandeliers, and floor covered with hand-painted tiles. It was just as well she was on her own. Lyall, she was sure, on seeing the ticket collector at the door and the souvenir seller in the anteroom would be tempted to show off his biblical knowledge, scant though it was, by muttering something about a den of thieves. Yet, she understood, with only a handful of worshippers left in the area that was still termed 'Jew town', the alternative to this measure of commercialism would be the lack of preservation. In that case she was happy to pay the entrance fee.

"You want to see temple?"

Of course they should. Didn't the signs say this was God's own country? In view of the fact they'd made visits to a church and a synagogue, it was fitting they offer equal obeisance to the varieties on offer. Besides, Ngaio felt duty-bound to repay the goddess for invoking the Devi in her recent time of need on the beach, and for the resulting deliverance from the multitude of postcard sellers.

The Sree Dharmanath Jainalay at which they alighted next, however, did not provide that opportunity as it proved to be one dedicated not to the deities of Hinduism, but to those of the Jain faith. Pigeons perched on points along the rooftops in the complex, perhaps appreciative of the fact that they were safer here than on any building in the city or elsewhere, given the Jain religion's strict policy of non-violence to any living thing. As they entered the gate Lyall detected a decided dip in the overhang of the roof on one of the buildings. Not a part of the design, he decided. Then he noticed that no pigeons favoured that particular spot. The rest of the roof hosted a row of roosting birds, but in the vicinity of the dip it was unoc-cupied. Lyall was intrigued. Perhaps the epithet 'bird-brain' was not such a slur as was usually considered, he thought.

The couple left their shoes at the place indicated near the gate and walked to the several buildings in the complex. A ceremony was taking place in one of them. A small group of people stood behind a priest as he gave reverence to the image of an Enlightened One – circling a flame and uttering verses while another man rang a bell hanging to the side. Behind them a woman knelt and painstakingly arranged coloured grains of rice to form an AUM symbol. Ngaio read the Jain dictum displayed on a wall –

NON-VIOLENCE, SELF CONTROL AND AUSTERITIES CONSTITUTE THE HIGHEST TRUTH.

She felt more moved than she had in the previous places of worship that day. There's something about a religion that not only welcomes birds to their buildings but sets up hospitals to attend to their care, she thought. That night at least she would select the vegetarian choice on the dinner menu.

Lyall leant forward to catch Abdul's words as they started back to the ship.

"You like temple?"

"Yes, it was very clean and peaceful." He thought a moment, then leaned forward again.

"You've taken us to a church, a synagogue, and a temple. Your name is Abdul – you must go to a mosque."

Abdul turned around grinning. "All the same in Kerala," he said with the characteristic Indian roll of the head that foreigners find so fascinating but can't imitate. A minute later as they headed towards the Thoppumpady bridge he throttled back the engine and pointed to one of the street signs they'd passed earlier – "Smile, you're in God's own country".

"All the same in Kerala," he repeated.

Back at the gate to the wharf Lyall pulled out his wallet, waiting for the predicted dispute over the agreed price.

"One hundred rupees, you said?"

Abdul nodded in agreement.

The unprecedented acquiescence checked Lyall momentarily. He pulled out the required note, then offered a little more. Abdul put up his hand with a gesture of refusal, adding that any addition was not necessary.

The couple walked back to the ship slightly perplexed.

"A hundred rupees and a tee-shirt," said Ngaio, "I hope he gets someone this afternoon who wants to buy something."

"A silk carpet," suggested Lyall.

"At least."

"I have Ferrari. Take you to Old Kochi."

— CHAPTER 13 —

Guests of the Goddess

Eduardo, stateroom attendant for the Yorkshires and their neighbours on C deck forward, said he was from Goa. That no doubt explained his name, thought Yvonne who had pondered previously about the reason why their steward bore a name more redolent of Mediterranean Europe than southern Asia.

"What a shame we didn't stop there," she commiserated, thinking of Eduardo's missed chance to break the long cycle of celibacy. Besides, recently she'd read a paperback romance in which the flaxen-tressed Marcia, prompted by her fiancé Richard who was laid up with a sprained ankle, had accepted the offer of their hotel manager's son to show her the sights of the old colonial capital. The memory of how the pair succumbed to animal lust after viewing the Church of St Francis of Assisi was still fresh in her mind. It wasn't as though Yvonne had any thoughts of replicating the event – far from it – but she would like to see the museum referred to in the book. Heavens, she asked herself, when had she got so old?

Eduardo – middle-aged, five feet three, and not at all likely to be confused for his fictional fellow Konkani or Goan who had so smitten the virginal Marcia – confided that his wife was at that very moment on the train to Mumbai, and if all went well he'd share a few hours with her at a hotel the following afternoon. A shy grin spread across his face as he told her.

Not everyone at the table in the Alexandria restaurant that

137

evening was as enthusiastic about the next destination.

"To me it's still Bombay – I can't think why they changed it." Harry Hampshire perused the menu momentarily before settling on the evening's "Best of British" selection – corned beef hash and mashed potatoes with baked beans.

"Because that was an English name," 'Sybil' explained, "and we altered it from a Portuguese term. Now it's named for Mumba Ai, the local goddess. I was just explaining that to you this afternoon, wasn't I dear?" she turned to 'Basil'. She wore a new pashmina over her shoulders, suggesting that at least one cruiser had pulled out their credit card in Kochi.

"In that case," Harry responded, "Bollywood should now be Mollywood, or Mummywood. I can't see that happening."

Anwen Cardiff broke in to say they hadn't booked a tour for the following day and could anyone suggest what they should see in the city.

"Stay on board, that's my advice," growled Harry. "I were here thirty years ago, then Zelda and I came more'n twenty years back. In that time you'd expect most places to go forward. Not here. It got bigger and dirtier."

"It's certainly bigger. They say four hundred families move to Mumbai from the surrounding villages every day of the year." There was a tone of amazement in Glen Henderson's voice. He still clung to the New Zealand tradition of each family owning a house set on at least a thousand square metre section, and couldn't imagine how so many new arrivals in the Indian city could all be accommodated. He found it hard enough to adjust to the knowledge that his home area was now a part of a metropolitan mass with a combined population of more than a million. The fact that it would take about thirteen Aucklands to

GUESTS OF THE GODDESS

make up greater Mumbai was rather too much to contemplate.

"There must have been a lot of progress," said Aled, "Mumbai's said to be the financial capital of India, and the I.T. capital of Asia."

"That'd be right," agreed Glen who knew first hand of the number of his country's institutions that had outsourced their call centres to this part of the world. "If we phone up a firm to ask a simple question we find we're not speaking to someone down the road in New Zealand who knows what we're on about – we're likely to be talking to somebody in Mumbai."

Harry nodded in agreement.

"That port lecturer – he didn't say anything good about the place. Take my advice," he repeated. "I'm stoppin' on board."

Lynn had also visited the city known as the gateway to India many years before and, despite her main memory being of the inside of a hospital ward and lying on a hard bed with tubes and leads attached to various parts of her body, had no intention of letting this opportunity slip by.

"Glen and I are going to hire a taxi for the day," she said quietly to Anwen who was sitting to her left, "would you like to join us? We could share the cost."

Anwen's response, expressing agreement, was cut across by Bradford Yorkshire.

"India were 'nother of our blumin mistakes in my opinion," he said in a tone that underlined his belief that it was the only opinion worth considering. "We spent all our money and energy on t' colonies and what did we get for 't? Blumin tea. They threw us out." He paused for effect before carrying on, "And blow me down if they didn't then all think they had a right t' move t' England. T'were a high price we had t' pay for

SEVENTEEN SEAS

cup of tea."

From the comments being exchanged around the various bars and lounges that evening it seemed there'd be more than the usual few electing to skip the chance of an excursion ashore.

At least Eduardo was looking forward to it, thought Yvonne as she lay in bed later that night. Fancy he and Mrs Eduardo being together for only four hours in eight months. She prodded Bradford whose snores had doubled from twenty-five to fifty decibels. He rolled over and the pattern altered to the explosive variety she particularly deplored. Four hours in eight months – well, there were some compensations for such an arrangement.

It seemed the port authorities at Mumbai had read the travel brochures too. As daylight dawned all aboard the vessel, which had berthed before sunup, could see the large banner painted across the white façade of the cruise terminal. "*Incredible !ndia*"

Tubs and planter boxes of shrubs and flowers were arranged either side of the doors that were standing wide open in welcome to the returning British.

The Hendersons and the Cardiffs made an early departure, eager to experience what they could in the day. Bradford Yorkshire had been influenced by Harry Hampshire's small tirade the previous evening and altered his plan in favour of a quiet day downing beer and watching television in Champions bar, which brought up the matter of a pair of coach tickets already purchased for a city tour. Perhaps the Cardiffs might like to help them out again, Bradford suggested to Yvonne, but his wife hadn't appreciated the previous such occasion at Port Klang when she was forced to spend the day aboard and miss

140

whatever the local area had to offer. She quickly came up with an alternative solution. Zelda Hampshire was even quicker to accept when Yvonne put it to her. While their husbands spent the day patronizing the bars on board the two women would enjoy theirs even more for the men's absence.

Less than an hour after disembarking the Hendersons and the Cardiffs, their cameras in hand, stood on a bridge providing a view over the area that accommodated dhobi ghat, but which Aled dubbed Mumbai Laundry Central. They jostled for a place among other tourists while attempting to fob off sellers of balloons, peacock feather fans, beaded purses, maps, and other apparent musts for every visitor to the city. Down below, the strip that accommodated the industry was packed bank to bank with small corrugated iron buildings, large tubs, and washing lines covered with pegged cloth. The couples looked down on the scene where a couple of hundred dhobi wallahs stood rhythmically dunking garments in the concrete tubs and slapping them on stone slabs.

"It looks like this family's got the contract for a hospital," noted Anwen pointing at an area displaying multiple white sheets and what looked like blue scrubs.

Lynn thought of the laundry room in their Auckland home, with its automatic washer and dryer and wondered if she took the washing outside and beat it on the garden steps she'd also look as lean and fit as the workers below.

Glen's attention was not taken for long by the sight of the dhobi pools, his gaze was quickly diverted by the comings and goings at the adjacent railway station. Trains that could hardly be more crammed unless the passengers were first liquefied and poured in, passed by with human body parts protruding from every window and door. Glen gazed in awe. Here was another nation that knew how to provide public transport to move its citizens en masse, even if not in comfort. It looked as though the facility provided transit for a good percentage of the population of the state of Maharashtra.

Lynn felt a tug on her arm and looked around, then reached into her bag to respond to a request. The girl standing at her side was small and dressed in only a skirt. Her top half was bare apart from a row of plastic bangles on both arms. She held out her hand and motioned to her mouth.

"Dollar," she said. Her eyes were dark, glittering and huge.

So far today, although a few others had put out their hands for money, they hadn't encountered any people who seemed as badly off and desperate as she'd seen on her previous visit. Perhaps they hadn't yet been to the worst places. But Lynn was ready for this.

Every night of the voyage their stateroom steward turned down their bed and left a chocolate, wrapped and bearing the wish "Sweet Dreams", on each of their pillows. After a dinner of seven courses – not that either of them had ever ordered more than three – they certainly didn't need a top-up so soon afterwards. So when Lynn reached them before her husband, who admitted freely that he lacked will power, she removed the small gifts and placed them in a cupboard beside the mirror. Over the previous weeks they'd formed a small tower that also served to illustrate the relative stability of the cruise liner. Now Lynn pulled out a portion of the chocolate mini Mount Meru and put it in the child's hand. It wasn't the dollar requested, but a smile spread over the girl's face. A few minutes later as the two couples walked back to their transport Lynn saw emptied

GUESTS OF THE GODDESS

wrappers bearing the message "Sweet Dreams" strewn along the street. At home she would have been embarrassed at her complicity in an act of littering but here the few squares of coloured paper barely registered among the rest of the rubbish. Anyway, that smile had made it all worthwhile.

The two couples' choice of taxi driver proved inspired, even though it had really been a case of coming to a quick agreement in order to curtail the clamour of a score of offers. Daljeet, turban-topped and bearded, spoke excellent English in a cultured tone and gave an informed commentary as they drove through the streets of the city.

"See that building there, with the clock on the front," he pointed, "it used to have a statue of the English Queen, Queen Victoria, on it. The statue was removed after independence."

Daljeet was not old enough to have seen it in situ. Anwen wondered why he had mentioned it and waited for him to make a further point, but no more seemed to be coming.

"Does it still exist?" she asked, though she didn't really care one way or another.

"Yes, it was placed elsewhere." Now he didn't seem keen to pursue it any further.

"Where?" she followed it up to be polite, though it didn't matter.

"It's at the zoo."

Even if Daljeet hadn't expected outrage from his car full of passengers, he was probably unprepared for the ripple of amusement that came from the back seat.

"I apologize," he said as he negotiated a large roundabout, "I did not mean to offend our English visitors."

Glen, seated next to him in the front of the cab, sought to

reassure him.

"It's okay – we're not English, we're from New Zealand," he indicated himself and then Lynn who was sitting behind him.

"And we're from Wales," added Aled.

"Excuse me, I thought Wales was in Great Britain," there was a puzzled tone in Daljeet's voice.

"That's right," but the Welsh aren't English. "We're proud to be British, but we're not English."

Daljeet thought for a moment and rolled his head in agreement.

"The same with some people in India," he said, "proud to be British, but they are not English."

At the next intersection Daljeet made a quick decision and a rapid change of lane. Glen braced for what seemed would lead to an inevitable clash of metal on metal, given the mass of traffic, but nothing came. The taxi, indistinguishable from the millions of other black Hindustan Ambassadors on the roads, slotted into line without any noticeable evasive action by the surrounding drivers. The traffic on the northwest motorway could learn a lesson or two here, thought Glen.

At that point the key to something niggling at the back of his mind occurred to him.

"Where are all the autoricks? The three-wheelers?" he asked.

"They are not allowed in the centre of Mumbai any more sir," answered Daljeet. "Further out in the suburbs you will find scooters still. You said you are coming from New Zealand, sir? Look." He pointed through the windscreen up to his right.

Glen bent down a little and followed Daljeet's finger. From a fifth floor vantage point a familiar face looked back at him.

Chris Cairns was known across many continents, including

this one, to be a giant when it came to hitting sixes over even the longest boundaries at cricket grounds from Eden Park to Trent Bridge. But he had never looked as large and formidable as he did here. Glen estimated the big man's face, uncharacteristically bearded, was a good five metres tall. Pictured alongside was an equally impressive Marvin Atapattu. "Will Atapattu's Delhi tame Cairns' Chandigar?" read the heading over the outsize billboard for the upcoming Twenty-20 challenge.

Another countryman, Lyall Wellington, seated on a coach on his way to join a heritage walk, also saw this and other billboards featuring his black capped heroes. A few minutes later a further banner landscaped across a twelve metre stretch of rough iron roofing showed the face of Craig McMillan for the Kolkata Tigers together with that of Inzamam Ul Haq and his Lahore Badshahs. Lyall found himself torn at the sight. It was a thrill to see his heroes honoured so highly, and largely, but he was unhappy that their own itinerary ruled out the opportunity of being present at this chance to see so many teams of the world's best perform. What was the chance of jumping ship to attend some of the matches? It was a fleeting thought only – the clashes on the cricket fields of the nation would be nothing to the one he'd have to face if he even let out a hint of what he was thinking.

At just the same time as Harry eased himself into a chair by the Riviera bar and signalled the waiter to bring the first beer of the day, Zelda and Yvonne were walking in the "Hanging Gardens" on Malabar Hill. The reason for such a descriptive name wasn't immediately clear when all they could see in the twenty minutes specified by their guide Padma were paths between sparsely-planted beds and some hedge plants trimmed into animal shapes. Others must have wondered too for Padma gave the explanation later as the coach load of cruisers drove off again en route for the next stop on the "Highlights of Mumbai – Best Seller" tour. The gardens were constructed on the slope of the hill, so appearing to give the illusion of hanging. Obviously they hadn't seen it all, including the best part of this particular highlight.

Whatever they saw, Yvonne thought as Zelda and she looked through the gardens, it was better than spending the day aboard the ship with Bradford. She was impressed when she learned that the area where they were walking covered Mumbai's main water reservoir. Zelda stopped to read a plaque attached to a stone pillar.

EXPERIENCE CONFIRMS THAT FRIENDS WHO REGULARLY MEET & WALK IN THE GARDEN HAVE REMAINED HEALTHY AND FIT FOR THE DAY. SPREAD THE MESSAGE OF GOOD HEALTH THROUGH FRIENDSHIP FOR GENERATIONS – M.C.G.M.

This reminded her of her previous visit two decades before when she delighted in spotting the wisdom-to-live-by homilies freely provided in various public places. She now shared some of them, long since committed to memory, with her companion.

"A ticketless travel is a social evil", displayed at a railway station.

"Please be kind to the keeper of the shoes", prompted a sign by the door to a temple.

And her personal favourite –

"It's nice to be important but it's more important to be nice".

MCGM, she pondered now. Mumbai Collected Good-living Maxims? Mottos Conveying Good Messages? Even, perhaps, Metaphysical Convictions of Gandhi (Mahatma).

Padma cleared up this mystery too.

"Municipal Corporation of Greater Mumbai," she said.

The coach moved on to the next scheduled stop where they were given a longer but still inadequate time to see a museum full of art. Yvonne realized the hopelessness of trying to do justice to all areas. While Zelda followed others in the group to the staircase that led to the upper galleries, she restricted her viewing to the halls of sculpture on the ground floor. She preferred three-dimensional figures to paintings anyway. Among the standing figures and stone friezes one showed a male deity clasping a round-breasted female consort. It reminded her of another couple – doubtless not so imposing or beautiful when shown in a state of nature, but more real. She thought of Eduardo and the woman who was prepared to travel in a train for a total of twelve hundred kilometres to see him for a few hours. She hoped they were, at this very moment, fully enveloped in the sort of ecstatic embrace freely depicted in examples of Indian temple art.

If they were, as the broader than usual smile the next morning seemed to indicate, the Canberra deck steward was much more fortunate than many of his fellow countrymen. Passengers remaining aboard and selecting to lunch at Café Bordeaux might have noticed the waiters casting longing looks through the windows that faced the city. The serving staff in the Orangery were doing the same. Had more of the cruisers taken the opportunity to leave the ship and go ashore those who served them each day of the voyage might have managed at least a precious hour or two on their country's soil.

The wooden stairway of the Mani Bhavan Gandhi Sangrahalaya was narrow, as the four sharing a taxi found after Daljeet delivered them to the famous door in Laburnum Road. Clearly its architects had not anticipated the fame that would come upon the house because of its most revered resident, and the resulting numbers who would visit what was now a museum in his honour. Sixty years after the death of Mohandas Gandhi, revered as the Mahatma, the feet that trod the stairs to each of the levels were measured in lakhs as people from all nations came to pay homage at the house associated with some of the 'Great Soul's' most distinctive acts. His four-day fast for peace in the city, the launches of the Quit India movement and the policy of passive resistance took place here, as well as some less auspicious times such as his arrest on a charge of sedition.

Aled was standing, his right leg on a step higher than his left, attempting to read a framed quotation – one of many that lined the walls of the display rooms and the staircases. He had already viewed the upper floors with their exhibits and was on his way down again. Lynn was absorbed in the detail of the diorama of the Mahatma's life and Anwen, as far as he knew, was still standing transfixed in front of the illustrious man's spinning wheel. Aled, the grandson of a non-conformist preacher who was a champion of the Welsh disestablishment movement and, according to family claim descended further back from a close supporter of Griffith Jones and his circulating schools scheme, had been raised with strong nationalist expectations and this place had prompted memories of much of the old rhetoric. Now, however, as he looked at the words in the frame he thought of the time that followed his early upbringing – the three years working in Belfast as a young man, then his return to Cardiff when he met Anwen who seemed a perfect match apart from her membership of an Anglican communion.

Glen came down the stairs towards him as a new group of tourists filed up. There was no room for further study of the material on the walls. The two men descended then waited outside the building till the women joined them.

"Religions are not for separating men from one another, they are meant to bind them," quoted Aled as they were all back in the taxi under the care of Daljeet.

Anwen was looking out the window at the row of closely-set houses, as they negotiated the lines of traffic that daily make a mockery of what was once no doubt a tranquil suburban avenue befitting its name Laburnum Road.

"What brought that on?" she asked.

"It's a quotation of Gandhi's that I saw on the wall."

Anwen reached out, took her husband's hand and squeezed it.

By late afternoon squads of coaches and taxis reversed their morning journey, returning their fares to their temporary home. The Cardiffs and Hendersons arrived at the gangway at the same time as Zelda and Yvonne. Yes, thanks, they'd had a great day, they assured each other. Others reboarding also reported positively, with those who were repeat visitors speaking of the number of visible advances made in the years between calls.

SEVENTEEN SEAS

For a city that was home to more than four times the number of people in their entire country, the Hendersons were pleasantly surprised at the number of open spaces with grass and trees they'd seen in the course of the day. True, the leaves of the trees were dark with the sediment of car exhausts and cooking fires, so much so that the pale green of new leaves stood in stark contrast to the deep grey of the older foliage. The wonder was that the trees survived. Zelda had noticed the attempts of the city's caretakers to beautify the city of Mother Mumba by the placement of planter boxes of flowers and shrubs along street kerbs and bridges. Highway flyovers, unaesthetic necessities in any country, were lined with brightly coloured tubs of greenery. It was just a shame, all agreed, that every building, be it tenement or marble wonder of a past time, was dark with accumulated grime.

"Someone's going to make their fortune here with a water-blasting business," predicted Glen. If he were twenty-five years younger, he thought, he might do something about it himself.

In his spare half hour between reboarding, showering, and preparing for dinner, Dick Napier downloaded his photographs onto his laptop. One showed a scene that illustrated Mumbai's inwards migration. A family of five – parents, two children and a grandmother – occupied a small triangular island in the middle of a city intersection. The area was raised less than ten centimetres above the streets, offering no protection from any side or above. The family's possessions were beside them – a small stack of bedding, plastic drink bottles, and a few other items. This was a typical sight he'd been told by his local guide on asking – more than forty years of searching for stories meant the habit was too deeply ingrained in his system to abandon now. Newcomers to the city would occupy any available space till they found more permanent accommodation – a process that could take weeks or months.

Four hundred families daily – Dick had heard the same report. Say there's only five per family, he calculated now, that's two thousand people every day. Two thousand times 365. Even if births equalled deaths among the rest of the residents, that was a nett gain of 730,000 through migration alone. In New Zealand that would be a large sized city all on its own. In fact, by far the largest if Auckland's population was broken into its constituent regions. It far outstripped the capital, Wellington, and was more than thirteen times the size of his own home area. He tried to imagine the small city where he lived, multiplied so many times, and shuddered. He liked it the way it was now.

He hoped the figures were misreported. Dick was about to close the photo file when something caught his eye. He'd missed it earlier when his attention was fully on the family, now with the picture filling the whole screen he could see that the group was gathered together sitting in a patch of shade cast by an advertising sign. The first thing that occurred to him as he read the words was that it was in English, but he knew that was one of the official national languages of India and there was no doubt that in the international world of commerce it was well in the forefront.

"Presenting LIC's Health Plus", read the words. Whether or not they were intelligible to those they sheltered from the sun, Mr Napier was highly dubious about the chance that the benefits of the policy offered by the Life Insurance Corporation of India would have held much relevance to them. However, he thought before clicking out of the program, the sign itself was serving some purpose to safeguard those in its shadow.

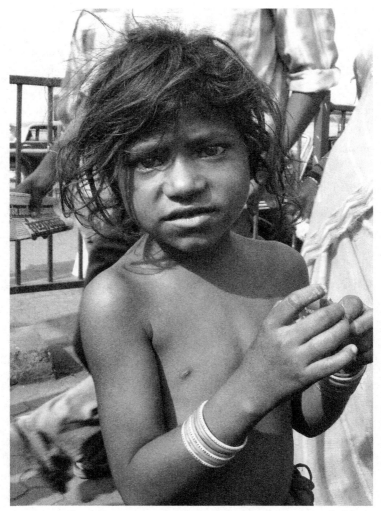

It wasn't the dollar requested, but a smile spread over the girl's face.

— CHAPTER 14 —

Arabian Days and Nights

With the former empire being left behind in her wake, the cruise liner sailed westward. If the hundreds of Indians among the crew felt bereft as the sea-miles between the stern and the sub-continent increased, they did a good job of hiding it, thought Lynn Henderson at dinner in the Alexandria Restaurant. Pratik smiled as widely as ever as they entered the room, and even more broadly when they told him how much they'd enjoyed their day. He recommended the fruit salad, promising it contained kiwifruit – to remind her of home.

"In India," he told her, "we have a fruit called chickoo. It is similar in size and colour, but it is smooth-skinned. So at home we call the kiwifruit 'chickoo with hair'".

The pair laughed. They could imagine how each other was feeling – away from their own land with the distance increasing by the hour.

Nine weeks earlier the ship had left its home port of Southampton in Europe. Since then she had negotiated the passage between the two continents of the Americas, sailed the Pacific Ocean to reach New Zealand then the island continent of Australia, turned north to visit ports in Asia including the Indian subcontinent, and now her bow was headed towards the remaining continent of Africa.

Five days of sea lay ahead.

Dick Napier consulted the map showing the route's

153

navigational plan, which was displayed near the entrance to the Crow's Nest bar and lounge on Sun deck forward. Ms Coolangatta, on her way to her Spanish lesson, stopped on seeing him.

"Got it figured out, Captain?"

Dick had been called a lot of things in his lifetime, Ed and Boss most commonly, but captain was a new one.

"This is our noon position," he pointed, "we're north of the Maldives, due south of Pakistan and Afghanistan..."

"It can't be far enough away for me."

Dick didn't follow up on the comment. He moved his finger to the left.

"We're heading west across the Arabian Sea."

"That'll take five days?"

"Three days across then we turn north and take two days up the Red Sea, by the look of it."

Caroline shrugged.

"It doesn't look far on the map. Gotta go to my class. Hasta luego."

She moved on again, entering the door to the Uganda Room nearby, and greeting her fellow estudiantes with "hola". At least when they got to dock at Barcelona she'd manage the opening and closing of any conversation. Anything in the middle was still very much in doubt.

Dick entered the Crow's Nest. He was in luck. A party of four rose, vacating one of the bays of seats near the centre of the panoramic window where he liked to sit. A good book and his journal beside one hand, a full glass by the other, and a great 180 degree view in the direction of travel, he could be set for hours. A waiter appeared at his side.

"Good afternoon, Sir. Coffee, black with one sugar?" His order was anticipated by a smiling Sunil. They both knew Dick's routine by now. Coffee after lunch, then at about three o'clock Sunil would reappear at his side for the expected order of beer.

As Sunil moved away to fetch the drink, Dick Napier was torn by conflicting thoughts – pleased at the good service, yet somewhat dissatisfied that he had fallen into a recognizable routine. One of the reasons he had decided to take this trip was to shake himself free of the groove he'd settled into so easily when he retired. He tapped his fingers on the cover of his journal, then relaxed with a small sigh.

"Darn it all, it's true," he admitted to himself, "I am a creature of habit." There were signs of it even in his childhood when he established a pattern of brushing his teeth that hadn't varied since.

"And that's not so bad..." he began to follow up his own thoughts when someone approached and stopped on his left side. Thinking it was Sunil back with the coffee Dick reached up, his pen in hand, ready to sign the docket.

"Hello Dick." He heard the voice of Lyall Wellington, closely followed by a greeting from Mrs W.

"Kia ora," said Ngaio.

She'd taken to using the phrase on board since she found most people asked as soon as they started talking if the couple were Australians. It was even worse when many didn't ask, but took it for granted. Ngaio didn't have any prejudice against Aussies – a statement she was quick to throw into any conversation that threatened to deteriorate into the half-joking half-serious banter that often arose at parties at home. It was particularly prevalent at gatherings of the social group associated with the cricket club that Lyall belonged to. Memories of the notorious 'underarm' episode and a whole list of dodgy umpiring decisions that had occurred on Australian soil were bound to arise soon after the beers were brought out. In fact, Ngaio was quick to add, she had relatives in that country. All the same, she was proud of her fourth generation New Zealander status and over recent years had gained increasing satisfaction that her given name was from te reo – "the Maori language", she translated for anyone who looked blank at the reference. When they got home again she was going to follow up on that recurring family rumour that her great-great-grandmother was Ngati Kahungunu with connections in southern Hawke's Bay.

"On your own? Can we join you?" Ngaio asked now. The couple sat on the other side of the semicircular bay seating without waiting for an answer. It saved Dick having to think quickly about what to reply. He enjoyed his times alone, but it was good to have company from time to time as well, and this couple of fellow-Kiwis had left a good impression when he'd met them earlier in the voyage.

Ngaio and Lyall, tempted by the aroma coming from the cup delivered by Sunil, put in an order for coffee also. The three sat and sipped, agreeing on the need to buy an espresso from one of the lounge bars if they wanted to satisfy their craving for a serious brew.

The discussion that followed began with Dick applauding the expertise of a particular barista at a café in Cuba Street in Wellington, and Ngaio and Lyall's quick promise to visit the establishment on their return. They were a little embarrassed that it had taken a non-resident of their city to bring the place

ARABIAN DAYS AND NIGHTS

to their attention. The conversation moved on by means of a trail that progressed through sharing opinions of the best brands, to varieties of coffee beans, and coffee-growing areas of the world, before halting at the mention of the fields of Sumatra. Dick Napier had obviously researched his topic – he now gave an appreciation of the characteristics of the product of the Gayo mountain region in Aceh. Medium roasted it was full bodied with low acidity, though he particularly favoured a darker roast that accentuated notes of papaya and chocolate. Since the tsunami and earthquake, he told them, he had sought to source his weekly pack from that part of the world in order to support the survival of the area and the continuation of its crop.

Ngaio felt a flush of excitement wash over her.

"You remember the tsunami?" she asked, "and the earthquake?"

"Of course. It wasn't long ago." Dick wondered momentarily whether he looked so ancient that his memory would be questioned automatically. But Ngaio and Lyall were of a similar vintage, he estimated, give or take a couple of years or so.

"Sorry, I didn't mean …" Ngaio let her sentence hang, then started again on firmer ground. "It's just that all the time and the area we've come through, there's been no mention of it."

"I've been thinking the same."

The three continued, sharing their surprise and their disappointment that few of their fellow travellers on the ship seemed to make the connection between the scenes of devastation that had dominated the world news for so many weeks so comparatively recently, and the seas they were cruising through.

Lyall told how the couple had asked the local Thai guide

escorting their shuttle-load of passengers from Laem Chabang to Pattaya what effect the tsunami had on the area, and received the response that they had fared well, unlike those on the western coast.

"That's right, " confirmed the ex-newsman. He opened his journal and withdrew a sheet of A4 paper. It unfolded to reveal a map printed, it seemed, from the internet. The ship's journey so far was shown by a line drawn by a blue ballpoint pen. He pointed to the spot off the west coast of northern Sumatra that was already marked with an asterisk.

"This was the epicentre of the quake that triggered it. And these were the areas that were hit most badly." He moved his finger over the coasts of Indonesia and Thailand, up to Sri Lanka and India via the Andaman and Nicobar Islands, jerking it a little southwards to include the Maldives and sweeping it across to the coast of Africa, stabbing at the islands of Mauritius and Madagascar before moving it to settle on Somalia.

"None of the worst-hit places are on our itinerary," said Ngaio.

"Penang," said Dick, "People on the beaches were swept away."

Ngaio hadn't realized. She thought back to their day on Penang Hill. Perhaps that had been a better idea than she appreciated at the time.

"Thousands in South India were caught, though only a few hundred in Kerala where we were."

Only a few hundred, thought Ngaio, but the newsman's elaboration confirmed he was not intending to dismiss the number lightly.

"The effect was more deadly on the east coast within the Bay of Bengal. Then there was Sri Lanka. There were between thirty and forty thousand lost there."

Ngaio felt a shockwave hit as he continued.

"But that was taken off our schedule."

"Are you saying that was the reason?" she asked.

"No, probably not," Dick said. "The political situation's enough for that." Lyall thought of interruptions in the international cricket calendar, and agreed. Dick carried on, quoting facts about damage from the Asian tsunami and death tolls in various places. Lyall was impressed, and Ngaio sat amazed.

"I handled the coverage myself for my paper," explained the retired editor.

Ngaio referred to the printed map lying on the table between them. She pointed to a spot on the western coast of north Sumatra. It was a place that had been in her mind particularly when they sailed up the Strait of Malacca.

"Aceh," she said.

"The worst place hit," Dick confirmed. "the epicentre was just to the west. The wave was ten metres there."

"There's an island off the coast," continued Ngaio, her finger still on the spot.

"Nias," said Lyall, "we've been there."

The couple told the newsman how they'd visited the Indonesian island for an unforgettable day that was for them the highlight of another cruise taken years before. After visiting a Nias Batak village in the central highland and dancing with people who, they were told, had been cannibals within living memory, Ngaio and Lyall had walked through the town of Gunung Sitoli and were approached by a young man who looked to be in his early twenties. He introduced himself in language that was understandable though far from fluent, as the teacher of English in the local school. His offer to show them around, including through one of the substantial traditional houses with its characteristic heavy wooden beams and high-pitched roofs, was too generous and appealing to turn down even though Ngaio, noting that he looked extremely tired, considered suggesting he go home to bed. They hesitated and he renewed his offer. The following couple of hours in his company was something they would always remember.

As they walked their new friend told them he had just become a father for the first time. After a very long night his wife had given birth just hours before. That explained the tiredness, thought Ngaio – she was well experienced in the matter of long night deliveries. Would they, the couple was asked, like to go to the maternity hospital to meet his wife and child?

Ngaio thought of the new mother and her overnight ordeal. She would hardly want to be visited by people she had never met, and whose language she could probably not even speak. She deflected the question. The young father, she noted, had referred only to a baby, without elaboration.

"Do you have a daughter or a son?" she asked now.

"It is a girl." The response seemed to lack enthusiasm.

Ngaio was aware of different cultural responses to gender from addresses given at a nursing conference she had attended, supported by her own experience with new parents. In the years since immigration from countries in Asia had increased, evidence of gender preference had risen accordingly. It was an attitude she did her best to discourage.

"A little daughter. That's lovely. I like little girls. You must be very proud." She made her tone as positive and enthusiastic as she could. "We have two daughters." She chose not to add the fact that their family also included a son, and was pleased that Lyall stayed silent on the matter.

After the promised visit to the traditional house, the invitation to come with him to the hospital was put to them again. Surely they'd be in the way – his wife would need to sleep. The young father dismissed their misgivings. For one who should be elated he looked rather depressed, but that was no doubt due to his tiredness. In the face of his repeated invitation, and his kindness in showing them around, they could not refuse.

Five more minutes walk took them to the hospital – a low single-storey building. They were led through the garden and directly into a room in which a young woman lay on a bed, a baby in a crib beside it. If the new father seemed tired, thought Lyall, it was clear the mother, who looked as though she should still be in school, was exhausted. As the young man explained to his wife who the unexpected visitors were – at least they assumed that was what he said – Ngaio looked at the room with a practised eye. This was obviously where the birth had taken place – it was far from the sterile delivery or operating rooms she was used to. The sheets on the bed bore bloodstains and several used hypodermic syringes still lay discarded on the table. She moved across to the crib and peeked at the little face, then conveyed her delight to the young couple with large smiles and enthusiastic use of the words "beautiful" and "lovely".

They made their exit from the room as soon as they judged it would seem polite, suggesting that if the new father wanted to stay with his family they could find their own way back through the town to the wharf. He insisted on accompanying them. On the way he related a sad account of how much the birth had cost. His wife had needed more drugs and they had to be paid for – the price was more than he had. The point of the lesson was grasped easily by the teacher's pupils and as they prepared to board the tender to take them back to the ship, Ngaio reached into her bag and pulled out a few items. Since there had been no advance notice she had to improvise. A tin of lollies was offered to help the young mother celebrate the sweetness of the new life, some toiletries for her comfort, and a pen bearing the ship's logo was gifted to the baby girl to symbolize their hope that she would grow up well educated. Then Ngaio opened her purse and put what Indonesian money she had into the man's hand. Though the notes bore figures in their thousands she knew it amounted to little in her own world. What it would buy in this island she had no idea.

"That is all I have," she said, then added the instruction "Please buy a nice gift for your little girl," though she knew it would be spent on more pressing needs.

When news of the Boxing Day tsunami was broadcast and pictures of the devastation in the area were shown, Ngaio and Lyall had thought of the family, probably increased by then by the addition of more children. In particular, Ngaio thought of the baby who would be a girl of nine. Was she playing with her friends, on her way to school, or helping at home when the water struck? If she survived, was she injured? She would most certainly be among the millions who became homeless.

"Then," added Dick, continuing his account of the region's misfortune, "three months later there was the Sumatran earthquake. The area still hasn't recovered from the effects of the two, so close together."

The three Kiwis stayed at their spot in the Crow's Nest for a further hour swapping thoughts about the destinations visited so far. As they talked a brilliant idea came to Ngaio.

She and Lyall had planned to go to the late afternoon quiz. On previous occasions they had teamed up with a couple from Nottinghamshire. Since Jim was originally from Scotland and Connie from Ireland, the pair proved good value since a good proportion of the questions concerned the United Kingdom. But teams could include up to six members and now Ngaio recognized that Dick's knowledge and memory would add further excellent areas of expertise to the pool.

She put it to him – would he come along and join the Brains Rust? Dick, often referred to as "Eagle Eyes" by a succession of reporters for more than two decades, swooped upon what appeared to be a mental typo, his virtual red pencil poised over Ngaio's words. But no, she assured him, that was the name the team had chosen, at her suggestion. As well as serving as entertainment, the quizzes helped to keep the mind polished and reminded the members at each session of the need to keep the internal grey matter free from degeneration.

Dick was onto his seventeenth book of the voyage. Not counting shore days when he was off the ship for as long as he could be, that meant he was going through the library offerings at a rate of more than one a day. True, he'd found that some of them warranted only a quick skim, but as well as the books he had his daily journal entries to keep up with, and each morning he picked up the day's sheets of sudoku and crosswords provided on A4 paper at the library. The idea of a 'Brains Rust', dedicated to a goal opposite to what its name implied, appealed as another weapon in the war to preserve his most personal computer. Besides, he was cheered by finding others on board

SEVENTEEN SEAS

who shared his concern for the magnitude of the devastation caused by the mega upthrusts. He made a decision – he'd join the team.

As the Wellingtons moved away, the PA system came alive and the Captain made a non-scheduled announcement. Over the past three weeks a series of news items in the *Britain Today* news-sheet – Dick couldn't bring himself to give it the full status of newspaper even though he'd have been hard-pressed to defend the judgement – had concerned the disappearance of a nine-year-old girl in England. It seemed it was another child-abduction case and every parent and grandparent on board, the great majority of the passengers, had followed the reports with growing gloom. Now the Captain announced the girl had been found alive and well. A ripple of relieved response sounded through the lounge area. Newsmen of all people were aware how rare such positive endings were, and Dick shared their satisfaction. This was a good day.

— CHAPTER 15 —

Ripples Aboard

For the course of the second and into the third day out from India the ship continued to cut through mirror-like water between the equator and the Tropic of Cancer on its way westward towards the African continent.

A huge block of ice was set up on deck and a kitchen worker with an artistic bent left the galley to carve a sculpture that was regarded with admiration for the first hour, and thereafter left to drip into a formless lump.

For the largely recumbent cruisers there was plenty of time to indulge in fantasy and another round of rumours swept along the rows of deck-chairs like a Mexican wave.

"Did you hear there was a man who climbed up onto the railing and had to be persuaded to get down?" By the time this one was on its third lap it was the Captain himself who had acted as counsellor – apparently after lesser officers had failed.

The apocryphal passenger who was cajoled to abandon his plan to disembark mid ocean might or might not have been related to the one who was then rumoured to be 'man overboard'. If there were such a one it seems the ship didn't stop for him for there was no back-tracking in the course, no slowing in speed, and no tender launched for the recovery.

Whether or not either of those flights of imagination had anything to do with another piece of scuttlebutt that shot through the staterooms after the second stop on the sub-continent was anyone's guess. According to current legend, a stowaway managed to make it on board at Mumbai and was living in one of the lifeboats.

Apart from the excitement generated by these possibilities life aboard was relatively uneventful. The group around the table by the Pennant Bar took up playing Pictionary – not with any great enthusiasm, and even less skill, but because they'd exhausted all the likely topics of conversation, at least for the time being.

Caroline continued to avoid Nola and Blue Rinse in case they suggested she try her luck at Bingo again and information about her defection to the dark side might somehow get back to her fellow members in AWAG – Anglican Women Against Gaming. One lapse could possibly be put down to research, more than that would be hard to justify. For their part, Nola and Blue Rinse were also avoiding Caroline for fear the woman was indeed a true daughter of 'the lucky country' and they'd turned her into a serious contender for the eventual jackpot.

The Brains Rust won the afternoon quiz for the first time, and followed up that success with others, to the growing frustration of a rival team of retired schoolteachers who called themselves Staff Room.

Bert Coventry was tiring of the routine of ordering breakfast in the dining room. Up till now Mona had turned down his entreaties to go "just for a change" to the Orangery where it was self-service, and a wider choice was available. No doubt thanks to the plaster patch she still wore behind her ear she had to admit the voyage so far had caused her no distress. As she emerged from the shower on the morning of day three of this

RIPPLES ABOARD

particular stretch between ports, she put a finger on the spot. It was time to replace it. Funny – she was sure her patch was on the left side. She checked the right.

"Bert," she said, lifting her hair so he could inspect her neck, "can you see my seasickness plaster?"

"There's nothing there," said Bert.

Mona's first instinct was to panic. She hadn't removed it. In that case it must have been dislodged – most likely when she had her hair done at the hair salon in the Oasis Spa. But that was five days ago. Its loss would also account for the fact that the characteristic dryness in her mouth no longer troubled her. She thought for a moment. The significance of the discovery hadn't seemed to register with Bert.

"Just for a change," she suggested, "we could have breakfast upstairs. Would you like that?"

Forty minutes later, well satisfied by the change of habit and diet, the couple ventured out of the Orangery onto the rear deck. Mona, with just a little trepidation, walked to the rail and looked at the expanse of the Arabian Sea. It was a part of the journey she'd not looked forward to, since it seemed from the map there was a lot of open ocean to be crossed, but now she was astonished. All around, as far as she could see, there wasn't a wave, or a whitecap. Not even the sign of a slight swell marred the mirror-like surface.

"Look at that. Not a ripple except where we've disturbed it," said Bert.

"It's as though we're gliding through a sheet of glass," she said.

"Not so bad after all, is it?"

"Not so bad at all," she confirmed.

That same morning Lynn heard, once more, that it was the

Germans who were monopolising all the deck-chairs. In her forays around deck, however, she had noted a decided lack of anything she recognized as a Teutonic accent. When finding herself sharing a lunch table with someone who mentioned his first origins as Hamburg, therefore, she picked up on the opportunity to check the veracity of the repeated information.

"How many Germans are there on board?" she asked him. The Cruise Director had read out a list of nationalities and numbers some time before, so even if she couldn't remember she was sure he would know. He did.

"I am the only one," he said with a certainty that made any further questioning unnecessary.

Lynn doubted seriously that one individual, even if representative of a super race, could single-handed be responsible for the lack of sufficient sun-beds. Furthermore, judging by the lack of brown tones in Klaus's complexion, if there were such a person, it wasn't him. She was more puzzled than before. Glen's theory must be right. The British fixation on the matter must be something to do with the war.

If there was anything that could disturb the peace on this leg of the voyage it was the apparent breaking of the well-established social rule that the Kiwis had agreed some time before could also have been a legacy of the war.

The announcement that passengers were to retrieve their passports from the Crow's Nest during set hours, had the majority of the eighteen hundred heading to Sun deck forward almost simultaneously. They began by forming the usual orderly line from the starboard side entrance. As numbers increased and the few crew members manning the table struggled to keep pace, the queue stretched serpent-like along the landing,

RIPPLES ABOARD

down the port side stairs to Lido deck, then started descending a further flight towards Arcadia deck. Other arrivals, perhaps unaware of their fellow-passengers' prior arrival and claim, or just taking the easiest route to the top deck, stepped out of the elevators to find themselves ideally placed in the queue on the landing. As each full lift deposited more people in an advantageous position, the ire of those forming the body of the snake warmed to overheat level. The demeanour of people who invariably wished "good morning" to everyone they met in the corridors changed. The coils down the stairwell rattled as each level hissed at those on the flight above, spitting out accusations of queue jumping.

As feelings rose to their height Dick Napier, unaware that his usual spot in the Crow's Nest had been commandeered as passport control by the purser's office, stepped out of the elevator with a group of others whose arrival was greeted by a further wave of invective from those lined dutifully on the stairs leading downwards. He looked at the mass and sought to make his escape. If everyone was up here, the library might be relatively quiet. He was still trying to come to grips with what he saw as an anomaly in the social rules of these northerners. It had been reinforced in his mind the evening before when a woman in the Curzon Theatre had yelled abuse at an able-bodied man sitting in seats reserved for handicapped passengers and their attendants. That was fair enough, Dick allowed, as was the unwritten rule about queuing in order, but these same people would stand in groups in the library, next to people seated reading, and engage in lengthy and noisy conversations. He stepped back into the lift and pushed the button to Devanha deck.

169

— CHAPTER 16 —

The Colour of Water

In the early hours of Sunday morning the ship passed through Bab Al-Mandab, or what was referred to in the log as the Straits of Bab El Mendab, and into the Red Sea.

When Dick woke that morning he lay still for some moments letting his mind catch up with his consciousness. There was no window through which he could check on the progress of what he assumed was a new day or the ship's position, so he looked for clues. A slight movement suggested the liner was still under way. The lack of any commotion in the corridor outside his door meant their passage had probably proceeded according to schedule over night. Either that, or everyone else aboard was dead or under armed guard in the Curzon Theatre, and he was the only one who had avoided a similar fate by fortuitously escaping the notice of the bandits who now controlled the ship. That alternative scenario deserved to be dismissed as soon as it appeared through the mental morning fog. He got up and headed into the closet that was his bathroom. He hadn't really been concerned, he told himself as he showered, but all the same he had found himself imagining different outcomes the day before. And he was the man who was quick to condemn conspiracy theories. He lowered the shower temperature and held his head under the water for six seconds.

Forty years in newsrooms as junior reporter, reporter, chief reporter, sub-editor, features editor, and finally editor in chief,

THE COLOUR OF WATER

had modified the natural Kiwi attitude of 'she'll be right' in Dick Napier. Thousands of stories over his working life had made him aware that things often were not all right – particularly on the international front. And, he had concluded on frequent occasions, they were often less all right on the African continent than elsewhere. As a features writer and editor he'd had to make publishing decisions about material that covered the full range of calamities that beset the human race in that part of the world – acts of God and afflictions of gods, colonization and disease, crop failures bringing famine and starvation, democracy denied by despotic heads of state, floods followed by epidemics, inter-tribal wars and imperialism, plagues and pests, racism and slavery. That continent, so rich in terms of natural resources, seemed to tread a rocky road to ruination. Africa held a fascination that both attracted and repelled him.

The previous afternoon he had sat in his most favoured spot orienting himself mentally to the geographic position. They were heading west through the Gulf of Aden. Off to starboard lay the Arabian Peninsula and the coast of Yemen, unfortunately too distant to permit even a glimpse. Only once did he recall meeting a native of the Republic, a representative of *The Yemen Times*, at an international conference of newsmen held in Bali. The event was ostensibly organized for the purpose of bringing the press up to date on changes that new technology would bring to the industry, but was regarded by most of the attendees who lined the hotel's pool as due reward for years of service and the collateral damage accumulated from associated stress. Dick and Yusef, both wearing rather more clothes than the majority of their colleagues – some of whom looked as though they'd misread the name of the resort as 'Bellihair' – sat in the shade of a verandah designed to resemble a Balinese split gate and swapped stories.

From his Yemeni friend Dick gained an appreciation of the tensions created in that country through interventions by a succession of outside powers over the previous century. Given Britain's inclusion in that list, a stop at Aden would have been an unlikely addition to the itinerary. All the same, Dick thought, it would have been good to pass through the strait in daylight hours. The passage between the coasts of Yemen and Djibouti was only thirty-two kilometres in width, so this had to be an opportunity to sight Asia to starboard and Africa to port simultaneously. Dick had considered assigning himself to the night watch in the hope of at least glimpsing lights on each continent but his enthusiasm had waned considerably as the time neared midnight.

From a newsman's point of view there had been an even more enticing reason to want to experience the transit and, even more so, its approach.

At the same time as Dick was considering the proximity of Yemen to starboard, he was also aware that further off the port side of the ship as it steamed through the Gulf of Aden, lay the coast of Somalia. He wondered if a fleet of speedboats under orders from a Somali warlord was heading towards them at that very moment. He knew that if he mentioned his thoughts to any fellow passengers they'd be dismissed with a laugh and comments to the effect that pirates wouldn't think of attacking passenger liners. Cargo ships yes, oil tankers maybe, but not cruise liners. Public memory, he knew, was short, especially for things people didn't want to remember, but a newsman's mental archive frequently threw up flags. The one that sprang

THE COLOUR OF WATER

up in his mind as they drew closer to that country bore the image of the Jolly Roger.

Granted, the *Seabourn Spirit* was a smaller ship. At ten thousand tons as against the seventy-six thousand that surrounded him now it could be classed as a mega-yacht, nothing like the super-liners now plying the world's oceans. But, Dick appreciated, when one was moving through an area notorious for attacks by pirates and saw boats closing in at speed, it would be enough to make the hardiest sea-goer experience a sharp rise in anxiety level. Add to that coming under fire from automatic rifles and rocket launchers and he was sure no size of ship would feel totally impregnable to those on board. His mind flitted momentarily to his morning routine in his bathroom. Yes, he had remembered to take his blood-pressure medication.

He knew that security measures against piracy at sea were not often talked about openly, so there was no point in questioning any of the crew. However, he felt sure full procedures were in place to counter any such acts of terrorism. In that case he could leave it up to those trained to man the water cannons, or the long range acoustic device, or whatever weapons they carried but would not confirm. Or deny.

As the evening progressed and any threat presumably intensified, conversely Dick's concerns decreased. Darkness, as well as bringing terrors, can also act to shut off visible signs of danger and give the impression of a contained zone of safety. Confidence came with the added thought that they had already navigated safely through several other potential danger spots on this voyage. The Malacca Strait, and the coasts of Thailand and India had all known instances of piracy in modern times and those had been passed without incident. The Barbary coast, once the most notorious stretch, was still to come but that no longer featured in anyone's areas of anxiety. Most reassuring, though, was the thought of the four engines below decks in the engine room working together to produce a total of eighty thousand horse power. That and the couple of whiskeys he downed between ten p.m. and midnight.

In earlier years he'd have been excited by the thought of being the correspondent right on hand to witness what could be a sequel to *Black Hawk Down* – all the more gripping as it would be more personally identifiable to a larger number of viewers. But as he made his way down to his cabin just after Saturday turned into Sunday, Dick was more than happy to leave any heroics in the hands of those less chronologically challenged. It was a shame to miss out on the syndication and serial rights to the story though.

These were the thoughts that passed through his mind on waking the next morning. It seemed all had gone well with the passage and they had passed through 'The Gate of Tears' without mishap. In ages long past it was most probably the point at which the prototype modern people passed from Africa to Asia to give rise to the different branches of the world's family of races.

For the next few days the two continents would lie on either side as the ship negotiated the narrow divide between west and east.

Even though almost all of the passengers missed the significance of the transit point of their very distant forebears and felt they were cruising through foreign waterways, the section

THE COLOUR OF WATER

of the voyage ahead could be seen as a form of homecoming for the ship itself. Several spaces within its interior – the Alexandria and Medina Restaurants and the Uganda Room – pointed clearly to the long-standing association between the company flag it flew and the region.

The breakdown of present passengers showed that only two could claim membership of a nation belonging to the continent off the port side and just seventeen to a single country situated on the huge landmass that lay to starboard.

The pair who held South African passports, or the seventeen who hailed from India on the sub-region that forms part of Asia, might have taken pleasure from the incorporation of influences from their home continents in the ship's decor, but since these designs reflected specific cities at the extremities, far removed from their own areas, it was a distant association for each group.

The majority of the passengers did not realize it, but they were more or less arbitrarily divided into two factions – an arrangement brought about by accident, whim, or according to the location of their stateroom. Each of the factions was represented by one of the two continents between which they were now passing. Few who entered either the Alexandria or Medina Restaurants by the impressive doors or grand staircases that led into each paid much attention to the fact, and even fewer made any considered study of the shapes incorporated in the interior design. As they sat and dined they concentrated their attentions on the social side of the experience; the bulk of the passengers enjoying the meals provided in either of the main dining rooms hardly gave the details of the chosen décor more than a passing thought after the first evening or two on board. However, if pressed to give an opinion, all would have judged the overall effect of the rooms in which they spent an hour and a half each evening as elegant.

Certainly Glen, and any of the other men at the dinner table in the Alexandria Restaurant, would have been hard-pushed to pick the correct response from a multi-choice selection relating to the décor of their dining room even if spurred by the possibility of becoming a millionaire by giving the correct answer. Their wives would have done a little better, by recalling the predominant tones of the carpet, walls and drapes. Except for those who remembered the descriptions in glossy brochures, the fact that the inspiration reflected the area of Egypt and particularly the culture of the ancient city after which it was named, largely passed by the consciousness of the cruisers.

Those seated in the Medina Restaurant were, by that process of allocation, associated with the continent presently slipping by to starboard. No passengers claimed to be citizens of Saudi Arabia, let alone of the room's namesake city which would lie a mere two to three hundred kilometres to the east, as the hoopoe flies, at the closest point of the voyage up the Red Sea.

Ngaio was among the few who had taken note of the design features of the dining room. This was partly because she was looking for ideas for her own home's renovation, which she was determined to begin as soon as they returned; but it also reflected the new awareness of art she was discovering through attendance at the auctions. By this time in the voyage the initial pleasure she had gained by getting to know the others at the table was being replaced by a growing sense of boredom as stories were starting to be retold. There was a limit to how many times she wanted to be informed about the cute sayings of

THE COLOUR OF WATER

Belinda and Billy Brighton's grandchild in Sussex, and the men didn't seem to tire from their talk about cars, ships and planes. She was particularly peeved that this was abetted by Lyall who frequently encouraged Bert Coventry by asking about the inner workings of the classic cars of Britain. Consequently, she now often took the opportunity to block out the chatter and look around as she sought some short-term relief from the small-talk into which the conversation tended to deteriorate at frequent intervals, and especially when it threatened to become an examination of the various physical complaints admitted to by those who occupied the dozen seats set around the circular table.

Mid Monday morning, on the second day of their passage up the length of the Red Sea, Ngaio completed her customary laps of the Promenade deck and climbed the outside stairs to the area of the Terrace Pool on Devanha deck. As usual, the sunbeds were fully occupied, but this was not a concern – she seldom looked for a place in the sun, and not on such a fine warm day as this. She looked around to see if she could find Lyall who had accompanied her on the first five laps then set off to find a spot to settle and read. He wasn't in this area – perhaps he was on one of the higher decks that curved back to form a windbreak for the recreation area at the stern. She climbed two more floors, then spotted a familiar figure.

Dick was standing at the starboard rail looking outwards.

"It's still so calm," said Ngaio as she moved to stand beside him. "What's to see?" she asked after he'd acknowledged her.

"Out that way there's Saudi Arabia."

Ngaio looked.

"You've got better eyesight than I have if you can see it."

177

SEVENTEEN SEAS

"No. We're too far offshore. I was just thinking it's a shame we can't stop at all the places we pass."

Ngaio wasn't sure this one would come anywhere remotely near the top of any list she'd construct. Some years before a nursing colleague had signed up for a three-year contract at a hospital somewhere in Saudi Arabia. On her return she'd recommended it for the money she'd managed to save, but the account of her life which was largely restricted to the hospital and the gated community in which she lived with other expats, held no appeal to Ngaio. She'd go stir-crazy, she thought, with so much time on her hands and not a lot of activity and variety to fill it.

"We must be very close to Jeddah."

Ngaio figured her countryman must have some connection with the place. Though it rang a faint bell, she couldn't bring anything definite to mind.

"You've been there before?" she asked.

"No. Not me. I had a Muslim reporter who made the pilgrimage. He wrote it up for the paper."

"Don't they go to Mecca?" Ngaio felt a moment of panic – that's the answer she'd have given with confidence if the question had been posed in one of the onboard quizzes.

"Yes, but Jedda's where a lot of pilgrims start. It's the nearest port, and also where they fly into."

"So we must be close to Mecca too."

"As close as we'll ever get. Unless we convert to Islam." Dick followed up the comment with a short explanation that the Holy City was reserved for members of the faith, then asked which of the restaurants she was allotted to.

"Medina, first sitting," answered Ngaio.

THE COLOUR OF WATER

"So am I, " responded Dick, "we must be on different sides. Well, Medina's not far away either. I figure we'll be sailing past that some time this afternoon. But it's further inland, so we won't be that close."

Ngaio thought for a moment.

"Medina's in Saudi Arabia? But the Medina Restaurant's supposed to be furnished in Moorish style, and I thought the Moors were in Spain and North Africa."

Dick looked at her expression. The lines between her eyes were accentuated in the way they became when they met for the afternoon quiz in Champion's Bar and she was trying to recall an item of information from her memory banks.

"Don't worry," he reassured her, "you're right. It's not a precise term for a specific race, and it's often been used for Muslims over a wide area. Why the restaurant's named for that place and not another, who knows."

Dick shrugged and turned back to gaze out to sea.

"See you later at the quiz," said Ngaio, feeling thankful yet again she'd got him to join the Brains Rust. She resumed her search for Lyall. No. She stopped. She'd go to the library and look at the large atlas on display. She found the stairs and started down.

Dick also felt slightly cheered. His countrywoman knew something of Saudi Arabia, the Muslim place of pilgrimage, and had some knowledge of the history of the Moors. Best of all, she hadn't remarked on the colour of the sea. He was still in a state of bemusement, bordering on slight shock, at comments he'd overheard more than once that morning.

"It doesn't look any different. I thought it would be red."

At least some people had laughed as they'd said it. What

179

disturbed Dick is that others hadn't.

The ship's staff must have met this one before too. Later in the morning the Duty Officer making his daily announcement dispelled any remaining ignorance – though not entirely, given the uncertainty of the designation. The name given to this stretch of water could be because of the red soil of the bordering countryside, or from algal bloom floating in the water. Or it might be from the direction southwards in which the water flows, as colours were sometimes used in past times to denote cardinal directions. Throughout that day and the next, however, people at deck railings continued to stare into the water. Even if it was only a matter of algae, it would be good to say they'd seen some evidence of a reddish hue.

Lynn handed a book to the staff member on duty in the library.

"I'm returning this," she said, then waited till she saw the relevant entry crossed out. "And I want this one." She offered a further volume and when it was recorded turned to go.

Ngaio, who had been waiting behind her, stepped up to the desk. While her choice was being checked out the two women chatted.

"Amy Tan," said Lynn, noting Ngaio's choice, "I've read one of hers."

"She's one of my favourite authors," replied Ngaio, speaking in a low voice. "I met her once. Well, I went to a talk she gave and she autographed one of her books for me."

Lynn displayed the title of her selection. She started to speak, and Ngaio gestured to the door.

"Let's find a spot out there."

They moved out of the library and stopped at a vacant

table in Raffles Court. The pair had met on the second day out when the ship was making its way across the Tasman Sea. Although the Hendersons and the Wellingtons had stopped to talk when their paths crossed, and had shared a lunch table at the Orangery on several occasions, both of the women had remarked to their husbands that they should make an effort to see more of the other couple. Now Ngaio and Lynn sat and talked. It was good to be able to start from common ground – to share ideas and experiences without having to stop to explain the context.

Forty minutes later, after they'd run through topics as varied as past ports, snippets of news from home, the general quality of the artists appearing in the evening entertainment, and their appreciation of the fact that this was an unprecedented seven week break from cooking meals, they rose to go.

"I must say, though," said Lynn, "by now I'm getting a little tired of lunches at the Orangery. They're really good," she hastened to add, "it's just I'd like a change, but Glen prefers it to the dining room because he can serve himself."

"I fancy being waited on while I've got the chance." Ngaio knew just how her new friend felt. "I sometimes leave Lyall to it and go on my own. Why don't we go to the Medina for lunch."

The two women were escorted to a table at which several people were also just being seated. Neither of them had met any of the others before. They made short introductions and sat, waiting for the menu.

The elderly lady in the place nearest the window on the opposite side of the table volunteered that she lived near Windsor. Lynn could imagine that. Her hair was sculpted in grey waves and she spoke in a cultured tone, vowels clearly enunciated.

Lynn confided to Glen later that she had to repress an urge to ask about Philip and the corgis.

The man directly across from Ngaio wore a black knit shirt and had close-cropped hair on his bullet-shaped head. He had left a chair vacant between him and Mrs Windsor. Ashwin, one of the pair of waiters who served the Wellingtons and their fellow diners each evening, appeared at his side with a request. Would he kindly move along one place so the table could accommodate another couple. Bullethead didn't move. The waiter repeated his appeal and still there was a lack of action. Ashwin employed a firmer tone, and this time Bullethead exploded.

"I can't understand a word you say," he shouted in an accent that Ngaio found much thicker than the one that had addressed him. "What language are you talking?" he stammered, groping for ideas before finally suggesting "mumbo-jumbo?"

Lynn recognized the man as one she'd encountered some days earlier, so was alone among those at the table who realized that what seemed like a bigoted slur was not primarily racially directed. On the previous occasion the same passenger was in one of the salons seated at the front table less than two metres from the English entertainment officer who was introducing the rules of a game.

"I can't understand a word of what you're saying," he kept repeating on that occasion too.

The officer was patient and reiterated her sentences. Finally Mr Sansaudio, as Lynn dubbed him, gave up and left the games room muttering about the Englishwoman's lack of clarity.

Contrary to Mr Sansaudio's opinion, Lynn had found most of the waiters, cabin stewards, and other areas of crew had an excellent command of English – spoken at least. Considering the low standard of written language in the compendium literature supplied in each cabin and in other printed materials, perhaps some of them could be consulted for the next review, she thought. And the British tour guide who repeatedly advised people to be "respective" of local customs might like to take some lessons in English from some of them too.

Now, seated at the table and witnessing the exchange between the waiter and diner, Ngaio cringed with embarrassment and sent a look of sympathetic understanding to Ashwin. Lynn thought once again that investment in a brace of hearing aids at the time of booking his trip would have increased Mr Sansaudio's enjoyment of it a hundred-fold. She gestured across the table, indicating the vacant chair, and was relieved when he moved a place over to his left. Mr and Mrs Suffolk joined the group and with order restored all turned to a study of the menu.

Most of the diners ordered the light option. Ngaio noted the fact with quiet satisfaction. Since coming to her early conclusion about the amount of food consumed aboard and the average size of the consumers, she had seen no reason to modify her view during the weeks since. Here, now, was a sign that some could be recognizing a correlation between input and outspread, and were making a move in the right direction. But wait – Mrs Suffolk was adding an instruction.

"Can you add chips to mine, please."

The other diners followed suit. Ngaio felt the sense of satisfaction ebb. She was to remember the moment a few hours later at the Captain's cocktail party.

Mr and Mrs Geordie, seated to Ngaio's right at the lunch

table, engaged her in conversation. To be more correct, they seemed keen to explain to her the details of their life at home. This gave her some further moments of embarrassment when called to respond, as Mr G's voice seemed to emanate from midway down his oesophagus. It was apparently fully intelligible to his wife, whose additions fortunately provided vital clues as to what he had apparently said. Mrs G's side of the conversation, on which Ngaio concentrated as it was much more accessible, centred on the five cats they had left behind at home – their breeding, medical problems, together with the names, details, and comparative advantages of the various catteries in which they were being tended. The Geordies had joined the cruise at Hong Kong. They decided to limit their trip to just four weeks away, explained Mrs G, in fairness to the furred members of the family.

When the two Kiwi women left the Medina Restaurant forty minutes after entering, Lynn looked at Ngaio and grinned.

"That was fun," she said.

Ngaio couldn't be sure how the comment should be interpreted, and decided not to pursue the matter.

"Have you and Glen been to lunch at Café Bordeaux?" she asked, "Why don't the four of us go there next sea day." That solution fitted the bill all around.

Ngaio and Lyall entered the Crow's Nest lounge early that evening holding their printed invitation to the Captain's party. A member of the entertainment crew took their names and introduced them to the uniformed man whose face they recognized from the portrait that hung in the ship's reception area. As he gripped her hand Ngaio had a close-up view of the

THE COLOUR OF WATER

spotless dress whites. Other equally immaculate uniforms were in evidence around the room, which was already crowded. Well, he had the ship's laundry facility at his disposal, she thought. She hoped she and Lyall passed muster.

Because this voyage was just the first part of a much longer trip they'd had to pack lightly. When they boarded in Auckland their single suitcases each weighed under twenty kilograms – no small achievement considering they had a variety of climates to consider. What's more, they intended to keep them that way. For a further couple of months after they disembarked from this temporary home they'd be moving their bags on and off buses, trains and planes to achieve their plans to visit a long list of further countries. Then there was the eventual flight home to consider. So Lyall's dark lounge suit, helped by the addition of a dress shirt and bow tie, had to do double duty as a dinner suit. For her part, a sparkly top transformed a long skirt on formal occasions. Now Ngaio looked around at the other guests standing chatting in small groups, champagne glasses in hand. The fiftyish woman in the evening dress with the fairly full skirt, she decided, was no doubt one of those who boarded with multiple trunks and was rarely seen wearing the same outfit more than once – there were always a few like that on board. She was probably on for the complete round trip. Or she could be one who had taken up the company's offer to transport additional suitcases 'out' in order for extra possessions to be available for those flying to make the voyage 'home'. Whatever, the Wellingtons didn't want the hindrance of further baggage. A further glance around confirmed their decision. They mightn't be the most glamorous in the room, but she was satisfied that they shaped up adequately in the dress stakes.

SEVENTEEN SEAS

A couple turned to greet them.

"We're Dave and Emma from County Durham."

Lyall shook the outstretched hand.

"Lyall and Ngaio from Wellington."

Ngaio could see the other couple trying to make a connection.

"Wellington New Zealand," she contributed.

"Ah," Emma had it now. "I was trying to place it. I'm sure we've got a Wellington too. I can't think just where."

Ngaio had once looked up the name and could have made suggestions but decided the occasion didn't warrant an examination of the alternatives.

"I think you've got more than one," she said. "We've been lucky with the conditions, haven't we?" she asked.

Dave agreed, adding it was just as well as Emma here wasn't too keen on sailing. His wife brushed the observation aside and addressed Ngaio.

"Your name," she asked, "how do you say it again?"

Ngaio responded, repeating the sound. "Ngaio. It's Ng as if you're saying the end of 'sing'." She repeated the syllables. "Ng-eye-or."

Emma practised.

"Is that it?" she asked.

"Close enough," Ngaio settled for a sound close to what most people at home produced.

"It's the same as that author, isn't it? The one who wrote the detective books?"

"Ngaio Marsh, that's right. She was…" Lyall began to talk when there was a signal that the speeches were about to begin.

The Captain took the microphone. All those gathered, appreciatively holding their complimentary drinks, already

THE COLOUR OF WATER

knew him to be a fount of knowledge about matters maritime. Each day he broadcast announcements from the bridge about sea and weather conditions and other useful information. This evening, though, they found the Master of the ship had additional skills as a raconteur, and at the cocktail parties he hosted he could afford to be more loquacious. Now the guests, attired in their ball gowns and tuxedos, listened attentively as the captain explained the science behind one of the dilemmas of a cruiser's life.

"We all know the oceans are salty, but what few realize is that when at sea the atmosphere is also salt-laden and this gets into one's clothes. When the salt evaporates, it has the effect of shrinking clothes. In regions such as the Red Sea even more salt evaporates. So that is why you find your clothes getting somewhat tighter on an ocean voyage."

Guests with drink in one hand and canapé in the other, smiled appreciatively at the wisdom. They popped the pastries into their mouths and tugged surreptitiously at their bursting seams.

"Good-o, is that the signal for dinner? Come on dear, we shouldn't be late."

The Crow's Nest lounge emptied again as the guests filed out and made their way towards the restaurants.

— CHAPTER 17 —

Respect Our Beliefs

Glen and Lynn looked from the rails of the Promenade deck to take in their first view of Egypt. This country had long been at the top of their most-wanted list. Surveying the sight now, they were struck by a pair of thoughts that came to them one upon another.

The first was a sense of the barrenness of the scene before them. Immediately below them a huge expanse of concrete stretched not only the length of the ship, but forward from its bow for what seemed hundreds of metres. Some two weeks earlier Glen had found himself a little short of fresh casual clothes during the part of the voyage where there'd been successive shore days in equatorial countries so had bought an extra tee-shirt from Piccadilly on Ellora deck. He was wearing it now. On the left breast, beneath a graphic of the ship's logo, was a short list of its specifications, which proved handy when one needed quick reference. Length 270 metres, he could confirm now. At most destinations the ship took up the full space of the wharf, and sometimes extended beyond so that the stern reached back into the open water. Here though, at Sharm el-Sheikh, in the south of the Sinai Peninsula, it was the wharf that made the ship look small. Several more liners of similar size could have found anchorage simultaneously. Well, thought Glen, this was a country that wasn't known for under-doing their amenities – this was a wharf of pyramidal

RESPECT OUR BELIEFS

size, if not shape.

The strip was comparatively unrelieved by buildings or other features, though a garage-sized room and a one storey high tower-shaped structure were situated beyond the width of the paving. Behind those rose a wall of brown – a cliff of bare rock and soil that supported no life on its face or top. Looking past the extent of the wharf to the land they could see a further line of barren brown hills, with some equally bare summits rising behind. The scene, thought Lynn, lacked only a caravan of camels in silhouette along the top. In contrast, the few houses in view a distance away to their left were painted in white, some with features of blue. A fleet of moderate-sized cabin cruisers was moored near the houses, suggesting that the arid nature of the natural surroundings was not necessarily repeated in the economic environment.

Thought two for the couple came with their realization that this sight also brought up another first. A first even more sizable than the pyramids – it was of continental size. In front of them lay Africa. Finally, they were about set foot on the remaining continent in their been-there-done-that register.

Thought two-point-five, which followed a minute later, was the sudden onset of doubt regarding the geographic designation of the location. Is the Sinai Peninsula part of Africa or Asia? The mental maps in their minds placed it right between the two, such as the length of rope that separates the two contending teams in a game of tug of war. Lynn tried to visualize a cut-out map of Africa. Did it include the peninsula as the northeast extremity? She wasn't sure. An attempt to imagine the outline of Asia in a similar way was much too difficult. Glen wondered whether the completion of the Suez Canal had made a difference. Did the fact of making a physical divide through the land cause the de facto severance of the two landmasses? Neither of them was at all sure whether or not a single country could lie comfortably in two continents.

The Hendersons stood at the rail and pondered these questions while watching the first passengers leave the ship and walk towards the row of coaches waiting to transport those pre-booked on excursions. The line of preferred passengers was shorter than usual. It seemed that most of the cruisers had elected to do their own thing around the local town rather than endure a daylong trip with a monastery as its goal – even if the destination did claim an historic connection with the burning bush of biblical times. An alternative option of a half-day sojourn into the desert for a close encounter with a camel had appealed to Glen a little more, but for the reason of the ride in the four-wheel drive vehicle rather than the chance of a voyage on a ship of the desert. In lieu of any more attractive option they decided to enjoy their day in the Middle East seeing what the area offered in the way of local colour.

Before booking this journey they had no knowledge of Sharm el-Sheikh, and had to check a series of maps before it was revealed nestling at the southern tip of Sinai. All the Brits on board, they soon found, were well aware of its location – the spot had boomed over the past decade as plane-loads of tourists took off daily from airports all around the UK bearing their nationals south east into the warm. The nearby beach resort of Naama Bay had been dubbed the capital of the Egyptian Riviera.

The information brought Lynn and Glen a degree of disappointment that the area had clearly undergone much

RESPECT OUR BELIEFS

adaptation as a consequence. They had come to see places that were different. But these misgivings did not override the thrill of their arrival at this spot – on no matter which continent it happened to be.

The announcement that passengers not booked on excursions could now disembark was broadcast and the couple set off down the gangway. The shore proper seemed a good hike away. Lynn put on her Cancer Society approved hat, a veteran of twenty-five previous countries, and Glen donned the wide-brimmed Barmah model he'd bought in Brisbane a month before. With the addition of sunglasses to combat the glare from the white concrete they were equipped to start on the trek to the gates of the port. They walked for several minutes and began to wonder if they should have caught a camel. At least the concrete paving was easier to traverse than sand. They caught up to and passed others also heading towards the gates to the outside, and Egypt proper. More trailed along in their wake, one complaining loudly that the ship should have put on a shuttle to take them from shipside to the gate.

Glen didn't mind the walk, any concerns he held were to do with the inevitable clash with the phalanx of taxi drivers they could see waiting. The number seemed to increase with every step forward. Glen didn't doubt their eagerness to assist the tourists – he'd met their counterparts in all quarters of the world. With extreme quotations rehearsed and ready, each one of the drivers was willing to convey the day-trippers to any place they wished, but preferably by way of his brother's shop.

As they approached, steeling themselves for the encounter, the pair were pounced upon by a couple they hadn't met

SEVENTEEN SEAS

formally but whose presence they'd noticed on the dance floor in Carmen's on rock'n'roll night. Glen had been somewhat surprised, and slightly envious if he cared to admit it, at how the largish man executed a body wave that pointed to his being a past master of the art. Now he found a further stereotypical thought challenged as the dancer addressed him in a broad Scots accent. Centuries of kilt-clad céilidhs had clearly laid the groundwork for this Hebridean Elvis.

Jim, as the man introduced himself adding the information that his wife was Connie, had managed to reduce the cost of a car to Naama Bay to half the first quoted figure. He was sure it was still too much, but it was better than the prices being agreed to by others who were piling into four-wheel-drive vehicles nearby. The car would take four passengers – would they like to share the cost? Why not? If Jim had spared them the effort of going through the haggling process, that had to be worth a dollar or two.

The slim young man with whom the contract had been made led them to an ageing saloon. He opened the driver's door and got in without a word. He didn't look overjoyed at the prospect of ferrying them for even the ten minute trip. Perhaps Jim had negotiated a reasonable deal after all.

The two women and Glen climbed into the back seat and looked in vain for seatbelts. Lynn had conducted the same search in many countries before with the same result. After thirty years of compulsory compliance in her own country it always came as a surprise to find others had not yet instituted similar laws. She hoped that the fact that three people, adult westerners at that, were wedged into the space might provide each other with some protection if it became necessary.

RESPECT OUR BELIEFS

She held onto that small measure of reassurance as the car passed through the town and sped up through an area that was just a little less congested though still fully built up. The driver ignored a question relating to the local area. It seemed the reduced price entitled them for the transport only – he wasn't about to act as a tour guide too. He turned up the volume on the stereo so the sound of Middle Eastern rhythms increased from mega to maxi decibels. Connie tapped her husband on the shoulder and Jim asked for the level to be lowered. After a short pause the volume control was turned counter clockwise, but only by a millimetre, then twenty seconds later it was returned to maximum setting. Jim reached out and turned the knob till it clicked off.

"No music," he ruled in a tone that made it clear the matter was not up for discussion.

Perhaps in retaliation, or maybe because he was missing his favourite radio programme and wanted to offload his charges without delay in order to restore the enforced break in transmission, the young man placed his right foot to the floor. Lynn grasped the seatback in front of her and again regretted the lack of reassurance offered by a secure tether. She also regretted that she had not undertaken the sort of inspection she had often carried out in other places, where she had walked around an offered taxi and checked the tyres. Twice before she had refused a car when at least one of its wheels had an inadequate covering of rubber. The memory of her indignation on those occasions was tempered just a little as she recalled another more recent event.

"There's plenty of tread left on that," she'd argued when the mechanic at the vehicle testing station rejected renewing the

SEVENTEEN SEAS

warrant of fitness because of insufficient depth on the Camry's left rear tyre. In future, she promised herself, she would abide by the rulings without dissent.

It was relief for the four, and possibly for all five, when the driver drew up outside a retail block and announced the spot as Naama Bay. They alighted and looked around.

"We said the beach." Jim, the original negotiator, had taken the role of continuing spokesperson.

The young man waved an arm in the direction forward of the buildings. Walk along there, was the instruction. Jim handed over the agreed amount and made it clear there'd be no renegotiation. The Hendersons reimbursed their new friends for their share. There was no doubting the status of their relationship, at least for the moment – one couldn't sit so intimately as the back seat of the small saloon required without acquiring a feeling of familiarity. The driver, on the other hand, obviously shared no such sense of fraternity. The tyres spat gravel in their direction as he swung the car around and headed back to where he'd pick up a few more fares from their fellow passengers.

Together the two couples made for the shade of the cafés and shops, but differing interests led them in them diverging directions within a short time. Connie entered a shop offering an array of jewellery and Jim followed. Glen and Lynn set out for the beach in the direction indicated, but got no more than a dozen steps when a man stepped from a doorway to greet them. Though he was not much more than medium height, the fez on his head and the spotless white dishdasha made him appear taller. The robe no doubt added to the overall impression of grace as he gave a small bow of the head and extended

RESPECT OUR BELIEFS

his hand in invitation. They were welcome on their visit to Naama Bay, he assured them, and he would like to show them hospitality by offering a glass of tea. If they would kindly step this way...

"Thank you," they replied, but they were not intending to buy anything. The look in response was one of mild reproach mixed with tolerant humour. There was no expectation of purchase, they were assured, but he would like to welcome them with tea – it was the local custom. Lynn had experienced such approaches before, and knew them to be part of a polished sales routine. She also knew the best defence was a matter of remaining polite but firm. She failed every time on the second count. On each occasion the aspect of politeness won over the option of firm refusal. It seemed rude to rebuff such courtesy, especially since to do so was apparently counter to local cultural behaviour. At home there was a word for it – kawa. The kawa of an area was to be respected. She passed through the relevant door and they sat where indicated to await the tea, which their host dispatched a boy to bring.

The room was lined with shelves containing jars, big and small, all marked with labels. Some signs in English left no doubt that the proprietor, their new-found friend, was a purveyor of perfumes. They sat, trying to convey an air of polite gratitude appropriate to their position as honoured guests, while simultaneously appearing not to pay undue attention to the presence of the shop's stock. It was not easy, and a moment's lingering look in a certain direction was enough for their host to whip a jar from a shelf and say he thought the lotus flower oil was a good choice. Not only was it a popular scent, but it would remind her of the visit. Was madame aware that the lotus was the national flower of this area?

Just as they finished their tea two women, also tourists, appeared in the doorway. Their host stepped forward with a slight bow of the head and an invitation to enter. Glen and Lynn seized their opportunity. They rose, extended their thanks for the hospitality, and left quickly. They hoped the manner of their sudden departure didn't violate local kawa, but perhaps their replacements would prove to be more profitable guests.

The distance past the remaining small shops to where there was access to the beach was not far, but the going was not unimpeded. Several more times they turned down offers of glasses of tea and the chance to view a variety of merchandise.

When they reached the beach they could see that more of their shipmates had found their way to the same place. Many of the tourists looked familiar, a perception confirmed by the giveaway presence of logo-ed lanyards hanging around a number of necks. The distinctive colour of the ship's towels could be seen draping a good number of the sun beds lined frame to frame along the frontages of one hotel after another. It seemed a good proportion of the usual suspects on melanoma deck had swapped the pool surround for the seashore. Lynn wondered if they'd left towels and belongings on the ship's deck-chairs so they could move right back in on their return. It seemed the lido-loungers had few scruples here either, as they claimed the chairs reserved for guests of the hotels situated along the shore.

Lynn and Glen had been careful to cover up, in deference to Egyptian expectations. Now, looking around, they saw they were on their own in this. All the bodies stretched out on display showed no regard for the local dress code – men

RESPECT OUR BELIEFS

sported briefs that didn't stretch to warrant even that name; the women's bikini bottoms couldn't be smaller and the tops were often non-existent. They wondered how the young male waiters on duty managed to reconcile the sight with the fully clad women in their own families.

Lynn spied an unoccupied picnic table on the boundary between two properties. As a bonus the spot included a small area of patchy shade cast by a spindly tree. They settled their belongings on the tabletop and Lynn pulled her one-piece swimsuit from her bag. In a poll of perfect swimming spots around the world this one would be pushing it to make the top thousand but right now it had several things going for it. One – the day was warm. Two – Lynn took pleasure in adding exotic stretches of water to the total of those in which she'd swum, and the Red Sea offered a new experience. Three – it was right here.

In spite of the beachful of bared bodies stretched out on sunbeds on each side, Lynn was mindful of local custom. She was even more conscious of the possibility of causing offence because a short distance away, within the domain of one of the hotels, three men attired in long robes, head-dresses and sporting dark glasses, stood talking together. As she revealed her intention by producing the swimsuit one of three walked down the sand and sat on the bench seat on the opposite side of the table. She waited. He stayed. She deferred her disrobing, opened her camera and took several shots of the scene, including one of a group of young Asian tourists receiving basic instruction in wearing and operating scuba gear. The man was still there. To indicate she was preparing to change, she made a show of removing further items from her bag – a towel, hair-tie, a tube of sunblock. He made no move. If she was trying to show sensitivity to the culture, it was beginning to seem a little one-sided.

Lynn, however, was not beaten yet. She was a seasoned traveller and pulled from her bag something she had learned was well worth the small space it occupied in her suitcase. She unrolled the long wrap-around skirt, draped its folds around her, and knotted the ties around her neck. Under her makeshift tent she extricated herself from her clothes and donned her one-piece swimsuit. If Daoud, or whatever his name was, was on duty as a defender of moral values he'd have to accept that, in comparison to other bathers in the vicinity, any part she'd displayed would have to figure very low on the transgression scale. If he was simply a voyeur, she was confident he'd be disappointed.

They'd crossed the Tropic of Cancer soon after the ship entered the Red Sea, so Lynn knew they were north of the line. All the same, she felt sure the water would have been warmer. She stayed in about ten minutes – more than ample time to be able to add this waterway to her count of seas-in-which-I've-swum. She returned to the table and carried out the manoeuvres needed to redress under the folds of her skirt. As she untied it to emerge once again decently clad the would-be voyeur rose and returned to his post in the hotel garden. She sat for a while warming up again. The young Asians she'd watched earlier were now in waist deep water putting their lesson into practice. A very short distance along the coast from here, she knew, was a spot called Shark Bay. If the name was at all indicative of the local sea life, the pod of young people she could see fiddling with their air tanks possessed much more courage than she did.

Naama Bay was a night-time destination, they decided an hour later when they'd walked into the town. The Hard Rock Café, with an outsized guitar stretched across its upper façade and a pink Cadillac parked outside, looked promising for a cup of coffee in the late morning, but on trying the door they found it was not yet open. Rows of other establishments that existed to ensure no one who ventured anywhere near this urban oasis would die of thirst, apparently also catered exclusively for the night shift revellers.

Glen and Lynn walked along wide streets paved with blocks of red and grey laid to create a meandering walkway pattern. Few other people were in sight. The street-cleaning crew must have finished for the day and gone home for lunch. Not a scrap of litter or dust could be seen. Whatever the ravages wrought by the previous evening's revelry no sign remained.

They walked by empty bars that couldn't differ more from those at home. Bays of floor-level seating were furnished with bright coloured rugs and cushions. This one favoured stripes of multi-colours, the next featured red with cushions in Zebra stripes They obviously catered for a younger crowd, thought Lynn – or for people much younger and more supple than she was anyway. Judging by the lack of walls and roofs the area received zero rainfall – that was another major difference between here and home. At night, she imagined, under the light of the few coloured globes that hung from a rough network of power cables overhead, the atmosphere would be even more exotic. It was a shame they wouldn't be there to see it. Glen, looking more closely at the state of insulation on the wires strung above, came to the opposite conclusion.

They walked on down the paved street. The shops in the market area, crammed full of raffia camels, hookahs, wooden figures of Bast and Anubis, and baseball caps, were just opening. A man standing at the door of one looked them over and grinned.

"Good morning, my queen," he addressed Lynn with a small bow, following it with a sweep of his hand inviting entry to the emporium. Then he straightened and greeted Glen in his Australian drover's hat.

"Hey cowboy, where's your horse?"

As midday approached the streets were still quite deserted. A few men went about their business connected with the bars or shops. The only woman in sight was a more than life-sized plaster figure outside the Bedouin Bar, posed holding a plastic-covered load on her head and displaying a bejewelled ankle.

In the more established shopping area – a block of modern design containing small western-style shops with a bias towards jewellers – the owners and operators were opening up for the day. As the couple walked through the arcade that offered pleasant shelter from the sun, their eyes were drawn to a notice taped on the inside of several windows or in the most prominent place on the glass door where it could not be missed by anyone entering. Along with the usual stickers assuring that the credit cards of AAIB, Amex, Diners Club, JCB, MasterCard, and Visa, were accepted was a statement printed on an A4 sheet.

NO FOR THE CONTEMPT RELIGIONS
WE LOVE MOHAMMED

RESPECT OUR BELIEFS

To some were appended a further handwritten sheet with an elaboration.

PLEASE RESPECT OUR BELIEFS
AND OUR PROPHET, MOHAMMAD.

Written signatures were added to the message.

Glen and Lynn stopped and studied the notice. They had some experience of encounters with the sort of people the statement seemed to be directed to. They recalled a visit to a Hindu temple when a group swept in brandishing crosses and Bibles and denounced the worshippers as idolators. And on more than one occasion they'd moved to dissociate themselves from other observers who made critical comments in various places of worship. The fact that so many of the shops here felt the need to display such a notice pointed to more than an isolated offence.

Their thoughts were interrupted by the opening of a door nearby. The owner of a shop that printed tee-shirts to order smiled and invited them to look at what he could offer. They declined – they had no need for further tee-shirts, they explained politely, and moved away. A few steps further on they stopped simultaneously as the same thought came into their mind. They turned back and entered the shop. Never before, they agreed later, had they met such extreme courtesy in a retail store. The owner went to such pains to help them select the correct size of garment in the right colour to match with their pick of the transfers. He was meticulous in its application, and wrapped the result in a double layer of tissue paper. Considering the very reasonable price that resulted when they converted it from Egyptian pounds by way of the British pound to New Zealand dollars, he was charging little for his time.

"I hope your granddaughter likes it and has a happy birthday," he wished them as they left.

"She will," they assured him.

It was not the price, and not the perfection of the small shirt, that made them think later that they should have bought one for each of the grandchildren. It was the memory of the utter courtesy and consideration that was extended to them in the twenty minutes spent in the small tee-shirt shop.

There was no need to entrust themselves to their earlier taxi driver or one of his cronies for the return journey. A small bus was offering a shuttle service to Sharm el-Sheikh. They climbed in, found most of the other occupants were shipboard companions, and alighted a quarter of an hour later at the entrance to the old market.

They couldn't mistake the place. An area of several blocks crammed with shops lay ahead of them. Its streets, in complete opposition to those they'd just left, were well populated. If any doubt had remained there was a further clue in the impressive entrance erected across the double carriageway street, made even wider by the addition of pedestrian portals on either side.

Four tall sculpted classical-style figures standing on stone plinths were on guard duty outside the short towers that flanked the roadway. Glen wondered idly if their assignment here would constitute a demotion from duty at more important sites – pyramids being the pinnacle, declining through a range of lesser tombs, to the market in a minor city. They deserved further downgrading of rank, he thought to himself, if these

RESPECT OUR BELIEFS

were the same ones on guard three years earlier when a car bomb exploded in the souq and killed so many. He didn't voice his thoughts aloud. He hadn't mentioned that incident to Lynn. If he had, she wouldn't be here now. And they wouldn't have enjoyed the morning at Naama Bay had she been aware of similar instances that had occurred there.

If the other signs hadn't been sufficient to identify the site, the clincher came in the blue wording across the horizontal beam connecting the short towers at either side of the road. On the left side as they looked read the words OLD MARKET, on the right was what Glen assumed was the equivalent in Arabic. For a moment he wondered why the order favoured the English, then realized that scripts in this part of the world read right to left, and in that case the English was the translation. He clicked the camera to record the scene for later study, and followed Lynn through the gateway.

If it was indeed an old market it had at least partially embraced modernity. The shops themselves, with their construction, awnings, and signwriting could have stood in the main streets of towns around the world. Though a few vehicles moved cautiously through the streets, the roads were primarily taken over by pedestrians. They seemed to be divided almost equally between locals and tourists. Lynn looked around. Something she had wondered about at Naama Bay came back to her. There they'd encountered so few people – local residents at least – that she couldn't be sure. Now as she scanned the figures walking about, shopping, working, she felt able to come to a more considered conclusion. Apart from the tourists, everyone was male. This was apparently a land without women.

Many of the older men were clad in long robes in shades

reminiscent of desert tones, but younger men wore western dress. One of the latter looked at Glen in his hat.

"Hello, cowboy, where's your horse?" he asked.

The couple walked through the streets observing. There was nothing they needed, and they didn't intend to buy. The vendors had other ideas. No thank you, their suitcases didn't need replacing. Souvenirs – they had all they wanted, thanks. Yes, we're off the ship, and no, I'm not needing another neck-lace. In a few blocks, thought Lynn looking into crammed shops while all the time trying not to look at all interested, you could buy anything you could possibly want. And even more you didn't want. A comprehensive stocktake would result in a papyrus printout kilometres in length. She made a mental start through the alphabet – alabaster souvenirs, belly-dancing outfits, cat figurines, dates, Egyptian cotton goods, fridge magnets, ginger, hookahs, internet services, jewellery, King Tut memorabilia. Really, it was too easy – she could give a list of alternatives for each letter. Lamps, melons, nutmeg, olives, persimmons, quartz (scarab shaped), rugs, star anise, tobacco, umbrellas, vinegar, water bottles… She paused as she reached the tricky end. It would just take a moment – she was sure the final three letters were also well represented.

Glen, however, had reached his limit. His tolerance for touts, no matter how politely they presented themselves, and not-withstanding the accompanying smiles, was fairly low.

"Let's walk back to the ship," he said, making towards the gateway.

By now Lynn was happy to follow.

The road back was downhill. It was good to walk with a 'ose – they could stride without stopping and without

RESPECT OUR BELIEFS

being stopped. At the gate to the wharf a clutch of taxi drivers waited, still hopeful of picking up a few fares. The couple passed through and started the long walk across the glaring concrete to where the ship lay at anchor. From behind they heard a voice call out.

"Hey cowboy, where's your horse?"

Lynn laughed. Egypt wasn't a land she had connected with westerns previously. But she would from now on.

The only woman in sight was a more than life-sized plaster figure.

— CHAPTER 18 —

The Price of a Free Keffiyeh

The alarm on Lyall's cellphone sounded. He turned on the bedside light and switched off the sound. Ngaio was still asleep, so he rolled over and shook her.

"It's half past three," he said.

Ngaio woke reluctantly and with bad grace – she hated being roused like that. She didn't have to open her eyes to know it wasn't morning. Though she was an habitual early riser such a time was pushing the limit, and she hadn't her full eight hours. Minimum. What such an awakening usually meant was that she had to get up, dress, and get to an airport in order to catch a flight. Of all the entries on her hundred-most-hated list that one hovered right near the top.

At the same time, she felt some relief as the remnants of her dream slipped away. There was something about the imagined scenario of snipers behind sand-dunes firing on a lone taxi that she found disconcerting. It was the fact that her viewpoint was from inside the cab looking out. She blamed that particular mental contortion on the conversation at dinner last night, and Willy Wolverhampton's reaction of horror when they told of their plans for the day.

"I'm stoppin' aboard," he said, "and I'll be keepin' my 'ead down and all."

By now Lyall and Ngaio were used to Willy's habit of settling for the inertia option, but it came as something of a surprise to

THE PRICE OF A FREE KEFFIYEH

learn that this time they had no supporters. In this case they were on their own. The general feeling around the table was that to take the overland option to Cairo was ill-advised. The Brightons were just as opposed, with Billy giving his opinion that "you'd need your head read" to do it now. He and Belinda were glad they'd made a trip to the pyramids years ago when it was safe to go, but since there was that "let's-kill-this-group-of-Israeli-tourists-oh-were-they-Greeks-oops-sorry" incident of some years back, you wouldn't get them going again.

Over the night the conversation had merged with Ngaio's own memory of an incident in dacoit country in India some decades before. She could see how imagined pictures from the one mingled with remembered scenes from the other. The earlier occasion had come out all right, and she trusted this one would too. She knew that since the occurrence that Billy also referred to repeatedly as the "let's-kill-the-tourists" incident, Egyptian police had handled the security of tour groups with a seriousness that couldn't be doubted. She had been assured by the fact that the two sources of revenue that keep the country running are the canal and tourism, and no small effort is expended in safeguarding the two. The worst part of the day, she was sure, would be this one – having to get up at 3.45 a.m. and get down to the ship's tender in order to go ashore.

Ngaio and Lyall walked down the stairs to the lowest deck and joined a small stream of others who were no doubt also rethinking their decision, made months or weeks before. At that time it didn't seem an unreasonable idea to wake at such an hour, get into a coach, drive for hours, see a pyramid or two, and then drive more hours to rejoin their fellow passengers who had spent the day at leisure watching the banks of the

SEVENTEEN SEAS

Suez Canal slip by on each side.

They took a place in one of the several tenders already launched and bobbing about in the water of Port Suez. As well as the necessity of getting off to an early start because of the distance to be travelled, explained a large man in a green jacket and matching hat on the same bench seat, this was something of a stealth operation. They were being offloaded out here in the bay to avoid the likelihood of an act of terrorism should they tie up at the dock. Glen thought it was much more likely the stopping place was selected to avoid both the time and port fees involved in berthing, since comparatively few passengers were alighting for the overland option and the ship was to continue on its way. And if there were any measure of furtiveness involved, wouldn't the liner be observing blackout? Yet there it was for all to see, festooned with more lights than a Christmas tree.

Whatever the fact, one piece of information seemed to be borne out – a launch on duty nearby was labelled clearly as belonging to the Egyptian police, and uniformed men stood on deck. The tender filled and moved away from the hull. Rather than setting out for the shore it hovered near the ship and waited till all tenders were occupied. Ngaio, still not to grips with the earliness of the hour, felt the confidence she had maintained in the presence of their Medina dining mates the previous night diminishing. What would happen, she wondered while they waited to get under way, if terrorists made a strike while they were out here? They were already in the lifeboats – what if those were sunk?

There was some small reassurance to be gained from the presence of the police launch stationed nearby. But not for long. A minute later it gunned its engine and headed towards the shore.

THE PRICE OF A FREE KEFFIYEH

There goes the escort, Green Jacket pointed out – they'd be setting out behind. They sat. The other tenders bobbed nearby. The lights of the police launch disappeared into the distance. So much for providing armed defence. Green Jacket produced another hypothesis. Perhaps it was acting as a decoy to draw any danger away – heat-seeking torpedoes had been launched in their direction and were now following their self-sacrificing protectors. No flash or explosion reached across the water so presumably the charges had misfired.

Eventually the small flotilla of tenders set out. On the stretch to the shore they passed close by a number of ships at anchor. Any of the looming hulls could have housed a colony of frogmen, any of the decks might have held a belt of machine gunners with weapons loaded and ready to go. If that were the case, however, it seemed the person detailed to give the order had slept through their alarm. Ngaio yawned yet again and wished she'd done the same.

By the time they reached the dock it was daylight. Ngaio couldn't help thinking they could have had another hour's sleep then set out in the light, which surely would have been a better safeguard. Small shuttle buses picked them up and transferred them a very short distance to where long coaches were waiting.

"Blimey," said Green Jacket, "we could have walked that – it's only half as far as the wharf at Sharm el-Sheikh yesterday."

The passengers were hurried into a customs hall where they went through a security check. It seemed as well as being kept safe themselves, the snipers who could be lying in wait had a right to be protected from the tourists.

Lyall and Ngaio were directed to bus number five. They took

a pair of seats near the front. The coaches filled, and an escort vehicle swung in to take up position at the front of the line. Four kalashnikov-carrying policemen occupied the canopy covered back.

In addition, each coach had a security police officer aboard. The one charged to protect bus five was introduced as Muhammad. He was dressed in a brown suit, so the effect of the pistol on one hip and the uzzi on the other was not too obtrusive. Bus five's tour guide, Rashida, was dressed in a light coloured top and trousers, her hair tied up with a muslim-style bandana. She referred to Muhammad as their "Guardian Angel" and introduced the driver as Mr Hamid.

Between the three of them, over the day Muhammad was to prove the least militant.

Lyall and Ngaio settled in for what was to be a two and a half hour drive to Cairo. If Ngaio thought she had a chance of catching up on some of the missed sleep she was soon forced to reassess. Rashida took up the microphone and hardly stopped talking all the way. It started with a lesson in vital knowledge for the day. She held up a lollipop sign with '5' on it – her charges were to remember their coach number and look for the sign, when following her.

A language lesson was next. "Mashi mashi", their word for the day, meant 'Okey dokey' and they were to use it to show they understood.

"Mashi mashi," responded Ngaio.

Rashida beamed at this evidence of aptitude in one of her pupils and said she might let her carry the lollipop at the head of the group.

She then launched into a twenty-minute history lesson on

how "we" – that is Egypt – was occupied by "you British". Because of their position near the front, the Wellingtons came in for more than their share of stern looks. This was not mashi mashi, thought Ngaio. She felt torn between explaining that Rashida should leave them out of the blanket judgement as their ancestors had left the accused country before such offence took place, and the alternative of maintaining a measure of solidarity with their fellow coach mates. She figured they might need that as a bargaining point in hostage negotiations, should it come to that, so she kept quiet for the time being.

A further admonition followed – a warning not to judge some of the sights they were to see as being backward or dirty. Since the evils of occupation had been thrown off there'd been only sixty years for the once mighty nation of Misr to accomplish all that's been done. Given that, the visitors had to understand, the achievements must be considered great. At last she moved onto a safer topic – a lesson on the ancient process of mummification.

Outside the desert passed by, kilometre after kilometre. But the outlook was not all bleak. Inside the coach Rashida assured her captives that in time "we" would forgive "you", and there was a way that atonement could be effected. The tourists were given a "holy mission". During the day they would be offered opportunities to increase the economic wellbeing of the offended country so it could regain the splendour it knew in past ages. They were urged not to neglect these chances – those who failed could expect to find their vital organs in canopic jars.

To reinforce the lesson, and so as not to waste any time in the fight for the travellers' assets, if not their redemption,

Rashida then produced a glossy brochure for personalized jewellery – your name depicted in hieroglyphs – and a batch of order forms. The tourists were to select their choice of style, she would phone the instructions through to Cartouche Central and the pieces would be delivered to the coach in the afternoon. No doubt the warnings had been heeded, for a good number of the Coach-Fivers signed up.

Shopping on the coach – what a brilliant innovation. Lyall was convinced that when other companies heard about the concept it was sure to catch on. He could imagine it growing to the point when tours wouldn't actually have to go anywhere. Tourists would just board the bus and make their purchases without the inconvenience of stopping along the way or ending up elsewhere. And it was environmentally friendly.

Meanwhile Mr Hamid drove, seeming to be determined to pass everything ahead. As other vehicles increasingly got between the coaches and the escort the tourists thought it was the matter of security that concerned him, but they were to learn better later in the day.

Muhammad occupied the seat in front of Ngaio and Lyall. He dozed most of the way. That was okay – they might need him to be alert later.

The desert sand gave way to scattered buildings settled on the local equivalent of what, at home, they'd call small lifestyle blocks, and then to more concentrated areas of housing. Then they swept onto a wide ring road, smooth and modern, with ornamented underpasses. Billboards lining the motorway advertised an assortment of overseas universities. With Cairo's Al-Azhar University counted among the contenders for the

THE PRICE OF A FREE KEFFIYEH

title of the world's oldest, it was a puzzle to Lyall why so many international institutions should be in such competition for this nation's students. Did the Egyptian universities, likewise, erect hoardings in other countries to maintain an equal exchange?

By now they were creeping through traffic that made the Auckland rush-hour look like the Otago plains on a slow day. Muhammad woke and sat up, observing the jammed roads. Trucks, cars, buses, vans so crammed with men that some were hanging out the open side panels inched through streets lined with establishments dedicated to depleting the country's supply of reeds in the pursuit of papyrus. If a detachment of gunmen or suicide bombers got near them here, there was no chance the tourists could get away. Lyall wondered if their Guardian Angel had a plan for such an event.

At nine o'clock they reached the hotel where breakfast was to be served. The triangle-shaped tops of two ancient wonders were peeking through the pall above the adjacent buildings. So close to their goal and there was to be a further delay. But they'd been up for more than five hours and missed out on breakfast. If the pyramids had stood for five thousand years already it was highly likely they'd still be there in another hour.

More instructions were issued by the redoubtable Rashida, the 5 sign was raised, and the tourists were marched inside the Giza Meridien.

The Wellingtons found themselves seated with two couples from Australia. They hadn't met before, but co-occupation of coach five, and the shared experience of being blamed for the sins of forefathers none of them claimed, meant they formed an instant bond. They agreed their guide was making some broad assumptions. Hadn't anything been learned from the

Israeli-oops-Greeks incident, asked Mr Geelong.

As good and as necessary as the belated breakfast was, all were keen to move on to the main object of the journey. When Rashida appeared with her lollipop they rose quickly to follow her back to the bus. If their guide was pleased at the degree of compliance she could apparently command, that would do no harm.

Muhammad was at his post in the front left hand seat, and Mr Hamid reappeared to resume his place behind the wheel. Finally, having again negotiated a few further congested streets, they were there. They and a multitude of others. Half the multitude were tourists, the rest were there to sell souvenirs to the first half.

The people who made up the complement of coach number five were seasoned travellers. At the very least they had already journeyed from the antipodes, passing through a succession of seas and surviving days ashore in a dozen previous places. For the majority it was double that number. And that was just for this trip. None, whatever their point of embarkation, were first time travellers. Some had even visited this spot previously. Rashida, however, gave out no credit points for frequent flyer status. Before the doors of the bus were opened, she laid out a detailed set of orders.

The pyramid experience would be in three parts. First she would take them to the place where they would get the best photograph of the three large pyramids together. Then her acolytes would begin their holy mission by buying any books they wanted at the bookstall situated at the viewing site because the prices here were better than in the shops to come later.

THE PRICE OF A FREE KEFFIYEH

Together that would take twelve minutes. It was good to learn that this economic form of holiness included the virtues of prudence and thrift.

Those of the Coach-Fivers who had over-estimated the value of their past-tourist credentials or, more likely had under-estimated the sheer persistence of the merchants of Giza as they alighted, were rather more respectful of Rashida's knowledge of local conditions on their return. The twelve minutes allotted stretched a little as they experienced the first lessons in balancing the requirements of a sacred mission with a measure of self-preservation. Then precious more minutes were expended as a search party had to be sent out to find a prodigal passenger wandering in the wilderness.

As they waited, a memory with its origin in the surroundings of the Curzon Theatre came back to Ngaio's mind. Some days before at the port lecture, the tour advisor warned that those going on the overland experience should try not to be too offended by the hawkers at the pyramids. "After all they are Arabs," he remarked, adding with paternal tolerance, "but we should try to be open-minded." At the time she and Lyall had exchanged glances of amazement and horror. It was a long time since they'd encountered such blatant bigotry, and she found this instance particularly offensive in the way it was couched in the guise of open-mindedness.

The next stop, the longest of the three scheduled by their guide, was the close-up hands-on pyramid experience – Cheops on one side, his son Kephren on the other. This was what they had anticipated for so long, and there was a heady fifty minutes allocated – time enough to get into plenty of trouble.

It didn't take much doing. Most of the tourists were here for

SEVENTEEN SEAS

just an hour or two of one day of their lives, but for the locals it was their livelihood. Over succeeding centuries since the initial skilled artisans crafted the incredible structures, their descendants had shown almost equally impressive ingenuity. Even if the original intention had not been a public works enterprise the long-term effect on the Egyptian economy was itself monumental. Previous generations had stripped the tombs of their treasures leaving their interiors empty and their exteriors unclad. Yet even with only the shells remaining the edifices were still huge economic assets that continued to provide employment. The most recent generations of descendants of the original architects and craftsmen had made an art form of salesmanship. Hundreds of these new Egyptian entrepreneurs were ready as the Coach-Fivers stepped onto the Giza sand.

"Hey madam, take my picture," came the call from atop camels as suitably attired men posed with flamboyant gestures.

"Have a photo taken of you on my camel, Sir."

Most madams and sirs knew better than to do so, but those who acted impulsively learned the service was far from free, even though that assurance was often appended to the invitation.

Boys, perhaps serving their apprenticeship years while saving for the necessary equipment to become the camel-sitters, walked around with shoulder bags crammed with wares. After asking where a tourist was from they'd pull out an item in a plastic bag and thrust it into the hands of their mark.

"Free gift for you," they'd insist, and only equally forceful tourists managed to press them back into the hands or bags of the selfless donors.

Even the tourist police stationed around the perimeter of

THE PRICE OF A FREE KEFFIYEH

the pyramids, presumably with the purpose of preventing the purloining of what remained of the resource one pebble at a time, were in on the act. A single strand of barrier rope was fixed at thigh height in the area where coaches disgorged the day-trippers in the shadow of the memorial to Cheops. Lyall and Ngaio accepted the restriction. It would have been good to actually lay their hand on the ancient stones, but they could see the necessity of protecting the massive blocks if they were survive a further five millennia. They paused at the barrier to take photos. One of the uniformed guardians approached. Rather than watching that they didn't leap over and make a run for the massive stones some metres away, as they expected, he put his foot on the cord to lower it to the ground. While they stood in some amazement, he motioned for them to step over to touch the stones they'd come to see.

With such apparent permission so forthcoming, who could resist? Without waiting to dwell on the possible reasons why they had apparently been singled out for special privilege, they crossed the expanse quickly, touched the stones, posed for a snap, and started back before their thoughtful guard could be upbraided by a superior for showing compassion to this pair of tourists who had come from so far to fulfil this ambition.

When they came to cross back it was made clear that their benefactor believed that one good deed deserved another. He held out his hand and it was clear that the intention was not in order to help them step over. Lyall was indignant and placed his own foot on the rope, lowering it to ground level so they could both pass. To the accompaniment of a low growl the couple retired a distance to observe. It soon transpired that far from being rewarded for their interest, they had been selected simply

SEVENTEEN SEAS

as potential payers of a tip for services rendered. It was not an exclusive offer – all likely-looking prospects who approached the barrier were being extended the same courtesy. In the viewpoint of the officer, no doubt it was a reasonable assumption, but in the Wellingtons' opinion there were two points of contention. First, their own country not only hadn't developed a culture of tipping, but discouraged it actively; second, it also engendered an expectation of honesty among its law enforcers. As they watched the actions of several other individuals and small groups who enacted similar scenes, it was clear that more nations than theirs also believed that police, even of the tourist variety, should be incorruptible. It did not appear to be a profitable day for the man in uniform.

The full extent of the deception was yet to be revealed. As the couple moved further away from the area where the coaches were parked, and rounded the corner to view another face of the great pyramid, a very different scene met their eyes. No barrier existed here. No rope was strung to mark any margin of protection around the monument. Not even a line was drawn in the sand. What's more, the stone blocks at the base of the monolith were well populated. People sat eating and children climbed upon them. The giant stones mined millennia before served as handy resting places for backpacks and cameras as visitors took a break from their viewing. If Lyall was indignant before, thought Ngaio, it was just as well she hadn't felt intimidated enough to slip the man a coin. He'd have been even more irate when he saw this.

All around the plain the couple witnessed instances of intercultural exchange. Mr and Mrs Derbyshire, fellow passengers on coach five, were unwise enough to accept the free gift

THE PRICE OF A FREE KEFFIYEH

bestowed upon them by a smiling young lad, and were quickly informed of the rule of reciprocity. When they demurred at playing their part, two of the tourist police were drawn into the discussion to arbitrate. Luckily, a man who introduced himself as "Ali from Sheffield" was lurking nearby and he too stepped in to help sort it out. At the end of the encounter the Derbyshires rather ruefully displayed the 'free' keffiyeh they'd scored after the help of two police at a cost of a dollar each, Ali for a further fee, and some consideration for the original donor. True, they'd paid a good deal more than the desperation rate of three for a dollar quoted to day trippers who were finally departing, they admitted, but perhaps it was worth it for an experience to tell down at the local back home.

After watching other tourists trying to extricate themselves from the clutches of insistent vendors, and working hard to avoid similar encounters themselves, the Wellingtons came across a clash with a somewhat different outcome. As they passed near one of the camels, a young Japanese woman raised her camera and snapped the fully garbed eastern rider. The instant the shutter clicked the camel slid to its knees and the rider dismounted to demand appearance fees. Ms Honshu was not counted among the number of Coach-Fivers but the circumstances demanded that all take sides – tourists versus touts. Ngaio and Lyall stopped, ready to lend support if necessary, but it seemed their assistance was not needed. Ms H responded to the repeated demand in a long stream of Japanese. She paused, the cameleer began to speak, and she began again with increased volume, length, and apparent eloquence. Whatever she said, the overall effect proved the match of her would-be beneficiary. He resumed his mount and went in search of a more amenable mark. Ms Honshu turned to the Wellingtons, grinned, and said in faultless English "That put him in his place". The couple walked off laughing. The score wasn't good but at least their team was finally on the board – touts untold, tourists one.

With stones caressed, mounds of mastabas marvelled at, photos taken, and feelings of awe indulged in, it was time to move on to do the same to yet another marvel of the ancient world. The third of the promised sights, the sphinx, was waiting – crouched in a nearby dip keeping its blind eyes on the activities of the further few thousand who clambered around it. Half of this horde held cameras, the other half moved among them insisting they depart with books, stuffed toy camels, souvenir pens, key rings, plates, model pyramids and sphinxes, and all manner of other goods apparently believed by their sellers to be essential to western living. A few tried to hawk rolls of film but found even fewer takers. Those rather more up with the play offered cards of replacement batteries.

Unlike their experience at the pyramids, the Coach-Fivers found there was no chance of approaching the figure of the human lion. Excavations surrounded the site and no tourist police were on hand to motion them through the gateway. They could only stand at a distance and wait for a chance to take the prescribed picture without including the heads of too many other photographers in the foreground.

The woman who occupied seat 8B went from vendor to vendor in a search for a memento to send home – anything at all, with the name Cairo on it. Sellers rallied to the challenge, but despite the variety of ephemera amassed in the area on that day, it soon emerged that she'd requested the unprocurable. A stuffed penguin with 'Egypt' on it might have been a stronger possibility.

"Madam," said an aggrieved salesman, "this is Giza, not Cairo."

As the bus rolled out of the arena Lyall looked down the aisle and contemplated the stock of souvenirs now being shown in most of the seat spaces. He'd arrived thinking that the skills and ingenuity of the builders of the pyramids were lost in the ancient past, but after this visit he'd changed his mind. Evidence of at least the ingenuity was present and fully developed in their descendants a couple of hundred generations on.

The Wellingtons were probably in good company with most of the others on coach five, in thinking Giza and Cairo amounted to the same place. Certainly they knew the pyramids were at Giza – well, the ones that tourists went to most commonly, anyway. As they crossed the Nile, however, it was made clear by their guide that they had left Giza and were now entering Cairo. No clear space separated the two – the city, or cities, continued without break on each side. It seemed to the couple that this place vied with hundreds of others around the world for the record for how many residents could be accommodated in how small a space. They had both grown up on the then standard Kiwi quarter-acre housing plot, and still enjoyed an outlook over scrub-covered hills from the kitchen window of their suburban house. Their own home city, the capital of their country, was a small town compared to this, and they prayed it would stay that way.

While one of the cities they were visiting had the pyramids as its top attraction, the other housed the treasures they once contained.

The Egyptian Museum, Rashida informed her charges, holds 250,000 exhibits. Lyall pulled out his cellphone and selected calculator. If they spent just one minute looking at each item, that would require a total of 4,166 hours to cover the lot. Allowing a forty-hour week, that worked out to 2 years full time work. The mere hour and a half allotted in their schedule was woefully inadequate.

There was no lack of experts on hand to provide commentaries to help them make the most of their visit. Each of the countless tour guides present, including Rashida, gathered their brood around their lollipop and delivered fluent explanations of some selected pieces – each shouting to be heard above the competition. That took up the first quarter hour, then each group was let loose to spend the remaining time at will – or at least contending with the hordes also trying to make the best use of their remaining minutes.

For Ngaio and Lyall there was no question as to what, from a quarter of a million exhibits, should be viewed. Predictable though it might be, the marvels of Tutankhamun's tomb had to be their top choice. Without discussion they headed towards the relevant galleries. Even though the items were so well known to them from studies and pictures, both lingered around the cases containing the major pieces. To see the real objects, so well preserved despite their three-thousand-plus years age, far outstripped any consideration of cost or discomfort the day brought.

It appeared that not all were so impressed.

"It's disgraceful," stated a voice nearby, "priceless treasures and just look at how they're displayed." Two women, most likely mother and daughter, were voluble in their criticism. There was no special consideration for keeping the relics in a controlled atmosphere, the security looked to be almost non-existent, and many of the items had little in the way of explanation.

"Look at this," Daughter continued, "for this one there's just a few words handwritten, on a piece of paper. And that's got a torn edge. They should be properly curated."

"Perhaps you should apply for a job, here," suggested Mother. Ah, that comment provided a clue. Daughter was still in full censure mode as Ngaio and Lyall moved on.

"I imagine she's right," said Ngaio, "but if the museum was that well ordered, we wouldn't have seen the treasures close up. Look at that – King Tut's death mask. We can almost put our hand right on it. It's just a sheet of glass away."

Their time up, it was back into the coach. The plan, according to Rashida, was to return to the hotel for lunch. With breakfast delayed till nine, and of a size that would have satisfied a pharaoh's full court, this didn't seem to be the best use of their time, but the schedule was fixed. This time Ngaio, occupying the window seat, could look down at the river as they crossed back over into Giza. There was still open green space on Gezira Island, she noted with a sense of satisfaction. It helped her complete the mental picture she'd missed earlier when she'd seen just streets of stone buildings. Upstream, she hoped, farmers still waited with anticipation for the annual flooding of the Nile. She'd like to think that somewhere they still set images of Hapi in fields, but there was no real chance of that.

They were back in the narrow road that led to the Giza Meridien. And they'd thought the congestion was bad in the morning! As they again crept along, stop-start stop-start in the traffic, Ngaio looked down into the canal they were following. Canal, or huge ditch, she wondered. As they made progress the litter that fouled the water became thicker till it formed a solid mass. She went to nudge Lyall, to bring it to his attention, then remembered Rashida's morning admonition about being judgemental. She'd seen sights like this in many countries, she told herself. But that was no consolation. In fact, if it was a global problem, that just made it worse.

It was after three o'clock as they stepped from the bus at the entrance. A band struck up a stirring march as they walked in through the doors and into the ballroom-sized foyer. It was anyone's guess how long the musicians had been waiting, but they performed with enthusiasm all the same. Lyall thought there was more than a modicum of irony in the fact that here they were being greeted like visiting dignitaries when about a kilometre or so away earlier in the day they'd been treated as gullible dupes. Though with good reason in many cases, he had to admit. It seemed Rashida was right – these Egyptians were a forgiving people.

So it came to pass that, with another banquet-sized meal over, the time for the redemption of the children of Rashida drew nigh. They were reminded of the "holy mission" they'd been given, to worship in a tangible way at the altar of the Egyptian economy. The people of coach five raised the cry "mashi mashi," and their leader was pleased with them and took them to the place of deliverance – a place of papyrus and other treasures. They poured forth from their transport and went into that place prepared to buy.

The thirty minutes allotted for this activity, as with others on the day's itinerary except for the two meals each of which was

THE PRICE OF A FREE KEFFIYEH

allocated ample time to consume more than an ample amount, was scant even for those who had no intention of adding to the national capital assets.

First, however, they were directed to a compulsory lesson on the art of papyrus making. Kadesh's demonstration was clear, brief and good-humoured. The steps of stripping the reed, soaking, pressing, and the use of the papyrus pounder, were explained in a pleasantly accented voice. Ngaio looked at the young man and wondered why, if there were gods like this right on hand among the reeds of the Nile, Cleopatra had lusted after the Romans.

While the Wellingtons went about the gallery admiring the intricate artistry in the works on display, others of their group could be seen making impulse purchases. It had crossed Lyall's mind that if they failed in fulfilling their set mission they'd be in for further castigation on the final leg of the journey. Now, seeing the zeal with which many of their fellow passengers were loading themselves with parcels, plastic bags and rolled tubes, he relaxed.

So, it seemed, did Rashida. She beamed as her charges climbed back on board bearing gold, frankincense, papyrus pictures, and heads of Nefertiti sculpted in resin.

Back onto the road once again – this time for the last stage of the journey. The Coach-Fivers looked at the city buildings as they inched by. To think they'd believed the traffic was bad a couple of hours earlier.

Ngaio looked at a splash of red in a concrete planter outside a large stone building. A row of hollyhocks made a cheerful sight. She was particularly pleased to see them, for that morning as

SEVENTEEN SEAS

the coach crept along crowded streets she had spotted some others growing in the earth beside the clogged canal. It had taken her some moments to identify the plants as they were grey with dust from stem to flower tip. It was good to see some now adding colour to the predominant concrete colour of the city.

An impression Lyall had formed during the earlier transits through the city now developed into a more substantial theory. He put a question to their guide who was sitting, uncharacteristically quiet. Not only was her mission largely filled, successfully at that, but after talking for more than ten hours with scarcely a break, perhaps she'd run through all the information she had to impart. Whatever, she deserved a rest. Lyall's question roused her and she responded with good grace, proving she was indeed a repository of much further knowledge.

"Most of the buildings look as though they're not completed – especially the tops. Is that so they can have another storey added?"

Rashida confirmed that was often the case, but it was more a secondary consideration. The primary reason, to do with tax payable, was one that appealed to Lyall as a reform that could be instituted by their own local body authority – their whole country, in fact. He could see their suburb transformed by the presence of uncompleted chimneys, extensions framed but not closed in, rooflines minus spouting systems and even lacking the full complement of tiles. It would be less attractive, true, and wouldn't improve the lamentable leaky homes phenom- enon that had come to light in recent years, but if you could hold off on paying tax on the grounds that your house was

THE PRICE OF A FREE KEFFIYEH

still a work in progress, well, this was an idea that warranted further investigation. He gave it more thought as coach five continued to work its way through city streets.

An hour later the 'city of a million minarets', as Rashida had informed them was an alternative title for Al-Qahira, the Triumphant City, was finally left behind and they were back on a comparatively open road. Ngaio looked her watch. It was now the time given for all passengers to be back aboard. No doubt the ship was waiting at Port Said for the adventurers to return.

Mr Hamid put his best foot forward. Or, rather, down. Perhaps, one of the English passengers surmised, he harboured a hope to be mistaken for Lewis Hamilton. Since their delayed lunch was scarcely digested, it's unlikely his concern was for fear his passengers would be late sitting down in their dining rooms that evening. His own meal arrangements were another matter. He too had been on deck, metaphorically, for as long as his passengers – no doubt longer as they had no idea from where he'd started his journey that morning. Maybe the thought of Mrs H, standing with papyrus pounder ready at the door was uppermost in his mind.

It grew dark. A police vehicle screamed up from behind, blue lights flashing, and pulled in ahead. Oh, that's all we need now, thought the Coach-Fivers – to be stopped for speeding. Mr Hamid's logbook would be examined and the fact that he'd been on the job for more than thirteen hours would be revealed. That would hold them up even further, if a replacement driver could even be found. They could picture their shipmates standing at the stern rail raising a glass in their honour as the dark continent disappeared over the horizon. But no, all looked to be amicable with no block of ticket forms being produced, no request for records. The truth dawned. The police had indeed caught up with them, but this was their escort – the cavalry had arrived to safeguard their passage. Two other buses drew up behind – numbers two and four of their contingent joined the line to form a small convoy. From this point on, coach five sped along mere metres from the pickup with its armed officers seated in readiness at the rear.

Ngaio wondered if the restored presence of the guard indicated an increase in the level of potential peril they could encounter, but Muhammad was slouched in the seat in front, apparently dozing. If he wasn't concerned on that score, why should she be? She could switch her full anxiety to the matter of the bus's speed, which was complicated by the fact that it had to be judged in relation to the set itinerary.

It was now well past the time that the ship was due to sail.

"Are we almost there yet?"

"No," replied Rashida, "Port Said's still two hours away."

There was nothing to do but sit back and take comfort in the thought that the top advantage of buying a tour organized by the ship was a guarantee against being abandoned. With five coaches of passengers still missing in the deserts of Egypt the captain had no choice but to sit at the dock and wait for them.

As they passed through different local areas of jurisdiction, designated by manned archways with booths, there was a changing of the guard. The current escort vehicle would pull off to the side, the kalashnikov-toting men in the back waving farewell, and a new crew would ease ahead to take over for the next sector. It seemed there was an orchestrated plan that was working fairly harmoniously.

There was, however, one note of discord. The presence of

THE PRICE OF A FREE KEFFIYEH

the pilot vehicle clearly goaded coach five's driver. No doubt the escort was doing the speed limit, but whatever that was it wasn't enough for Hamid Hamilton. He tailgated them, blew the horn to hurry them along, and kept pulling out as though to pass. The men with the assault rifles were apparently of lesser concern to him than Mrs Hamid. Fortunately they also proved to be of more equable temperament.

At last they passed under a sign that proclaimed they'd entered the Port Said region. The road ran alongside the canal where large ships lay waiting their turn to transit. Almost three hours after the ship was to have sailed, the brave little convoy reached the town. Ngaio allowed her fingers to relax their grip on the grab handle fixed to the back of Muhammad's seat – their speed would decrease and all would be well.

It was a momentary respite only. The lights of two other buses could be seen just ahead. With numbers two and four still behind, they had apparently caught up with one and three. Hamid Hamilton pressed his foot down again. Houses and shops on each side became harder to focus on as they were passed with increasing speed. Coach three was now dead ahead and it was clear that it was not the bronze medal that was in their driver's sights. At a small intersection he seized his chance. If his counterpart was cautious enough to ease back on the accelerator he was shrewd enough to seize the advantage. Ngaio couldn't see how they could possibly have got by, but there they were in silver position.

As they tailed the remaining contestant for line honours, the houses and shops gave way to the dock area. Dead ahead they could see their home away from home was waiting, lit up at the wharf. No doubt, they thought, the rest of the passengers, having been held up since berthing at five o'clock, were lining the decks and tapping their feet at the delay. Wrong again.

Once more, it was a case of if-you-can't-get-to-the-shops-the-shops-will-come-to-you. Under a long row of awnings stretched along the dock, stalls were piled high with merchandise. If the ship's schedule had been put out by their late arrival that hadn't been an upset to the local businessmen. Savvy & Serial Shopper, Rhoda Retail, Mrs Bling Festooned, Con Sumer and a good proportion of the rest of the passengers were on the wharf making the most of this bonus opportunity.

Surely, thought Ngaio, as she felt herself being pressed against the back of the seat, their driver wouldn't think of passing here, not with all these people about. But this had been a day for under-estimations. It seemed he would, and he did. In a manoeuvre that any grand prix great would be proud of, Mr Hamid swerved to the right and slid coach five into pole position. After all that had happened over the course of the day Ngaio wouldn't have been at all surprised to see a local official whip off his black and white chequered keffiyeh and prescribe a figure eight pattern in front of them as the bus pulled to a halt.

She stepped down onto the dock. It was seventeen hours since they'd left the ship a distance of ninety nautical miles away. Those who had overlanded, however, had covered something like four hundred kilometres. Even though she wasn't behind the wheel herself, it was no wonder her legs felt a little wobbly. She could only imagine how Mr Hamid felt after his even longer day, and she presumed he had still to get home – wherever that was. She and Lyall climbed the short ramp to re-enter the ship.

With the steel structure enclosing them, the various tensions

THE PRICE OF A FREE KEFFIYEH

generated by the day dropped away. Rashida's patriotic concerns could be understood, the artifice of the pyramid peddlers admired, the workings of Egypt's security system appreciated, even the frustrated Formula One wannabe, Hamid Hamilton, she now found funny. They headed for the lift – the stairs could wait for tomorrow.

What a great day. They'd started out with high expectations and these had been exceeded. It was more than mashi mashi, it was mighty mighty.

So it was that the people of coach five parted from their leader at this point. Leaving her on the shore they passed out of the land of Egypt and crossed the sea to the next promised land.

He put his foot on the cord and motioned for them to step over to touch the stones.

— CHAPTER 19 —

Justice Human and Divine

A Mediterranean cruise – along with everyone else who ever breathed Glen and Lynn had been saying for years they'd do it one day. Now, finally, there they were.

The couple had grown up with stories of the perils associated with crossing the Tasman Sea, and they had survived two such voyages in relative comfort. They'd also crossed other larger oceans and seas, so the sliver of blue that marked the Mediterranean on the world map appeared to pose no problem. After all, it was an enclosed space – almost land-locked, with a bonus in the surrounding continents giving their protection. It was with confidence that they looked forward to experiencing unfamiliar places around the heart of the classical world in the European spring.

As the ship left the shore of one continent and steamed northwest to another, some of their fellow travellers were not so optimistic.

"It's cold," complained 'Basil', "we must be getting near Britain."

"News is tha's snow in England," added Bradford Yorkshire, following it up with "Ah can feel it from here."

The grumblers seemed to be concentrated in the cabins that had been occupied for the full trip. In the lead-up to their own departure, Glen had worried about being confined to such restricted surroundings for six and a half weeks. Now, with

JUSTICE HUMAN AND DIVINE

only a week to go, he was pleased to find that his misgivings had not been realized. All the same, when the ship docked for the final time he'd be happy to leave – it was time to move on. Several others he encountered, however, were showing signs of increasing depression at the prospect of reaching the last port. Strangely, it appeared to be those who would be completing the round trip after eleven plus weeks who were least looking forward to the arrival.

Harry Hampshire was already talking about the next time. He and Zelda would be home for less than a month before joining another cruise around the Norwegian fjords. Norwich Norfolk, a frequent patron of the Pennant Bar on Lido deck, felt the air and moved inside to Champions, referring to the two as his summer and winter palaces respectively.

"You can tell we're back in Europe," he remarked, "didn't I say that as soon as we passed through the Suez Canal and into the Mediterranean the temperature would drop by five degrees? We'll be back in our woollies next."

It seemed there was some truth in Harry's forecast. Already the Greek gods into whose territory they were heading were proving less merciful than those who ruled the Arabian Sea. Their equivalents to the south had treated the travellers with benevolence. On the previous days Ra had bathed his territory in the golden warmth tourists usually associated with sand and sphinx, yet even more kindly had held back his full force. Now, though, the closer the ship steamed to Olympus the more the Nephelae nymphs could be seen to be active in the sky readying their water pitchers, and the less Helios seemed to want to peer through their ranks to interrupt their work.

SEVENTEEN SEAS

Ngaio Wellington found the briskness in the sea-breeze gave a certain impetus to her circuits of the Promenade deck, though she and the others striding out found their gaits less steady than usual. On more than one occasion that morning she'd found herself executing impromptu dance steps while passing other pedestrians. She reached her circuit marker, lifeboat two, for the fifth time and went inside. Though there was still ten minutes to the scheduled start time a good number of the regular morning quizzers were already seated waiting. Ngaio took a chair at one of the tables. She'd given her physical body a reasonable warm up with the walking, now it was time to attend to keeping her brain in condition. Today's appointed member of the entertainment crew arrived and the questions began. For the first half of the twenty questions she was reasonably happy. She was confident about her answers to the highest waterfall, the medical term for the kneecap, and the actress who played Scarlett O'Hara – but she was sure everyone else would know them too.

"In which county is Stonehenge?" She could answer that one.

"In which year was Queen Elizabeth the Second born?" She could work that out, but who was the host of a radio programme she'd never heard of – that would be a cross on her scoresheet. Why couldn't they ask about the morning programme on National Radio at home?

"Who is the current poet laureate?" About half the pencils were employed as contestants wrote on their papers. Ngaio knew the New Zealand one but if she wrote that it would be marked wrong. There was a strong assumption being made here. She experienced a moment of irritation. "Of what country?" she asked. Her question didn't receive an answer.

JUSTICE HUMAN AND DIVINE

The others at her table gave her an odd look, but she didn't mind – she hoped she had made her point.

"I scored only one point less than the winner and more than most people there," she told Lyall a little later as they made their way down the stairs, "under the circumstances that was pretty good."

Lynn and Glen Henderson stepped out of the midships lift at Ellora deck just as the Wellingtons reached the same landing. It was clear both couples were bound for lunch in the Medina dining room. It was a fortunate meeting – each pair had been thinking they should get together with the other more often, but with their slightly different interests and habits their paths had not crossed as often as they'd have liked. They walked to the entrance together and were shown to a round table where five people were already seated.

"Where in Australia are you from?" asked 'Basil' after the usual greetings were exchanged.

Lynn and Ngaio exchanged looks of frustrated resignation and Glen added a slight upward roll of the eyes. The signs were picked up by 'Sybil' who took the opportunity to both chide her husband and make amends.

"I think you'll find they're from New Zealand, dear," she said. Susan Plymouth, aka 'Sybil', felt relieved that it was not she who had made the error this time. She had done so before and learned how tiresome Kiwis found it when almost everyone from the northern hemisphere made the wrong assumption. It was like Canadians being identified with the United States – she knew that one as well from past travel, and now asked anyone with a North American accent what part of Canada they were from. She'd learned that Americans didn't take offence when she made the wrong call while Canadians, more sensitized by fears of imperialism from south of the border, often did.

'Sybil's' correction gave Jovial Joe a toehold. It was a tiny niche that really wouldn't provide a purchase point for even the metatarsal minimus, but Joe was adept at taking advantage of even the smallest opportunity. He pulled a proven audience-pleaser from his mental files and made the appropriate adjustments to fit the occasion.

"I was talking to a Kiwi girl on my last cruise," he started off, at sufficient volume for others to break off their small talk and pay attention. "She was telling me how she'd met an Australian fellow on board and they'd had the odd drink together. Then the chap started upping the pressure – you know what I mean. He followed her back to her cabin one night and started to turn on the charm.

'How do you like your eggs in the morning?' he asked her in a seductive tone.

'Unfertilized,' she told him, and shut the door."

The men gave the punch line enough of a chuckle for Joe to make a mental note that this joke had scored again. He must remember to cross that one off the list in the notebook he kept in the drawer he'd designated for stationery in his stateroom on Formosa deck. The standards to which he kept, in his self-imposed comedian's code, included a rule against repeating a gag on any one cruise, even when he was sure the company was not duplicated. It helped him keep his act top class.

Mrs Liverpool-Lancs waited for the men to settle, then posed a problem that had given her cause to ponder.

"Tomorrow, when we dock at Athens," she began.

JUSTICE HUMAN AND DIVINE

"Piraeus," put in 'Sybil'. "The port is at Piraeus."

"Piraeus for Athens," elaborated Mrs LL, using the term repeated by the Ports Advisor in his address. "We're going in to the city, aren't we dear?" Mrs LL glanced at her husband but didn't wait for confirmation before she continued.

"It has crossed my mind that tomorrow is Good Friday." She paused for the outcry that she thought her revelation would bring. Should bring. A moment later, in case the full significance had not been grasped, she added, "Everything will be shut!"

Ngaio, looked across at Mr LL, and thought she detected a slight lifting of the eyebrows and lightening of his expression.

"It's the acropolis we're going to see," was the man's response, "they can't shut that."

"The tour takes in the Plaka."

Lyall wasn't at all concerned about the lack of further opportunities to shop – that was a matter on which he and his wife were in complete accord – but he wondered if this was another instance of unfortunate pre-planning. The removal of Colombo from the original itinerary was still a disappointment, though he had no complaints about its replacement. Ngaio, however, was pursuing another line of thought.

"Hold on," she said, still thinking, "It's Good Friday in our calendar. The western calendar," she added, in case there was some doubt. "But is it the same in Greece?" There was a short silence. "The Greek Orthodox calendar is different. I'm sure Easter's later in that."

Mrs LL looked dubious, but Ngaio's degree of certainty was increasing. She was sure she remembered a question about it in a TV quiz show once. 'Sybil', meanwhile, had spotted a further

SEVENTEEN SEAS

potential sticking point.

"If it's our Good Friday," she asked, though not with great conviction, "should we be going ashore at all?"

"If you were home," answered 'Basil', "you wouldn't be going to church anyway." It seemed to settle the matter.

Mrs LL brightened. If Ngaio was right, there was no threat to the anticipated Plaka experience. And just in case anyone considered such an activity was unsuited to the most significant day of the Christian calendar that objection had been covered too. It was clearly a case of 'when in Rome…' Or in this case, Athens.

Her husband, on the other hand, felt his mood descending again.

"The weather gets worse the closer we get to home," he remarked.

Jovial Joe saw his chance again.

"There are deck-chairs available all around the pool. Even the Germans aren't bothering with them."

There was a titter of laughter from the diners on the opposite side of the table, but Lynn noticed none came from her left where Ngaio and Lyall were seated. On the contrary, they too seemed a little puzzled. That was a clue. She resolved to get to the bottom of the mystery, but the conversation moved on to people's plans for the next day in Athens. Her chance came as the group filed back out through the Medina's doors. Lynn moved in front of Joe and turned to face him.

"What's the story of the Germans and the deck-chairs?" she asked, "I seem to be missing something."

Jovial Joe's comedian's code also covered the matter of explaining the point of a joke – he abhorred the practice of

JUSTICE HUMAN AND DIVINE

some less principled humorists who stopped to elaborate to those who remained blank, then demanded "Get it, get it?" till they concurred. In the face of Lynn's question, he sought to slip around her and move on.

"It must be a British, thing," said Lynn, "None of us get it," she indicated Glen and the Wellingtons. They agreed.

Joe stopped. If there was ever a case to make an exception, this was it, but he was still uneasy. He hesitated. No, it was a matter of principle. With a polite excuse me, he moved on not relaxing till he had rounded a corner and was out of sight.

Mrs Liverpool-Lancs, had no such scruples. Besides, she was appreciative for the information that her planned trip to see the Parthenon, and just as importantly the Plaka, was not in jeopardy. She was only too happy to step into the breach.

"You're right," she confirmed and outlined the facts, or at least the perception, that a battle of the deck-chairs was being fought by British tourists throughout the resorts of Europe. The claim was that their German counterparts rose before dawn to place their towels on the sunbeds in order to reserve them for the day.

"They do it the night before, more likely," her husband interjected.

It seemed Glen's theory of it being something to do with the war held a modicum of truth, because even mention of the battle of the beach towels was enough to raise certain Brits' xenophobia to levels unknown since V.E. day. However, Mrs LL added with undisguised glee, the supremacy of the sovereign nation was recently illustrated in a television ad in which a Bond-like hero, to the accompaniment of the *Dambusters* theme, throws a Union Jack patterned towel from a hotel balcony to claim a deck-chair ahead of a contingent of sunbed-bound Germans. The pair laughed yet again, and departed humming the strains of the march in unison.

When Lyall pulled back the curtains to the balcony next morning the ship was passing abeam of the breakwater. Ngaio emerged from the bathroom wrapped in a towel. He did the same five minutes later as his wife was replacing the telephone handset.

"Glen and Lynn called. I said we'd meet them in the Orangery for breakfast in twenty minutes."

The two couples had discovered, to their mutual delight the afternoon before, that not only had they booked the same excursion tour – "The Acropolis and The Plaka: Best Seller" – but they'd been allocated seats on the same coach. Great – they'd go together. Unlike Mrs LL and others, they agreed the priority was the part billed as being rich in beauty, architectural splendour and historic importance. Every piece of travel advice dealing with the city named for Athena that had ever been printed rated viewing the Acropolis as the experience par excellence, the most memorable of any tourist's trip or, less lyrically, that which cannot be missed. Even without such recommendations neither couple could contemplate returning home to admit they had missed this priceless opportunity to stand on the sacred rock of the upper city and drink in the history-soaked surroundings in an attempt to recapture some sense of the glory of the golden age of Greek history.

The drive-by sights included in the tour – the Old Olympic Stadium (traffic permitting), Hadrian's Arch, Statue of Lord Byron, Temple of Olympian Zeus, National Gardens, Academy

JUSTICE HUMAN AND DIVINE

and the University Library – might be a bonus. The "tempting shops" of the Plaka were of no interest at all.

Back in their cabin after breakfasting, Lyall opened the glass sliding door and stepped out onto the balcony. The ship was completing its approach to the berth. The floor of the balcony showed there had been rain but the clouds were breaking up in the distance.

"It's looking a lot clearer, and the Captain's forecast was good," he announced, "I don't think we'll need these." He proceeded to pull the matching Kiwistuff weatherproof jackets from the backpack where Ngaio had placed them. The two folding umbrellas followed. Ngaio opened her mouth to suggest a more cautious approach, then shut it again. He was the one who carried it. She hung the "Please make up my room" notice on the door and the couple set out for the day.

The lettering displayed on the frontage of the building facing the ship was in three lines, two of which were readily readable to everyone on board. The second level, under a row of Greek script, read "Welcome to Piraeus". Below that, the words "Cruise terminal". Ngaio had already noticed that "Blue Star Ferries" and ships of "Hellenic Seaways" crisscrossed the bay. As the coach set out through the streets of Piraeus she saw, a little to her surprise, that she could read a lot more even though she didn't know an Aleph from an 'Ayin. The car in front had a "Baby on Board" sign hanging in its back window. Billboards for a variety of products were readily readable. If she were of a mind to she could stock up on burgers, cigarettes, cosmetics, and a variety of technology with no difficulty at all. It was more than she expected. The presence of English in Hong Kong, Singapore and India was understandable, given their

SEVENTEEN SEAS

histories as British colonies. In Pattaya and Sharm el-Sheikh the beach resorts existed to cater for tourists, most of whom had English as one of their spoken options. Greece, she had thought, would be another matter. Apart from petition sheets soliciting signatures urging the return of the art treasures now further anglicised and alienated under the term 'Elgin marbles', she had not anticipated that they'd encounter much written English during the day.

There was another sight beyond the windows of the bus that was more eye-catching in a rather different can't-miss-it kind of way – conspicuous but certainly not classic, attention-getting but far from aesthetic. Mounds of rubbish were heaped up all along the streets they were navigating. Memories of a small item of news amid more momentous global issues some weeks before popped into the travellers' minds. The strikes that had hit the country as millions of Greek workers protested against projected changes in pension plans evidently hadn't been resolved. Skip-bins placed on the pavements were packed, with the stacks reaching well above the rims. Outside the containers further hills of plastic rubbish sacks in black and blue, bulging supermarket bags, cartons and other packaging rose and sprawled across the footpath leaving just a narrow walkway for pedestrians to access entrances to shops, banks, and other businesses. So far the road itself remained clear, but unless the issues were sorted out soon that too would be inundated with waste. The people of the cradle of democracy were making their will known.

Gina, the local guide for the group, had shoulder-length chest-nut hair and a pleasant accent. She pronounced the name of the

JUSTICE HUMAN AND DIVINE

city as Arthens. Ngaio made a mental note to remember that – it sounded nicer than with the short 'a' sound she'd always heard before. When the bus halted at the foot of the hill Gina held up a rolled yellow umbrella and instructed them that it was their beacon to look for and follow. She led them up a series of wide flights of shallow stairs to the plaza area that fronted the entrance and approach path to the acropolis.

They stopped to wait for the more infirm members of the party and those who had paused during the ascent to buy souvenir guidebooks and sets of postcards from elderly men clad in foustanella and fermeli. Lynn and Ngaio stood together looking down the hill onto the theatre of Herod Atticus which, Gina had told them, was built in the year 161 and was still used sometimes for classical concerts.

"Going on for two thousand years," Lynn found it hard to come to grips with the fact. There was nothing at home that could rival that, even remotely. It was only half that time since the first people had voyaged to the shores of their country, and they didn't have a culture of using permanent materials. The oldest building in New Zealand wasn't even two hundred years old – let alone ten times that much. Ngaio's grandfather was a builder, and she remembered he often referred to his apprenticeship years working on the construction of the capital's Town Hall. The clock tower, which was his particular pride, had been demolished after only three decades as a precautionary measure for fear of a large earthquake. In previous travels she'd often regarded streets of old buildings with a mixture of awe and dread.

In the few minutes while they waited it seemed there was a changing of the divinities detailed to guard this gathering place of the gods. Whoever it was who guaranteed fine weather apparently finished his watch and flew off, taking with him what would be the last patch of clear sky for the day.

Light rain began to fall, causing a crop of anoraks and umbrellas to pop from packs all around the plaza. Gina unfurled the beacon so it provided a bright spot among the predominantly dark colours. The drops increased to a moderate downpour so the group delayed their ascent and took shelter under a tree to wait till it had passed. Ngaio cast a long stern look at Lyall as her flattened hair formed a freeway for the rainfall from crown to collar. This spot, she remembered, was the setting of *Lysistrata*. That gave her an idea, but she couldn't do much about the Captain and his part in the favourable weather prediction. She and Lyall were not the only ones under-equipped. Many others among the assembled tourists, including Lynn and Glen, were almost equally without protection.

The group moved on – up the further flights of stone stairs to the real acro polis – the top of the city. The rain moved on too – keeping up with them for the following hour. Gina's instructive explanation of the wonders of the ancient architecture largely washed over the two women who couldn't see much past the lamentable fact that none of the remaining marvels of the ancient world had an intact roof. Lynn looked at the draped maidens of the caryatid porch of the Erecthion and thought that supporting the roof on one's head wasn't such a bad deal if it meant one had refuge from the elements. She looked so chilled and bedraggled that Gina handed her the yellow umbrella. At the time, it seemed to Lynn it was an offering almost on a par with Athena's gift of the original olive tree. In sisterly concern she shared its shelter with Ngaio so that

JUSTICE HUMAN AND DIVINE

from this time on each had only one side that was saturated, the other merely soaked.

Zeus and his underlings seemed in no mood to move on from their sport, and the dripping foursome found that over the course of the morning they experienced a dramatic change of heart. The cafés of the Plaka now sounded much more inviting than the open-topped Parthenon. Without so much as a backward glance at the remains they had so long anticipated they started down the hill.

It was a day for abandoning principle in favour of expedience. One of the souvenir shops that had topped Ngaio's to-be-avoided list was found to have an air curtain across the door. She stood circulating in the stream as on a kebab spit till comparatively warm and dry. Then the appealing plan of coffee Mediterranean style in an authentic kafeneio was set aside without hesitation as a Starbucks was spotted – the demitasses of kafes varys glykos switched for Americano grandes. Collapsible umbrellas of inferior quality, offered by an opportunist street seller who had customers queuing, seemed a solid investment at two for five euros.

The regrettable thing about visitor information, they agreed as the reclaimed coach retraced the route to Piraeus, was its reticence to engage with the full range of possibilities. Along with references to the mythology of classical times the advice given in tourist texts laid strong emphasis on the wisdom of timing visits to the hill to avoid the heat of the day. Early morning or evening were to be preferred, and spring and autumn visits were recommended. Guarding against sunstroke, sunburn, and the necessity to take shade and water all featured prominently in each account. Every photograph backed up the modern-day myth-making that cerulean skies always overspread the spot where Poseidon and Athena strove to gain ascendancy and claim patron status of the city. The goddess won and passed on the gifts of her portfolios – arts, civilization, craftsmanship, justice, strategy and wisdom – to those she protected. They had learned those lessons well. But this bus full of visitors would have appreciated it if the craftiness and strategy had been balanced by the inclusion in the tourist information of a picture or two of the ruins-topped rock under a leaden sky and captioned with a warning that cold and rain were also distinct possibilities.

Gina pointed to a large modern building on the left side. Its roof prescribed a rolling curve that put Ngaio in mind of a beret worn so it was a little raised front and back. At the same time, Lynn was thinking that if it was a sponge cake she would have returned it to the oven for a further few minutes baking. Its name in English translation, they were told, was the Peace and Friendship Stadium. Being a venue for many events in the recent Athens Olympics, and for world championships of a variety of sports before and since, it was a well-used facility. An all-weather venue, it was stressed. Ngaio and Lyall felt their earlier feelings on the hill subside a little. Wellington's Westpac Stadium had a seating capacity three times that of the one they were passing now, but it wasn't fully covered. From personal experience Lyall and Ngaio knew that its lack of a roof meant its patrons frequently left feeling just as miserable as they'd been themselves a couple of hours earlier.

Some hours later Ngaio had to reassess once again. It was mental discomfort she experienced this time as she realized

JUSTICE HUMAN AND DIVINE

this was not the first time today her preconceptions had been challenged. It seemed this had been a day for it. Now Belinda Brighton, who was sitting directly across from her at their usual table in the Medina Restaurant, had taken her up on the comment she'd made about a paucity of ethics in the Greek pantheon.

Ashwin removed the entrée plates and Belinda explained her view of divine justice as it related to the human world. Ngaio looked at the other woman with growing surprise. They had shared a table on this ark for forty days and up till now the two had exchanged few comments, and small talk at that. It pushed her to think.

An hour later when the coffee cups were also cleared away the two women had found parallels in the practices of two geographically diverse peoples as Ngaio had contributed examples from her own area of interest. What earlier today she might have viewed as frivolous fun, and perhaps a little spite, in the actions of the deities, she was now relating to concepts of mana and tapu in her own homeland. She had to admit to herself that until tonight she'd underestimated the woman who usually sat at the far end of the table out of easy conversational range. Now she felt challenged and inspired by Belinda's lead. When she got home she'd look into what was offering in continuing education herself.

SEVENTEEN SEAS

*A crop of anoraks and umbrellas popped from packs
all around the plaza.*

— CHAPTER 20 —

The Gods Must be Angry

The tradition of the cruise company was to give their liners names inspired by mythology. Perhaps the purpose was to give additional assurance to the safety and comfort of the passengers choosing to cruise under their colours, but as this one left the Port of Piraeus and steered a westerly course back into the Mediterranean Sea some aboard wondered whether this was always a prudent policy.

The ship's approach to the home of the Hellenic gods the day before suggested that the welcome being prepared was a little less than civil. Then the ceremonial dowsing of the worshippers she brought to their mountain tended to confirm that all was not well in relations between the cruise company and the celestial realm. Now, a day later, as the sea-miles increased between stern and shore those of a superstitious nature had reason to wonder whether any of their number had caused further offence while ashore.

On the evening of the first of two full days at sea between the ports of Piraeus and Barcelona, the ship scudded through the Malta Channel, past the southern coast of Sicily and towards the Sicilian Channel.

As it did so, four couples were seated at their usual table in the Medina Dining Room, though their order was somewhat altered. Ngaio and Belinda had enjoyed their discussion on the morals of the Greek deities the evening before so arranged to sit together again. Mona Coventry had seen the two apparently engaged in what looked to be a lively conversation but was not able to pick up much of it from her usual position, so tonight she changed places with Bert. Wilma Wolverhampton was keen not to be left out of what looked to be the setting up of a sisterhood and switched with Willy. The shuffle meant the usual seating arrangement of couples in pairs side by side was abandoned, replaced by a women's end and men's end of the table.

Ngaio began the conversation with the light observation that the Greek deities didn't seem any more pleased with them since they'd left that country. In fact, it appeared the maritime highway of the heroes was developing more and more potholes as they proceeded west. With Belinda as classical advisor the four women explored the possible scenarios. Though the wielder of the thunderbolts hadn't yet put in an appearance himself, the Harpies certainly seemed to be sporting with them, perhaps on his behalf, and it appeared Poseidon and Amphitrite were partying with their multitude of co-deities. When Wilma wondered why they had not received a warmer welcome, in any sense, when their ship was named for the Dawn Goddess, it became clear. The Greek pantheon included its own Goddess of Dawn in the form of Eos, so the arrival at their shore of a Roman rival was bound to cause offence. And then, to add insult to injury, the ship's Captain was Italian. The gods must be angry, they agreed.

The women were delighted at their cleverness in coming up with what was clearly an inspired answer to the enigma. It was validated when those who were on board for the full voyage recalled that the ceremony enacted in the mid Pacific on the

THE GODS MUST BE ANGRY

outward journey honoured the Roman deity Neptune. It was no wonder the Greek divinities had taken offence at the preference given to their rivals, and were now making their displeasure felt. Belinda recalled stories from her study of the epic tales of how Poseidon had responded to insults made by those who travelled his waters without making the due offering.

There was no doubt they'd hit on the right reason, and the four women were sure the confirmation would be received very soon. By now they had passed beyond the domain governed from Olympus and must be in the territorial waters of the Romans – the province of Neptune to whom they had already shown allegiance. Their champion would surely drive his chariot to their rescue and overcome the petty spite of his counterpart to the east. Just watch how the waves would subside from this point on. Right then the ship rose and fell – the movement coinciding with the serving of the main course. Any moment now would be good.

Sometime later when the coffee cups were cleared and Ashwin was hovering, Mona noticed that they were among the last diners of the Medina's first seating who remained. This new arrangement seemed good for all. She had learned long ago to understand the purpose of the various components of the internal combustion engine and the importance of such things as cylinder compression ratios and ignition timing. It was a matter of self-defence, but she was particularly happy that tonight, thanks to the complete change of topics, she had managed to remain focused and interested for the full extent of the meal. The men had also enjoyed the range of subjects that had dominated their starboard side of the table. Without any of the group commenting on it directly, each one favoured the new arrangement and was happy for the pattern to be repeated for the remaining days of the voyage.

The ship passed by the Italian coast and continued on her course to the west, but the expected smoothing of the sailing conditions failed to eventuate. Perhaps it was the turn of the Roman divinities to take offence – possibly because this vessel, dedicated to one of their own, failed to turn north and to spend at least a day at Civitavecchia. Or maybe they were busily engaged in their own sports at the time and so neglected to mount a challenge to their Eastern counterparts who were usurping their waters. Whatever the reason, the effects were set to last some time yet.

The Medina lunch group was minus a member on the Sunday. 'Basil' and 'Sybil' were first to arrive at the door of the restaurant. Mrs Liverpool-Lancs was right behind them, bearing the message that Mr LL wouldn't be joining them today – he'd had a late breakfast and what with the choppiness of the sea he thought he'd be better off staying in their cabin with a book. She'd run into Mona Coventry on the way and brought her along to join them as Bert had also opted for a quiet afternoon. In his case it wasn't a matter of breakfast overload – he'd had only two thin slices of toast with marmalade, a change from his usual full English.

Jovial Joe also arrived with another in tow. It was almost literal in this case as Dick Napier seemed a somewhat less than enthusiastic recruit. Joe had found Dick occupying his favoured place in the Crow's Nest as he was doing one of his regular rounds of the lounge areas in search of fresh prospects for his humour. He'd seen this man on his own before and

THE GODS MUST BE ANGRY

recognized him as a fellow single. They could well be the only two such men aboard – he hadn't come across another – in which case they'd welcome each other's company. He was right on one account.

Years of dealing with the variety of people encountered in a newsman's working life, had developed Dick's disinclination to suffer fools gladly – a phrase he recognized as deriving not from Shakespeare as a co-worker had once claimed, but from the Second Epistle of Paul to the Corinthians. At the same time he had no desire to be impolite, so when Joe slipped into the seat opposite with a light-hearted remark about two bachelors needing to join forces in order to repel the advances of the army of unattached women apparently occupying a good number of the cabins, he had merely smiled. It was sufficient, he calculated, to acknowledge the attempt at friendship, but not broad enough to suggest he was desperately needing company. It proved ample, however, for Joe to settle in and introduce himself. In only a couple of questions he learned of Dick's background. The ex-editor could have used him to tutor many a junior reporter in skills of interrogation.

"We have something in common," Joe claimed, delighted at finding a perfect opportunity to employ one of his favourite jokes. Even better, it was one he hadn't used so far this trip. He could have worked it in to other conversations, but had saved it in the chance of the optimum occasion – in his scoring system those were awarded double points.

"I'm a linotype setter." He paused for a counted two beats. "At least I was. I used to sit at a linotype machine setting type, now I prefer to sit on a liner. I guess you could say I'm set on being a liner type sitter."

SEVENTEEN SEAS

In the six months before retiring Dick had twice felt exasperated enough to tell a colleague to piss off and stop wasting his time. He'd taken it as a sign, and shortly after the second occasion made the decision to put in his resignation. Now there was no excuse to be brutal to someone who was obviously well meaning. After a further half hour of talk he had allowed himself to be persuaded, even if not convinced of the wisdom of it, to join the Medina lunch group. Wherever he ate he had to go through the same round of introductions and subsequent small talk anyway.

The majority of the core luncheon group, together with Mona and Dick and a further couple who arrived at the same time, were shown to a table near the staircase that curved upwards to provide access from Promenade deck above. Jovial Joe sat and waited for a comment on the condition of the ocean and its effect on the ship. He had been hoping a patch of rough sea would occur during the cruise. It wasn't so much that he was immune to mal de mer – he too had experienced some queasy moments – but it would give rise to a debut delivery of his most ambitious act to date.

On his annual cruise the year before, Jovial Joe had observed the various gaits of some of his fellow passengers as they navigated the passageways on the accommodation decks in different degrees of bad weather. At a point in the North Sea that ship, at fifty thousand tonnes being two-thirds the size of this one and not equipped with such efficient stabilizers, was rolling like a pastry cook – a simile he'd made up himself, and another thing he was quite proud of.

Joe had stood outside his cabin, bracing himself against the doorframe, and watched as a number of his fellow passengers

THE GODS MUST BE ANGRY

worked on solving a navigational problem involving the length of the corridor multiplied by the effects of fifteen-foot waves hitting the hull. He had, he realized in a moment of insight, hit upon the original inspiration for the Monty Python Ministry of Silly Walks sketch. Mental images, augmented by a dozen or so digital, provided him with the raw material for the routine he rehearsed over the intervening months in front of the full-length mirror at the end of his short hallway. He had every hope the performance would develop into the pièce de résistance of his repertoire.

It, however, relied on what he termed an optimum occasion to make the well rehearsed situation seem spontaneous. He could afford to wait. On any day at least a passing remark in small talk was a reasonable bet, on one such as today it was inevitable.

Mona Coventry led into the topic by expressing a fervent hope that the present level of pitching was at its peak. She confided that she found it strange that so far she was coping all right, touch wood, but her Bert on the other hand wasn't quite so shipshape.

Joe had planned to deliver his joke as a performance piece, embellishing the script with at least some appropriate footwork. There wasn't a lot of space between the tables, and waiters were passing to and fro, but if he didn't take the opportunity now and the sea subsided to restore the smooth passage his chance would be gone. Or there was always the chance a change for the worse would leave him without an audience – that's if he himself were up to giving his best. He elected to make the most of this opening.

The premiere performance of Jovial Joe's corridor

demonstration, as Wilma later described it to Willy, was a triumph. He hadn't anticipated utilizing the aisle in the dining room as an acting space, but found it was ideally suited to his display of the various styles of listing and lurching to be observed in times of high seas. It also had the advantage of extending the audience beyond the immediate group. Diners at tables in each direction put down their tableware to look on and appreciate this unexpected variety act, then added to the applause.

Joe sat down again as a waiter distributed the soup bowls – containing a lower level of fluid than usual in consideration for the linen tablecloths and the clothes of the passengers. He decided to mark himself with an almost unprecedented triple score. The glow of achievement lasted throughout the meal, just ebbing momentarily some forty minutes later as he left the dining room and a woman at another table grasped his arm as he passed by.

"You should be on television," she said. As Joe turned towards her and started to respond, she added "when you see all the rubbish they put on TV, it's a wonder you're not on it."

"Ah – thank you." He could see the comment was meant as a compliment. And he could rework that one and add it to his repertoire. It had been a great day so far.

The members of the newly formed women's branch of the Medina dinner group reported only slight disappointment that their conjecture was taking some time to be confirmed. For the second day the sea conditions failed to subside. In fact, as they continued on a north-westward course towards Barcelona the south-westerly increased from force four to nine on the

THE GODS MUST BE ANGRY

Beaufort scale. For almost the first time in the voyage the deck-chairs on Lido deck couldn't attract a full quota of bodies even though the clear roof of the Skydome was drawn across the midships area surrounding the Crystal Pool.

To Mona Coventry it was a double denial of theory. Not only had she been a willing participant in the classics-based speculation the women had delighted in constructing the evening before, but she remembered her own premise that supposed a perpetually serene Mediterranean Sea due to the protection of the surrounding landmasses. Yet here they were, closing in on the coast of Spain, with the strong gale conditions causing twenty-foot waves to crash around them. Even more astonishing than that was the realization that she was not only feeling well but almost enjoying it. The Waterworld scenario didn't seem quite so daunting after all.

Bert was another matter. Even after missing lunch, in the late afternoon he decided he wasn't in a mood to go to dinner either. Mona wasn't inclined to stay in the cabin with him. Right when she had cast off her multiple fears – seasickness, the vastness of unrelieved expanses of ocean, being entombed in her cabin in a sunken ship, and the horrors pointed to in remembered lines such as "full fathom five my father lies" – she was determined to enjoy to the full what remained of the voyage. She pulled out the lower drawer in her bedside table and extracted a toilet bag. This one, in lilac, was in addition to the pink one in the bathroom. From its roomy interior Mona pulled out a variety of medication that looked sufficient to top up the stocks in the ship's infirmary should that be necessary. Thanks to the calm conditions in the Arabian Sea, and her resulting revelation after the accidental removal of her medicated patch, she still had

SEVENTEEN SEAS

five of the plaster circles unopened. Even if things changed she wouldn't need all of them now. She peeled back the covering and without waiting for approval stuck the disc behind Bert's ear. She followed it up with a tablet offered with a glass of water.

"Take this," she ordered. If one of the treatments didn't do the job, the other might. Bert was a belt and braces man, so it seemed appropriate.

So it was that a full complement was present at their table that night. It wasn't the case all around the dining room as fewer tables than usual were occupied fully. Two of the waiters at the nearby service console were taking the opportunity to fold napkins ready for the next sitting.

Mona, Belinda, Ngaio and Wilma resumed their conversation of the previous evening. It seemed other passengers had also stopped to wonder whether one of the cruisers had offended any of the divine beings with influence in the area. Ngaio considered giving her opinion that the average age and condition of most of the passengers made it unlikely any of them were up to emulating the antics of the immortals but with Belinda's mini-lecture in mind, added to the thought that she and Lyall looked to be the best part of a decade younger than their table-mates, decided to keep it to herself.

Meanwhile, Wilma had a further theory that deviated from the earlier line. Mrs Wolverhampton, who hadn't been able to contribute much to the discussion about the personalities within the Greek and Roman pantheons, now came into her own. This was Easter Sunday, she reminded them.

The new penny dropped in the mind of Mona then Belinda. Ngaio, whose imagination was still wrestling with images of any of her shipmates as heroic figures or even minor divinities,

THE GODS MUST BE ANGRY

came in last. That could be it, the four agreed. They were guilty of ignoring Good Friday. Any defence along the lines that the calendar of the eastern branch of the church deviated from that of the west was unlikely to produce a pardon. In this case it was more a matter of 'when in Rome' than in Athens. Even worse, they had increased the sin by using the day to pay homage to pagan deities whose dispensation had been ended two thousand years before.

Wilma said she had considered attending the church service advertised for the Playhouse that morning, an admission that had Mona and Belinda looking slightly uncomfortable. The event hadn't even registered with Ngaio.

"Barcelona tomorrow," she said, "we can all do penance there."

Many of the cruisers might well have started on their atonement far before they reached port. A good number went straight from the restaurant to their staterooms, resolving to retire early for the night. For a change there were plenty of seats available in the theatre where the billed entertainer did a heroic job singing while the stage continually rose and fell a couple of octaves.

Over the course of the night, conditions worsened even further. Lyall and Ngaio lay awake in their stateroom positioned on Canberra deck forward listening to the noise and feeling the thuds as the bow of the ship crashed down to meet the water at a point that seemed directly beneath them. There were several decks below them where it must be even more pronounced. Lyall had never heard of a ship breaking in half. However, it was disconcerting during the dark of such a night to spot the flaw in lifeboat procedure. If the worst did occur

SEVENTEEN SEAS

you certainly wouldn't want to have to put to sea in small boats in those conditions. At least they had a balcony door through which they could escape if necessary. He rolled over and went back to sleep.

— CHAPTER 21 —

Lucky to be Here Today

Easter Monday in Barcelona dawned fine and cold. The ship slid into the dock an hour ahead of the scheduled time and a waiting ambulance transferred a prone patient towards the city.

Lynn and Glen boarded a coach for a half day highlights of the city tour. They looked at the clear sky with appreciation. It was something they missed in most other places they visited – on this and other trips abroad. Almost everywhere away from home they found a pall of grey covered the expanse where they expected a stretch of blue. Here though, it was clear and bright, with a crispness that suggested it was just washed. The blue was in keeping with the tourist brochure image even if the cool temperature wasn't.

The bus reached the top of a hill where they were promised a view over the city. The passengers pulled on their jackets and alighted.

"You're lucky to be here today," said their guide, a local woman with brightly hennaed hair and an accent so thick Glen thought it needed a litre of olive oil to slide past his ears. "We've had a week of wind, so it's blown all the pollution away. You usually can't see the city from up here." She seemed proud of the fact.

It must have been the same force nine wind they'd encountered at sea because they could see the whole city nestling in a natural bowl of hills, and snow on the peaks in the distance. They had heard there was snow in London – but here it was stretching right down to Spain.

Senora Henna pointed out they were lucky for another reason too. Being Easter Monday and therefore a holiday, the traffic was much lighter than usual. Just as well, they thought a half hour later, while driving through the streets. On the other hand, being held up by longer lines in some spots would have allowed more time to pass judgment on the distinctive Gaudi buildings which were the city's main claim to fame.

"So idiosyncratic," came a female voice from the seats behind Lynn and Glen.

"You've got a couple of syllables too many in that," responded a gruffer tone.

Two rows further back Ms Coolangatta was also enjoying her introduction to the city that had been an anticipated highlight in the itinerary. In the friendly company of other learners in the Spanish language class she had amassed pages of notes, and learned phrases that would be a great help if she happened to take un gato a un restaurante para una comida. At least she hoped she could use at least a word or two, even if it was just hola. Their tutor had prepped them on to the fact that she was giving them Castilian dialect, as opposed to the Catalan of Barcelona, but Caroline didn't imagine that any of the few words she'd be able to muster if pressed would be out of the range of the locals' vocabulary.

Now Caroline was intrigued to find that Senora Henna did indeed say "Barthelona". She lisped it at frequent intervals when imparting the sort of facts that tour guides the world over learn from their local tourist offices and feel impelled to pass on to all visitors. The city is said to have been named by either Hercules when on his voyage with Jason in search of the

LUCKY TO BE HERE TODAY

Golden Fleece for the Barca Nona or Ninth Ship in the fleet, or alternatively, by Hamilcar Barca, always further elaborated as father of Hannibal, after his family; however it is more likely from the ancient village of Barkeno. It is also sometimes referred to as Ciudad Condal, the City of Counts, from the former aristocracy of the area. At least, thought Caroline, that topic was more interesting than the figures that preceded it as a time-filling exercise between the passing of the site of the Olympic water sports on Montjuïc and when they rolled into mid-city and were alerted to Gaudi watch. There could be some people, she acknowledged, who would not only take in but appreciate the facts that Barcelona laid claim to being the tenth-most populous municipality and the sixth-most populous urban area in the European Union, but she wasn't one of them.

The pièce de résistance of the morning tour – Ms C was aware she was borrowing the term from north of the border but her un poco of Spanish wasn't up to a more appropriate phrase – was Antoni Gaudí's unfinished church, Sagrada Familia. They'd already passed by several of his houses and the general buzz around the bus seemed positive, with a woman in the seat behind remarking that she'd quite fancy living in the Casa Batlló. Caroline agreed, with one reservation. She appreciated the artist's desire to design something different, and his incorporation of forms from nature, but she would like it transported to her Gold Coast home. She could feel the effects of the snow on the hills that surrounded the city and decided that if this was the vaunted Mediterranean climate she wasn't keen to relocate.

As they approached the much anticipated temple of the Holy

SEVENTEEN SEAS

Family she was prepared to like it. After all, if the Master had devoted forty-two years of his life to its construction before his unfortunate encounter with a tram, it had to be something really worth seeing. Even before the coach found a place to stop among the dozens of others and the passengers had added another fifty persons to the throng of milling pedestrians, it was clear that most viewers found this another matter altogether. Caroline took the obligatory pictures and listened to the comments being contributed freely by tourists doing the same. Uneven, hotch-potch, maybe when it's finished/cleaned, were recurring comments. On the other hand, she noted that lines of people at the entrance were queueing to pay and enter. Their own group, under orders from Ms Henna, walked in a group around the edifice. It seemed no one in their party was greatly disappointed to be told there was no time on this tour for an internal view.

The great churches of Barcelona were not at their best on this Easter Monday. The neo-Gothic façade of the Catedral de la Santa Creu i Santa Eulalia was blocked by a huge hanging sign proclaiming –

TELEFÓNICA
DÓNA SUPORT A LA RESTAURACIÓ
DE LA CATEDRAL

with another hanging above the entrance –

CAMPANYA "PATROCINA UNA PEDRA" AJUDA'NS!
CAMPAÑA "PATROCINA UNA PIEDRA" ¡AYÚDANOS!
"SPONSOR A STONE" CAMPAIGN. HELP US!

LUCKY TO BE HERE TODAY

Ms Henna had all the facts on the building's history. The construction was begun in 1298 but the western façade was not completed till 1892. Caroline could hear the voice of her late husband commenting,

"Yeah, we've got some builders like that in 'Stralia too."

Deliberately she turned her attention back to the commentary as their guide talked of the crypt of Santa Eulalia, and the altar of St George.

"Have you any questions?" Ms Henna had apparently imparted all her facts about la Catedral.

Sally Sale was quick to respond.

"Yes. Where is the duty free?"

For those few who showed sufficient quantities of the virtues of faith and courage to negotiate the obstacles to entry, a greater reward was forthcoming inside the structure. Caroline looked up into the nave and marvelled at the fact that workmen were able to construct such a building in the fourteenth century. She could make no comparison between this and the modest wooden suburban church she attended, either in architecture or activity. At home on this day there'd be a reasonably simple one-hour service attended by a very depleted congregation – those who hadn't taken the opportunity to get away elsewhere for the Easter break. Here the main area was being well utilized by worshippers who didn't seem too concerned with the hundreds of tourists passing by. Young girls and boys dressed in white were being addressed by a priest in what she assumed was a confirmation ceremony. Other people, singly and in pairs, lit candles in small chapels along the length of the nave.

When she emerged again, the activity in the Plaça de la Seu was also impressive. A group of local musicians was performing, and

SEVENTEEN SEAS

dancers in Catalan costumes circled with hands joined at head height, taking small steps in set patterns to the instructions of a caller quietly giving notice of change from one set to another.

A couple of hours later she stopped to watch another circle of dancers as she, with Ngaio and Glen, walked down las Ramblas. This troupe, however, wore everyday clothing, and by the look of the faces there could have been an over-sixties age requirement.

Between the events, the coach tour under the guidance of Ms Henna had returned to the ship in time for lunch. At a table in the Orangery the Hendersons and Ms Coolangatta agreed it was a comfortable walk between the wharf and Barcelona's most famous street. They set out as soon as they'd eaten.

The day had warmed to a welcome seventeen degrees Celsius, the shops along Las Ramblas were closed for the holiday, and alternative activities were in full swing along the length of the 1.2 kilometre-long avenue. They couldn't have ordered better. Flea market stalls selling all manner of household and novelty items could be examined without any intention to buy, street entertainers watched and applauded, art and artists-at-work admired, and living sculptures posed with for a small donation.

A real statue caught their eye for several reasons. The figure of Christopher Columbus, cast four times human size, stood atop a sixty metre high ornate monument. It was here, they learned, that the European voyager to the new world landed when he returned with the news. The three companions gazed up at the image so far above. From what they could see the man looked justifiably proud. His right arm was extended straight out indicating the direction of his triumph. But was it? Glen

266

looked at the sun, the shadows being cast, and calculated. It certainly wasn't to the west that the explorer was pointing. Columbus evidently hadn't learned much since his original error when he sailed west in an effort to get to the orient. Here he was, proudly pointing east. After all the intervening centuries he still had it wrong.

At the end of the afternoon they started the walk back. After the rough weather over the past two days, and particularly the crashing interruptions to their sleep the night before, to spend a day walking on firm ground was just what they needed. The streets were spotlessly clean, though perhaps made so by the fierce wind of the previous days. Even the advertised 'seedy' end looked inviting in the daylight before the red light area lit up for business; and all the warnings to beware the pickpockets and opportunist thieves were apparently not necessary.

Or were they? Other passengers were also making their way back to the dock. A couple catching them up from behind asked about their experience, and the three responded with enthusiasm. The pair looked less than keen, as well they might be, given they'd spent much of the time at departamento de policía making a statement about the most memorable event of their day. This man's was apparently just one of a number of pockets picked that day in the central city. He was particularly unimpressed that there was apparently no chance he'd ever see his wallet and its contents again, even though he had caught hold of the woman who lifted it from his pocket and held her till the arrival of the police. Given the fact he'd done their work for them, he thought restitution seemed a reasonable outcome. Apparently not.

"Lo siento, Señor," but it was a common crime. The woman

had thrown the wallet to a young lad who took to his heels and vanished into the crowd. He would never be caught.

Caroline agreed with the others that it was an unfortunate occurrence. Her personal feelings about the day, however, remained high, thanks particularly to a small but significant success she had experienced.

She had the opportunity to share it the following day. As the members of the Spanish class gathered the next afternoon in the Uganda Room their tutor asked if any had tried out the language they'd learned. Yes, she had, she was pleased to report. At a stall on Las Ramblas she had purchased a postcard of La Sagrada Familia she intended to send to an architect friend back home, and handed over a five euro note. From the vendor's look and the odd word, she recognized his response as equivalent to "Do you have anything smaller?" Now, relating the incident, she paused, then told of her triumph. Thanks to the lessons she was able to respond suitably.

"No, nada."

There could have been an over-sixties age requirement for this troupe.

— CHAPTER 22 —

Separate Ways

Dick Napier rejected the term 'creature of habit' in relation to himself. The fact that he tended to follow a daily and weekly pattern, he argued, wasn't a matter of habitual behaviour because that might imply he was acting without thought. He, on the other hand, had developed a routine that was planned and deliberate, formulated to make the best use of his time. In that case, he had an established system. Since he wasn't averse to deviating from it when there was good cause he also considered it, and himself, flexible.

The problem with such a programme was that in the non-flexible times it was predictable to others. Dick was just finishing a post-lunch long black in the Crow's Nest when Jovial Joe entered by the port door and walked straight to where he was seated.

"Talk about déjà vu," said Joe, "I had a premonition, and here you are in the very spot."

There were several answers Dick could give to that statement, and would have once – especially if it was a case of 'as the young reporter said to the editor' – but those days were over. He responded with his number two smile, a grade given when he wanted to give the impression of friendliness, yet not go so far as to encourage ongoing contact. That was where he'd gone wrong two days before. He'd given a four points rating – broad smile with light chuckle – in response to Joe's impression of passengers negotiating the passageways in rough seas. It was no wonder the amateur comedian had turned up again, no doubt in the hope of giving an encore performance.

This was a case for using a variation on the exit strategy he had perfected over years to remove people from his office without their catching on to the fact they were being moved along – at least until the operation was completed. He stood and stepped away from his chair.

"I was just going to check our position on the chart," he said indicating the starboard door with his left hand, while the right moved in an 'after you' gesture. He was sure Joe hadn't seen him examine it fifteen minutes earlier, and it was worth another minute's study if it meant he could divert Joe from his intention of taking more of his time.

That manoeuvre worked well, but ten minutes later when he was making notes in his journal another voice interrupted his work.

"Good afternoon Richard." He recognized the Queensland accent, but didn't look up. He had a good reason why he shouldn't.

"Afternoon Richard." Caroline's face appeared in front of his own as she bent down. He couldn't ignore her this time.

"Good morning Caroline. Are you talking to me?"

"If your name's Richard," she said, sitting down.

In that case he could have continued to overlook her greeting, but now she was sitting right across from him he couldn't do it with any measure of comfort.

"As a matter of fact, it's not," he said.

Her eyebrows raised.

"No? Don't tell me you're a real Dick." She clapped her hand

SEPARATE WAYS

over her mouth at the same time as she laughed. "Sorry, I didn't mean it to sound quite like that," she continued.

"A Dickens, actually."

"Dickens? As in Charles? Or what the…?"

Evidently it was his morning to encounter comedians. But Caroline wasn't too bad. In fact, a little to his surprise, Dick found he didn't mind her company. He sensed a match between them in the sense that, like him, she was not interested in anything more than friendship. Since her cousin Briar's departure at Singapore it was understandable she sought some companionship.

"Dickens as in Charles." He left it at that. Anyone in his hometown who knew might have asked if he were called after the main street but since that was named after the novelist, the original derivation didn't matter. He'd long since come to appreciate the fact that his parents' choice could have been worse – neighbouring streets in the centre-city honoured other English literary greats, and he could have been Chaucer, Tennyson, Thackeray, or Shakespeare.

"Do you mind?" Caroline indicated the empty seat on the other side of the table. She carried a thick novel with a bookmark at the halfway mark.

"Help yourself," he said, using an expression he disliked the first dozen times he heard it. His standards were slipping, he told himself. He reopened his journal and the two settled into a comfortable silence.

In mid afternoon Caroline closed her book. Dick looked up.

"What did you think of that?" he asked.

She shrugged. "Okay," then qualified it with "I wasn't expecting much."

SEVENTEEN SEAS

He took the volume as she offered it. He had noted earlier her choice from the ship's library – *Children of Hurin*, Tolkein's unfinished manuscript. The two began to discuss the Master of fantasy's previous books and the recent films. Dick found himself telling her more than he intended – anecdotes related to him by a young relative employed in the shooting of the *Lord of the Rings* trilogy. Everyone in New Zealand had stories to tell of how they were connected, if only remotely, with the making of the movies or the locations. 'God's Own' had readily opened its embrace to include hobbits and elves.

It was a further twenty-five minutes later when Caroline stood.

"I've taken your time," she said "sorry – I know you're busy."

"Not at all," replied Dick, and realized he meant it when he added "I've enjoyed talking with you."

She started to move away.

"We'll be passing through the Straits of Gibraltar, soon," he said.

She stopped again, and he continued.

"We're due there at seven o'clock."

"I'm at dinner then."

"So am I, but I don't want to miss it. It should be still light enough to see each side. I'm going to be in here – then I'll have dinner in the Orangery."

Ms Coolangatta paused. Was he suggesting she join him? Dick carried on.

"Eighty thousand ships a year pass through the straits, you know. That's two hundred and twenty per day. The watchman might need another pair of eyes. How's your eyesight?"

"Pretty good."

SEPARATE WAYS

"Then it's a bit better than mine," Dick admitted, "would you like to help out too?"

Caroline grinned.

"See you here," she said, and moved on.

Dick looked at his watch. He'd forgotten about the afternoon quiz and his appointment with the Brains Rust. If he went right away he'd just make it.

Two and a half hours later, still satisfied after the team's winning performance in the day's round of the progressive quiz, Ngaio and Lyall walked into the Crow's Nest by the portside entrance a few seconds after Dick's entry via the starboard door. They met again in the middle of the curved window that provided a panoramic view from the top of the ship. Caroline was already seated – her camera on the table.

"We decided to join you," said Ngaio, "It should be quite a sight from here."

The Wellingtons settled themselves in the pair of lounge chairs on the left. Dick took the one next to Caroline.

Glen and Lynn arrived soon afterwards, and took seats nearby. It seemed the residents of Australasia were taking the opportunity to view this passage from the Mediterranean to the Atlantic.

The Hendersons had also decided to skip dinner in the Alexandria Restaurant. Though they had no problem with their allotted dining companions, a change would be welcome. And if the menu in the Orangery included something spicier that would be an added bonus. Over the past weeks the couple had found the fare in the dining room much blander than they were used to.

The Plymouths and the Hampshires frequently ordered from a part of the menu headed "Best of British". Some of the dishes listed in the section were familiar to the Kiwi couple by name at least – cottage pie, Cornish pasty, steak and kidney pudding – and they knew the 'mash' that accompanied a good number of the listings. But other items remained a complete mystery. 'The London Particular' had them stumped till Harry identified it as thick pea and ham soup and happily added it to his order. Lynn had often felt Glen was less than willing to try a new recipe, but now found herself reluctant to ask for 'Cullen Skink' or 'Haggis, Neeps & Tatties' without knowing just what was likely to be delivered. As for 'Black Country Pork and Liver Faggots with Mushy Peas & onion gravy', the name itself was enough to warn her off asking for details.

Glen was intrigued by the frequent recurrence of such an unpretentious item as baked beans on the finely printed menus. At home baked beans might be offered in cafés as an extra with a full cooked breakfast, but he'd never seen them featuring in a serious restaurant, especially as accompaniment to items such as 'bubble and squeak cake with fried egg', 'corned beef hash and mashed potatoes', 'scotch eggs with a creamy mustard sauce', or other unlikely sounding combinations.

The couple from Auckland had also decided that the chance to see two more continents simultaneously was not to be missed. After their Africa-on-the-left Asia-on-the-right experience some days before, they were looking forward to seeing Africa-on-the-left again but this time with Europe-on-the-right.

The five New Zealanders and one Australian turned the event into something of a viewing party, moving as a group from the forward lounge to the restaurant aft as the famous rock had passed astern. Two days at sea lay ahead, then they would go their separate ways. The Hendersons were taking a train to Scotland to visit relatives, then planned to hire a car and go where the mood took them, though the Southwest region of England was what they had in mind. The Wellingtons were heading back to the Mediterranean immediately, to spend time in France, Spain, and Italy. Dick was taking the opportunity to do some research in libraries and parish offices for his sister who was constructing a family history, and Caroline intended to travel to Ireland with a cousin who had left Queensland twenty five years ago on her OE and never returned.

The plan they all had in common came to light a little later when they'd moved on yet again, to Anderson's Bar on Promenade deck. It was with initial surprise that they found all were, to some extent, filling in time till the European tour season started in a few weeks time, and that they were all booked on bus tours around Europe. They compared dates and routes to find that the coincidence ended there – none of the tours were the same though many had destinations in common.

On the other hand, it should not be such a surprise, they all agreed. For Kiwis and Aussies it was a long way from home to this side of the globe – half a world away east to west and south to north as Lynn put it – so once they were there it made sense to make the most of it. Lyall's idea was to "do it all" while they were here, then they "didn't have to come back". Ngaio, agreed – her roots were more in the Pacific region than the northern hemisphere. Their grandparents' generation might have regarded Britain as 'home' because of ancestral links, but time, history, and different cultural experiences had eroded that sentiment so only mere remnants remained.

— CHAPTER 23 —

Time To Say Goodbye

Bert Coventry still wore the plaster patch behind his ear. He was aware it was readily seen through his thinning hair, but that didn't worry him. They were now in the Atlantic Ocean and the crossing of the notorious Bay of Biscay was yet to come. He was sitting in Masquerade with a glass when Mona entered, looked around, and spotted him.

"Ah there you are." She was holding a handful of paper. "I went to all your usual places. What are you doing on your own?"

Mona sat down. She was a little out of breath. She'd been to the cruise desk on Formosa deck and picked up some written information. Though she'd walked through the reception area and the balconies around the Atrium many times before, she now realized she had not stopped to examine the artwork that formed the central feature of the ship. She stopped and looked up at the 35-foot sculpture and waterfall. Really, it was stunning, she decided. She ascended the first flight of the staircase so she stood at its base, and looked up at the entwined figures depicted behind the falling water. She walked around the balcony on Ellora deck viewing it from half way up. The tours desk was situated here, and she picked up more information. Then she set out to find Bert to lay it all before him. On Promenade deck she looked through Charlie's and Anderson's, through Raffles Court on Devanha, then checked out the

TIME TO SAY GOODBYE

various bars on the upper open deck areas. Coming back down again, she'd eventually found him, sitting alone, away from the windows, in this spot where she hadn't seen him before.

Never mind, here he was. Mona put the papers onto the small round table and pushed them to him.

"This is where the ship's going next," she said, "and this is the list of places it's visiting over the summer. I've been thinking, there's no need for us to even go home if we don't want to."

Bert picked up his glass and drained it.

"What are you drinking?" asked Mona. It didn't look like his usual. She picked up the glass and sniffed it. She knew that smell – it was what she'd ordered herself throughout most of the voyage.

"Ginger ale?" She stopped and thought, then laughed to herself. It was ironic, she had to admit. Bert had tried for years to get her to consider a cruise, and she had blocked the idea for fear of seasickness. Now it seemed it was she who was the sailor – she, who thought ocean views were well over rated and would have been quite happy if she never saw a coastline. Perhaps Bert's move all those years ago was a good one for yet another reason – this development meant he might not have had much of a career in his first choice of marine mechanics.

"We will do it again some time, won't we?" she asked.

Bert patted her hand.

"Sure we will, love. Just let me get back home for a while first."

Mona tucked the pamphlets into her bag and leaned back. A platoon of male staff began stacking large pictures against the chairs around them. The art auctions were well advertised through the daily printed programme and additional announcements. Early in the cruise an invitation to attend a private reception and exhibition of art works had been delivered to their stateroom addressed to Mr Robert Coventry. Bert had opened it and dropped it onto the desk with a "humph" similar to the one he used when asked in the street at home to buy a raffle ticket. Mona looked at the card. Why send it just to him, she wondered. She wouldn't mind going, but they didn't stand a chance with Bert. It seemed, from a casual conversation with another woman also viewing a painting hanging in one of the foyers earlier in the voyage, she was not the only woman aboard who was not impressed.

"It's no good asking my husband," said Mrs Gouache, "If I wasn't there to tell him how, he'd as likely as not hang paintings upside down."

The room filled quickly and waiters moved around offering free glasses of champagne. Mona took one, then claimed one for Bert too, even though he said he'd keep to his ginger ale. One of the art assistants placed a ticket from a roll on the table in front of each of them. A man – she presumed he was the Art Director – began to talk. He posed six questions about artists to warm up the potential buyers. Mona finished her champagne and picked up the second glass. Really, she decided, this was more interesting than she had anticipated. Perhaps she should have come to sessions earlier in the cruise.

A waiter paused by their table to pick up the empty glasses. There was one full flute remaining on the tray. Mona picked it off, rewarding Udai with a wide smile. The Art Director was addressing the audience. He kept referring to them as "you guys". All the answers to his six questions had been male artists, and he used only the pronoun 'he' when he referred to artists in general. Apparently all artists were male – or at least all whose

TIME TO SAY GOODBYE

paintings the company sold. Mona downed the contents of her glass. She put her hand on Bert's leg.

"Shall we buy one, dear."

Bert looked more than unconvinced. He hadn't been paying much attention to what was going on at the front of the room, but now he heard the Director introduce a large painting as a stunning work by Martiros and start the bidding at a sum for which he could buy a Mark II Jaguar 340 – a model he'd long coveted.

"No we won't," he ruled.

Mona resumed watching. Bert would rather have gone back to their stateroom but he stayed beside her in case she raised her hand during any succeeding auctions.

A woman she remembered meeting over lunch the week before bid successfully for what was introduced as a Pepoloni.

"Funny," Mona giggled, "I thought that was a pizza."

Bert looked at her. That was the second time on this trip she'd become tipsy on a few drinks. For someone who didn't drink much, it didn't take much. He looked at her leaning back in the seat smiling. He didn't mind – she was happy and it had been free.

Two more women bought paintings and the auction came to a close. Tickets were being drawn from an ice bucket. The couple at the next table expressed disappointment.

"One off," said the woman. She looked towards Mona and Bert. "It could be you." She pointed to the tickets on their table then, as Mona was slow to respond, picked them up.

"Over here," she put up her hand on their behalf. "You've won a painting," she said.

Mona sat in awe. This cruise just got better and better. There was no doubt about it – she'd be taking another one, as soon as she could get Bert to agree.

On day 80 of the full 81-day circumnavigation of the globe, the public areas were less populated. To the relief of many, the waters leading to the ship's home port were behaving with benevolence, but the cool breeze ensured the outside areas were largely abandoned. The bars did best as men sat and talked together – carefully avoiding their cabins where their wives were packing and repacking suitcases. Savvy and Serial Shopper left their stateroom on two occasions during the day to visit Mayfair Court and Piccadilly in search of further bags to hold their purchases. On the first such foray the sisters found the sales table offered enticing bargains on even more goods than they'd seen before, so an hour later when it became clear that even the new bag couldn't stretch to contain it all, the second trip became necessary. This time Savvy kept her hand on Serial's arm and steered her past the tables, while keeping her own eyes averted from temptation.

The task of packing didn't take Dick Napier or the Wellingtons long. When they met in the Crow's Nest both of the men were viewing printouts of their statements. Dick was surprised at how much his coffee habit added up to but considering the alternative available didn't regret the expense. Lyall wouldn't have bothered with the photographs Ngaio had bought from the ship's photographers, but his bar tab amounted to a little more. On the whole, the couple agreed, their bill was very reasonable – not like those of others they'd talked to, who had bought jewellery in the shop, paid for courses called 'computers for the not so terrified' and the like, or frequented the casino.

TIME TO SAY GOODBYE

Lyall was all for user pays. Every player at the blackjack table, each shampoo and set in the hair salon and seaweed wrap in the spa, lowered his bill for the voyage. The company was entitled to make money where it could, he allowed. Dick agreed, with one reservation.

"But do they really need to run advertisements before showing films in the movie theatre?"

Jovial Joe passed through the lounge area on the lookout for last-day opportunities to cross off another joke from his list and saw his opportunity.

"Looking at your statements to see what's tax deductible?" he asked. "I don't know about your tax office, but when I have to deal with ours I put perfume on the letter. I figure that considering what they're doing to me I might as well get them in the mood."

The men shook hands assuring each other it had been good to meet, and Joe moved on in search of further quarry.

In the Orangery he found a thin woman alone at a table. He was sure to be able to get her to bite with one of his lead-in strategies. His first attempts were all but ignored as her attention was fixed on demolishing the contents of a plate laden with food. Joe tried once more but it was clear that when she finished the main course she'd be starting on the plate of cakes that lay waiting. He knew when to cut his losses and moved on again, leaving Ann O'Rexia to the meal she'd denied herself for so long.

Had the liner's home port been yet another day-stop, records would have been broken for cruisers staying on board and the ship's dozen bars would have done a roaring trade. No one

281

lined the outside decks for a glimpse of Southampton – the view through the falling rain didn't extend past the closest buildings, and they'd be out in the midst of it soon enough. Rather, they sat in every available chair in lounges and theatres waiting their turn to disembark, clad in sweaters and jackets that hadn't seen duty for weeks. Furled umbrellas were waiting with day-bags.

Eighty-one days away avoiding the worst of the weather had seemed a good idea to Liverpool-Lancs when he booked their passage in the depth of the previous winter.

"Mind you," he'd grumbled at the time, "I don't know if I'll handle twelve weeks cooped up in a tin box."

Now Mrs LL listened quietly as he complained the voyage was ending before the spring weather was established. There was no point reminding him of his earlier fears.

The Hendersons had made their farewells to their Alexandria dinner companions the evening before. At the time, 'Sybil' pulled a pen and pad from her beaded evening purse and wrote an address and phone number.

"If you're coming through Plymouth, you must call," she instructed, calling on 'Basil' for backup.

Harry & Zelda, not to be outdone, assured them it was no more than a three-pound taxi ride to their home from the port. Apparently they'd be welcome there too except, Zelda recalled, they'd be leaving again on the eighteenth. Anwen Cardiff pushed a printed card into Lynn's hand.

"If you get to Cardiff…" she said.

"Yes, do," Al added, "I could take you to a rugby match," he promised Glen, "and show you how it should be played."

When the Wellingtons had deposited their packed suitcases

TIME TO SAY GOODBYE

outside their door on the final night aboard they were amazed at the sight along the corridor. Their two modest-sized bags had to compete for space outside their own cabin as the selection belonging to Serial and Savvy encroached on their space. As far as they could see both fore and aft it seemed a similar situation as trunks, cases, zippered holdalls, and an assortment of packages tied together bore testimony to the raised GDP of twenty-six ports situated in so many seas around the globe. The couple seemed to be almost alone in their unwillingness to add to their possessions.

They vacated their cabin early on the final morning. Despite the chill and gloom waiting outside, they were keen to move on. They had nothing but good memories of their weeks on board but, as the previous evening's entertainers had reminded them yet again, it was time to say goodbye. They were ready for it. During the voyage Lyall had sat in on a total of twenty-four lectures given by a platoon of senior men with stiff backs and trimmed moustaches before he decided he'd heard more than he ever needed to know on the subjects of British military and associated topics. He had skipped completely the series on a year in the life of a red grouse and, to his own surprise, found the most enjoyable talks were by the one woman speaker permitted a place in the phalanx of men – an actress and singer he'd never heard of but who was apparently a household name to most of the passengers. Ngaio still felt the remnants of the glow of delight that came from the Brains Rust's final performance, in which the team had beaten their closest adversaries by a good margin.

Their plan to fly straight out to the south of France seemed an even better one now than when they'd planned it. In three

SEVENTEEN SEAS

weeks time when they returned to the UK to join their booked tour, the season should be more advanced, and they were looking forward to a further three months of travel to come. The call for their coded disembarkation time was made and they headed for the stairs.

Dick Napier, descended to the vast area of the arrivals hall alone. Was that his name being called? Perhaps it was Caroline who had spotted him. But the crowd was dense and the noise level high as hundreds of departing passengers searched the numbered rows for their luggage, so he could have imagined it. The small band of Kiwis, with the addition of Ms Coolangatta, had met up again the night before and said their goodbyes. There was no need for anything more. He picked up his case and walked to the exit sign without looking around. He hadn't come on this trip looking for company, so it was with some surprise that he found himself regretting that he wouldn't see any of these people again.

Printed in Dunstable, United Kingdom